Jewish Women in the Medieval World

Jewish Women in the Medieval World offers a thematic overview of the lived experiences of Jewish women in both Europe and the Middle East from 500 to 1500 CE, a group often ignored in general surveys on both medieval Jewish life and medieval women.

The volume blends current scholarship with evidence drawn from primary sources, originally written in languages including Hebrew, Latin, Aramaic, and Judeo-Arabic, to introduce both the state of scholarship on women and gender in medieval Jewish communities, and the ways in which Jewish women experienced family, love, sex, work, faith, and crisis in the medieval past. From the well-known Dolce of Worms to the less famed Bonadona, widow of Astrug Caravida of Girona, to the many nameless women referred to in medieval texts, *Jewish Women* tells the stories of individual women alongside discussions of wider trends in different parts of the medieval world. Even in texts written about women by men, the intelligence, courage, and perseverance of medieval Jewish women shines through to modern readers.

With the inclusion of a Chronology, Who's Who, Documents section, and Glossary, this study is an essential resource for students and other readers interested in both Jewish history and women's history.

Sarah Ifft Decker is Assistant Professor of History at Rhodes College, USA. Her work explores intersections between gender and religious identity in the medieval Mediterranean. She is the author of *The Fruit of Her Hands: Jewish and Christian Women's Work in Medieval Catalan Cities* (forthcoming 2022).

Introduction to the series

History is the narrative constructed by historians from traces left by the past. Historical enquiry is often driven by contemporary issues and, in consequence, historical narratives are constantly reconsidered, reconstructed and reshaped. The fact that different historians have different perspectives on issues means that there is often controversy and no universally agreed version of past events. *Seminar Studies* was designed to bridge the gap between current research and debate, and the broad, popular general surveys that often date rapidly.

The volumes in the series are written by historians who are not only familiar with the latest research and current debates concerning their topic, but who have themselves contributed to our understanding of the subject. The books are intended to provide the reader with a clear introduction to a major topic in history. They provide both a narrative of events and a critical analysis of contemporary interpretations. They include the kinds of tools generally omitted from specialist monographs: a chronology of events, a glossary of terms and brief biographies of 'who's who'. They also include bibliographical essays in order to guide students to the literature on various aspects of the subject. Students and teachers alike will find that the selection of documents will stimulate the discussion and offer insight into the raw materials used by historians in their attempt to understand the past.

Clive Emsley and Gordon Martel
Series Editors

Jewish Women in the Medieval World
500–1500 CE

Sarah Ifft Decker

Routledge
Taylor & Francis Group

LONDON AND NEW YORK

Cover image: Sarajevo Haggadah, Barcelona, 1350, Family Celebrating Passover Seder © Album / Alamy Stock Photo

First published 2022
by Routledge
4 Park Square, Milton Park, Abingdon, Oxon OX14 4RN

and by Routledge
605 Third Avenue, New York, NY 10158

Routledge is an imprint of the Taylor & Francis Group, an informa business

British Library Cataloguing-in-Publication Data
A catalogue record for this book is available from the British Library

Library of Congress Cataloging-in-Publication Data
Names: Ifft Decker, Sarah, author.
Title: Jewish women in the medieval world: 500-1500 ce / Sarah Ifft Decker.
Description: New York, NY: Routledge, 2022. | Series: Seminar studies | Includes bibliographical references and index.
Identifiers: LCCN 2021057594 (print) | LCCN 2021057595 (ebook) | ISBN 9780367612771 (hardback) | ISBN 9780367612726 (paperback) | ISBN 9781003104964 (ebook)
Subjects: LCSH: Jewish women—History—To 1500. | Jewish women—Social conditions.
Classification: LCC HQ1172 .I44 2022 (print) | LCC HQ1172 (ebook) | DDC 305.48/8924—dc23/eng/20220114
LC record available at https://lccn.loc.gov/2021057594
LC ebook record available at https://lccn.loc.gov/2021057595

ISBN: 978-0-367-61277-1 (hbk)
ISBN: 978-0-367-61272-6 (pbk)
ISBN: 978-1-003-10496-4 (ebk)

DOI: 10.4324/9781003104964

Typeset in Sabon
by KnowledgeWorks Global Ltd.

Contents

List of figures

Acknowledgements

Due to both my long-standing interest in the history of medieval Jewish women and my own lived experiences navigating communities as a Jewish woman, I am deeply grateful to have had the opportunity to bring this project to fruition. Thank you to Morwenna Scott, who first approached me about the possibility of publishing in the Seminar Studies series; to Laura Pilsworth, who worked with me in the early stages of this project; and to Isabel Voice, whose patience and attention to detail have been crucial as I completed the manuscript. I am deeply grateful to the reviewers who gave thoughtful feedback on this proposal; they have without doubt made this book a better one.

The mentorship, formal and informal, I have received from other scholars has been deeply valuable in making this book possible. Special thanks are owed to Paul Freedman, Alexandra Guerson, Marie Kelleher, Eve Krakowski, Dana Wessell Lightfoot, Ivan Marcus, Stefanie Siegmund, Paola Tartakoff, Francesca Trivellato, and Rebecca Winer. The conversations we have had over the years have helped to shape this project in many ways. I have also been fortunate in enjoying two excellent institutional homes during the time I spent working on this project. My colleagues in the Borns Jewish Studies Program at Indiana University and in the Department of History and the Program in Jewish, Islamic, and Middle Eastern Studies in Rhodes College have encouraged and supported me through the challenging process of staying dedicated to research and writing during my job search and my transition to a tenure-track position—all in the midst of a global pandemic.

My students have been a constant source of inspiration for me as I sought to create the kind of book that I felt was missing from my courses. I am especially thankful to have had the opportunity to work closely with the graduate students in my Gender and Jewish History seminar at Indiana University and with the advanced undergraduate students in my Sex, Gender, and Religious Identity in the Medieval World seminar at Rhodes College. Their thoughtful questions and deep engagement with both medieval texts and modern scholarship have informed this project in so many ways. I especially thank Patsy Wardlaw for her excellent work as my research assistant in the summer of 2021.

The support of my family has been vital. My mother, Beth Greenfeld, has been a particular source of inspiration; she taught me from childhood that gender mattered in Jewish life. I dedicate this book to her.

Thank you to the copyright holders who have permitted for material to be published in this book. All care has been taken to contact copyright holders where appropriate. Please advise the publisher of any errors or omissions, and these will be corrected in subsequent editions.

Chronology

66–70 CE	First Jewish Revolt against Rome; culminates in the Roman destruction of the Temple in 70 CE
c. 200	Redaction of the Mishnah
312	Constantine goes into the Battle of the Milvian Bridge with a sign of Christ marked on his soldiers' shields; they win
313	Edict of Milan, which extends toleration to Christians in the Roman Empire
325	Council of Nicaea, which distinguishes between Christian heresy and orthodoxy
c. 400	Compilation of the Palestinian Talmud
476	Romulus Augustulus, the last Roman Emperor in the West, is deposed; this is considered the end of the Western Roman Empire
c. 570	Birth of Muhammad in Mecca
c. 600	Compilation of the Babylonian Talmud
612–633	Visigothic rulers of what is now Spain pass a series of anti-Jewish laws, including forced conversion
622	Muhammed leaves Mecca for Medina, where he establishes a community of believers
632	Death of Muhammad
634	Muslim conquest of Palestine from the Eastern Roman Empire
711	Muslim conquest of the Iberian Peninsula from the Visigoths; the territory in what is now Spain under Muslim rule becomes known as al-Andalus
750	'Abbasid dynasty takes control of the caliphate from the Umayyads
756	Abd al-Rahman I, last survivor of the Umayyad dynasty, establishes quasi-independent emirate in the Iberian Peninsula (al-Andalus)
800	Charlemagne takes the title of Holy Roman Emperor
909	Shi'ite Fatimids declare an independent caliphate in North Africa

929	Abd-al-Rahman III declares an independent caliphate in the Iberian Peninsula, based in Córdoba
969	Fatimid conquest of Egypt
1031	Fall of the Caliphate of Córdoba and rise of the *taifa* kingdoms, independent city-states
1066	William the Conqueror, Duke of Normandy (r. 1066–1087), conquers England; establishes Jewish community in England in 1070
1085	Christian King Alfonso VI of Castile-Léon conquers Toledo
1086	Almoravid conquest of al-Andalus
1096	Pope Urban II calls for a crusade to conquer Jerusalem; crusaders massacre Jews in the Rhineland
1099	Crusaders take Jerusalem, massacring Jewish and Muslim inhabitants
1144	First blood libel accusation in the town of Norwich, England
1146–1173	Almohad conquest of al-Andalus; Jews and Christians subject to expulsion
1171	Blood libel accusation in Blois (northern France)
1190	Massacre of Jews at York, England
1204	Death of Maimonides
1215	Fourth Lateran Council
1240	Public disputation between Jews and Christians, debating whether the Talmud contains anti-Christian content, held in Paris
1263	Public disputation between Jews and Christians, debating whether the Talmud secretly proves the truth of Christianity, held in Barcelona
1290	Edward I (r. 1272–1307) expels the Jews from England
1306	Philip IV (r. 1285–1314) expels the Jews from France
1346–1353	The Black Death spreads across Asia, the Middle East, Europe, and North Africa
1391	Massacres of Jews across the Iberian Peninsula
1453	Ottoman Turks conquest of Constantinople, bringing the Eastern Roman Empire to an end
1475	Blood libel accusation in Trent (Italy)
1478	Establishment of the Spanish Inquisition
1492	Ferdinand II of Aragon and Isabella I of Castile, rulers of a newly united Spain, defeat the last Muslim-ruled Iberian kingdom of Granada and expel the Jews from Spain
1497	Expulsion of the Jews from Portugal

Who's who

Rabbi Akiva (c. 50–135 CE): Important rabbinic sage quoted frequently in the Mishnah and Talmud. He died in the Bar Kochba Revolt and was venerated as a martyr.

Augustine (354–430): Theologian known for his "doctrine of witness," which mandated Christian toleration of Jews but only on the grounds that Jews' preservation of their shared scriptures demonstrated that Christians had not falsified parts of the Bible, which Christians interpreted as prophecies foretelling the coming of Christ.

Beruriah (2nd c. CE): Woman sage quoted in the Talmud. She was the daughter of Hananiah ben Teradion and the wife of Rabbi Meir. According to a legend that arose in the Middle Ages, she was seduced by a student of her husband and subsequently committed suicide.

Constantine I (272–337): Roman Emperor (r. 306–337), who in 312 claimed to have had a vision which inspired him to go into battle with the monogram of Christ marked on his soldiers' shields. After his victory, in 313, he passed the Edict of Milan, which formally instituted toleration of Christians. Constantine eventually became a Christian, and during his rule presided over church councils and patronized churches.

Dolce of Worms (d. 1196): Wife of the rabbi Eleazar of Worms, Dolce worked as a moneylender and businesswoman to support her household financially while her husband pursued the study and teaching of Jewish texts. She was murdered, along with her two daughters Bellette and Hannah, by Christians.

Dunash ben Labrat (c. 920–990): A poet based in al-Andalus, who is credited with introducing Arabic meters into Hebrew poetry. His wife, whose name is unknown, wrote the only surviving example of a medieval Hebrew poem authored by a woman.

Rabbi Eleazar of Worms (1176–1238): Leading Talmudist and figure in the pietist movement in Central Europe. Eleazar also studied Kabbalah. His best-known work, *Sefer ha-Rokeach*, "Book of the Perfumer," offered a guide to Jewish law and ethics for a general readership. Born in Mainz, he later became a rabbi in Worms. He wrote elegiac poems for his wife, Dolce, and his daughters, Bellette and Hannah, after they were murdered by Christians.

King Ferdinand II of Aragon (1452–1516): Ruler of the kingdom of Aragon. Before he acceded to the throne, he married Isabella, heir to the throne of Castile. When they both became rulers of their countries, they presided over the effective unification of the two kingdoms under a shared monarchy. Ferdinand and Isabella were nicknamed the "Catholic Monarchs" for their deeply held faith. They received papal permission to establish the Spanish Inquisition in 1478. In late 1491, they completed the conquest of the last Muslim kingdom in the Iberian Peninsula, the emirate of Granada; Granada formally surrendered in early 1492. Ferdinand and Isabella expelled the Jews from Spain later that year.

Rabbenu Gershom ben Judah (c. 960–1040): Known as the "Me'or ha-Golah," or "Light of the Exile," Rabbenu Gershom was a highly respected rabbi in medieval Ashkenaz and the head of a rabbinic academy based in Mainz. Communities throughout northern Europe and beyond accepted as authoritative his ban on the practice of polygyny.

Glückel of Hameln (1646–1724): Author of the first memoir in Yiddish written by a woman, intended to be an ethical guide for her children. Her memoir demonstrates that she was an active businesswoman. Scholars have used Glückel's memoirs to gain insight into everyday Jewish life, including business, family matters, and the ways ordinary Jews reacted to news of pivotal events.

Innocent III (1160/1161–1216): Pope who presided over the Fourth Lateran Council in 1215. The regulations instituted by the Fourth Lateran Council solidified Church doctrine on matters including transubstantiation, strengthened ties between the Church and individual believers by requiring confession, supported efforts to combat heresy, and reinforced boundaries between Christians and non-Christians. Canon 68 of the Fourth Lateran Council was the first attempt in Christian Europe to require Jews to wear a distinguishing badge or clothing item.

Queen Isabella I of Castile (1451–1504): Ruler of the kingdom of Castile. Before she became queen, she married Ferdinand, heir to the throne of Aragon. When the two acceded to their respective thrones, they presided over the effective unification of the two kingdoms under a shared monarchy. Isabella and Ferdinand were nicknamed the "Catholic Monarchs" for their deeply held faith. They received papal permission to establish the Spanish Inquisition in 1478. In late 1491, they completed the conquest of the last Muslim kingdom in the Iberian Peninsula, the emirate of Granada; Granada formally surrendered in early 1492. Later that year, Isabella and Ferdinand expelled the Jews from Spain.

Licoricia of Winchester (d. 1277): A wealthy Jewish woman moneylender from England. After her first husband's death, she married another wealthy English Jew, David of Oxford. This marriage required a protracted legal battle, as David had to divorce his first wife, Muriel, against her will. After David's death in 1244, Licoricia took over his business. She loaned money to many members of the English aristocracy and even the royal family; through her work, she developed ties with King Henry III. In 1277, she was found murdered, along with her Christian maid; her home had also been robbed.

Maimonides (1138–1204): Also known by his name Rabbi Moses ben Maimon and by the acronym RaMBaM, Maimonides was known as a rabbi, community leader, physician, and philosopher. Born in Córdoba, he and his family fled to escape persecution under the Almohads. After a sojourn in North Africa, he settled in Egypt, where he would become the *ra'is al-yahud*, the head of the local Jewish community. He is well known for his extensive writings, especially the *Mishneh Torah*, an organized synthesis of Jewish law, and *The Guide for the Perplexed*, a philosophical work in the medieval Aristotelian tradition. Both works received criticism, and in some places the *Guide* was even banned.

Rabbi Meir of Rothenburg (c. 1215–1293): Central European rabbi, born in Worms, who later established an academy of Jewish learning in Rothenburg. He is sometimes referred to with the acronym MaHaRaM, "Our Teacher, Rabbi Meir." He was a leading *halakhic* authority in the region. He authored numerous responsa, along with commentaries and overviews of the *halakhah* on particular topics.

Muhammad (c. 570–632): Founder of Islam and believed by Muslims to be God's final prophet, or the "seal of prophecy." His divine revelations, considered the basis for the written scripture of the Qur'an, attracted many followers during his lifetime. Muhammad and his followers would also establish political control over much of the Arabian Peninsula.

Rabbi Solomon ibn Adret (1235–1310): Also known by the acronym RaSHBA, ibn Adret was the leading rabbi in Barcelona in the late thirteenth and early fourteenth centuries. He authored thousands of surviving responsa, sent to him not only from Catalonia but also from Castile and France, which represent important sources for the study of medieval Jewish communities and of Jewish law. Ibn Adret opposed extremism in both Kabbalistic mysticism and in philosophical rationalism. During the Maimonidean Controversy, he defended Maimonides but banned anyone under 30 from studying philosophy.

Rashi (1040–1105): An acronym used to refer to Rabbi Solomon ben Isaac, who was educated in the centers of Jewish learning in central Europe but based in Troyes. His commentaries on the Bible and the Babylonian Talmud are still read today. He also issued halakhic rulings in the form of responsa; additional rulings preserved in other collections were attributed to Rashi, although it is not always necessarily clear whether these attributions should be considered accurate.

PART I
Introduction

1 Introduction

Scholars of the medieval world have long understood the crucial importance of gender as what historian Joan Scott termed a "category of historical analysis" (Scott 1986). In the past, as to some degree remains the case today, ideas about gender shaped social expectations. How should a person behave, in public and in private? What kinds of relationships should they have? What types of jobs should be available to them? In the medieval world, gender also determined legal status. Laws about control over financial resources, sex and adultery, and guardianship of children, to take only a few examples, differed for men and women. Medieval historians have long since abandoned the view that women in the Middle Ages suffered from such grave oppression that they utterly lacked agency. We know that women made decisions about their own lives, sued people in courts of law, worked outside the home, ruled territories large and small, and wrote poems, prose, and prayers. However, women tended to be disadvantaged in relation to men of their same status. Men and women had very different experiences when they worked, married, went to a court of law, or exercised power.

However, gender did not exist in a vacuum: ideas about gender affected different women, and men, in varied ways. Some scholars use the term **intersectionality** to describe analysis that considers the intertwined impact of factors like gender, race, and class. We can better understand the complicated dynamics that shaped people's lives in the medieval past if we consider their gender identity in combination with other factors. What socio-economic stratum, or class, did they belong to? Did they live in England, or Italy, or Egypt, or somewhere else in the world? Did they reside in a city or in a rural area? Were they married? What faith did they profess? This book will address many of these points of difference between women, but it will focus on the experiences of Jewish women. As members of a religious minority community, how did they experience the medieval world differently from either Jewish men or from women of other faiths?

Religious identity, like gender, was a legal category, not only a matter of personal faith. During the medieval period, Jews generally lived as a minority

DOI: 10.4324/9781003104964-2

community under the rule of another faith—usually either Christianity or Islam. As a minority community, Jews were typically subject to legislation designed to create and reinforce boundaries between people of different faiths as well as to affirm religious hierarchies. Medieval understandings of Jewishness at times blurred the boundaries between faith and ethnicity. While Christians, in particular, pursued efforts to convert Jews to the majority faith, they also expressed concerns that baptism could not in fact fully wash away Jewishness. Jews, for their part, deplored conversion out of the faith but also believed that converts remained part of the Jewish people.

The focus on Jewish women in this book reflects the assumption that we can enrich our understanding of both Jewish history and women's history through an intersectional approach that incorporates religious identity alongside other forms of difference. Women experienced Jewish life in fundamentally different ways from Jewish men. Jewish law makes divisions based on gender in both religious and social life. Gender also shaped the economic options available to Jewish men and women: Jewish communal and religious authorities had different expectations, rooted in ideas about gender roles, for men's and women's work and their control of financial resources. Jewish men and women may have experienced attacks on the Jewish community differently. The institution of Jewish self-governance—usually understood as beneficial to Jewish communities—might not have seemed so unequivocally positive to women, who at times sought justice outside the community. A richer, fuller, and more nuanced Jewish history requires that greater attention be paid to this other half of the Jewish population. Women's history, too, benefits from a more extensive assessment of the similarities and differences in how gender shaped the lives of women who belonged to a subordinated minority group.

Previous works on medieval Jewish women

Although a growing body of scholarship has focused particularly on medieval Jewish women the specific experiences of Jewish women still tend to receive short shrift in broader surveys on both medieval women's history and medieval Jewish history. Most surveys on medieval women and gender, even fairly recent ones, have primarily emphasized a Christian European religious and geographical context. Patricia Skinner's *Studying Gender in Medieval Europe: Historical Approaches* (2018) incorporates a few passing references to Jews, including a brief discussion of how religious and ethnic identities intersect with gender (Skinner 2018: 140–143). The vast majority of the specific examples that Skinner uses, however, are drawn from Christian European society and culture. *The Oxford Handbook of Women and Gender in Medieval Europe* (2016), edited by Judith M. Bennett and Ruth Mazo Karras, includes two articles focused on Jewish communities and one on Muslim communities, out of a total of thirty-seven. Bennett's *History Matters: Patriarchy and the Challenge of Feminism* (2006) calls for intersectional approaches that address religious difference in both teaching and research (Bennett 2006: 142–145). However, the examples Bennett draws on throughout the book mostly come out of her own research area of late medieval England, a time and place with no significant Muslim or Jewish communities.

Similarly, overviews of medieval Jewish history and even specialized monographs focused on specific communities usually devote little attention to the distinct ways in which Jewish women experienced the joys and tribulations of pre-modern Jewish life. Surveys often assigned in undergraduate courses, like Mark R. Cohen's *Under Crescent and Cross: The Jews in the Middle Ages* (2008), Robert Chazan's *Reassessing Jewish Life in Medieval Europe* (2010), and *The Jews: A History* (2019), a textbook authored by John Efron, Matthias Lehman, and Steven Weitzman, include little discussion of Jewish women. The same can be said of most regionally focused monographs on Jewish communities, including magisterial multi-volume works. General medieval history textbooks, to their credit, include more and more references to Jews and to women, but little or nothing on the specific experiences of Jewish women. All the works mentioned here are excellent surveys—but those interested in Jewish women in particular might be left wanting more information.

However, the overview of medieval Jewish women presented in this volume is only possible because the last several decades have witnessed the development of an increasingly rich body of specialized scholarship focused on Jewish women and gender in the medieval world. In a monumental five-volume study (1967–1993) of the Jewish community of medieval Egypt based on documents from the **Cairo Genizah**, S.D. Goitein offered a much more comprehensive discussion of women than found in most local and regional studies of medieval Jewish communities. The third volume, entitled "The Family" (1978), focused largely on women's experiences. In *Jewish Women in Historical Perspective* (1991), an edited volume containing essays on Jewish women from the Hebrew Bible through the twentieth century, editor Judith R. Baskin called for historical perspectives to inform current understandings and conversations about the role of women in Judaism. Contributions from Baskin, Renée Levine Melammed, and Howard Adelman offered crucial early overviews of medieval Jewish women's experiences in different regions. All three scholars have also authored other works that have contributed a great deal to our understanding of Jewish women's lives in the medieval world. Avraham Grossman also published extensively on Jewish women, particularly as seen through the lens of rabbinic sources, in the 1980s and 1990s. In 2001, he published in Hebrew an extensive survey, which was subsequently abridged and translated into English as *Pious and Rebellious: Jewish Women in Medieval Europe* (2004). This survey has been of great value to students and scholars alike.

Meanwhile, the last two decades have also seen the dramatic growth of the field. Scholars have produced excellent monographs on Jewish women focused on different regions throughout the medieval world. Elisheva

Baumgarten's *Mothers and Children: Jewish Family Life in Medieval Europe* (2004) and *Practicing Piety in Medieval Ashkenaz: Men, Women, and Everyday Religious Observance* (2014) both offer insight into the experiences of Jewish women in **Ashkenaz**, the Hebrew name for a region comprising what is now Germany and northern France. Those interested in the women of **Sepharad**, the Hebrew name for what is now Spain and Portugal, can turn to works like Melammed's *Heretics or Daughters of Israel: The Crypto-Jewish Women of Castile* (1999), on the experiences of women who practiced Judaism in secret, after they or their ancestors had converted to Christianity under duress. In *Women, Wealth, and Community in Perpignan, c. 1250–1300: Christians, Jews, and Enslaved Muslims in a Medieval Mediterranean Town* (2006), Rebecca Lynn Winer compares the gendered social and economic norms experienced by Jewish, Christian, and Muslim women in the city of Perpignan, which today is located in the south of France but in the thirteenth century belonged to the same political and cultural orbit as the northeastern part of the Iberian Peninsula. Several publications by the late Elka Klein detail aspects of Jewish women's experiences in Catalonia (2006a; 2006b). Eve Krakowski's *Coming of Age in Medieval Egypt: Female Adolescence, Jewish Law, and Ordinary Culture* (2018) crafts a nuanced portrayal of ideas about gender and adolescence in the Jewish communities of the Muslim-ruled Middle East. Works of scholarship like these, as well as numerous articles that explore medieval Jewish gender and women's history from a variety of perspectives, have made it increasingly possible for general readers and undergraduate students to learn far more about medieval Jewish women than ever before.

The limitations of this work

This work is a synthesis, which means that the amount of detail it can offer is limited, although every effort has been made to distinguish between regions and identify change over time whenever possible. This study also cannot provide a fully comparative perspective relating the experiences of Jewish women to those of their Christian and Muslim counterparts. However, occasional comparative discussions are incorporated. In addition, the Guide to Further Reading includes recommendations for related scholarship focused on Christian and Muslim women's lives.

The work focuses on the period between 500 and 1500, which in the European context is referred to as the "Middle Ages." All surveys must take a beginning and end point, and there are certainly pivotal moments around the years 500 and 1500 that justify those as cut-off dates—for example, the 476 fall of the Western Roman Empire, on one end, and, on the other, the 1453 Ottoman conquest of Constantinople and the 1492 conquest of Granada, expulsion of the Jews from Spain, and European exploration of the Americas. Historians have often used these dates to draw boundaries between different historical eras in textbooks and undergraduate courses.

However, it is important to acknowledge that this traditional periodization has its drawbacks. Early modern Europeans coined the Latin term *medium aevum*, from which are derived the English terms "Middle Ages" and "medieval," in order to distinguish themselves from their recent ancestors and emphasize their connection to a more illustrious antiquity. They saw themselves as partaking in a "Renaissance"—literally, a rebirth—of classical Greek and Roman culture. Periodization always requires some amount of oversimplification, and in this particular case our periodization relies heavily on how a particular group of intellectual elites saw themselves and their own culture. Today, historians recognize that there is arguably much more continuity than change in the transition from the Middle Ages to the Renaissance or early modern period. In addition, certain developments associated with the Renaissance—for example, a passionate interest in classical antiquity—are also characteristic of the medieval world, and claims that religious intolerance diminished with the Renaissance are patently false.

In this particular case—and many others—the other problem with our traditional periodization is that the boundary dates we choose are fundamentally Eurocentric. Neither the fall of the Western Roman Empire nor the Renaissance, the standard start and end dates for the Middle Ages, is a particularly meaningful turning point in the Islamic context. The more obvious starting point in the Middle East might be the rise of Islam in the early seventh century. The year 1500, meanwhile, falls in the heyday of the Muslim-ruled Ottoman Empire. Moreover, Muslims of the sixteenth and seventeenth centuries probably would have viewed the intellectual culture of their ancestors in the seventh to fourteenth centuries not as a "middle" period, but as the dawn of Islam and the classical era of Islamic learning and arts.

However, particularly when acknowledging interconnections and relationships between Europe and the Middle East—connections which included the Jewish communities of both regions—it has become accepted for scholars to employ the term "medieval" when referring to a wider geographic span. Following the example set by recent scholarship on the "global Middle Ages," this work will refer on occasion to events or individuals dating slightly before and after this period, in tacit acknowledgment of the fact that historical periodization can be better thought of as guidelines than as strict boundaries.

Sources for the study of medieval Jewish women

The growing body of scholarship on medieval Jewish women has drawn on a wide range of source material. Rabbinic sources have offered fruitful insight into communal ideas about gender and—when used carefully—women's lived experiences. Some of these sources are prescriptive: legal codes that worked to define what women's role should be in religious life, in the family, and in the economy. However, it is at times difficult to determine the extent to which these laws were followed and enforced in practice.

Rabbinic **responsa**—questions sent to rabbis and their legal rulings—are particularly compelling sources, in that they shed light on real issues faced by women and their families. However, they should be used with caution due to the fact that they often represent unusual cases. A standard legal conflict would not necessarily require the intervention of particularly learned rabbis, rather than local authorities. Even if a well-known rabbi were consulted, it is possible that their collected responsa do not necessarily preserve all the questions sent to them. When read carefully, responsa can reveal broader ideas about gender roles and norms and illuminate some of the challenges faced by Jewish individuals and communities. But students and scholars should hesitate to assume that an issue described in an individual responsum was common or normal.

Scholars working on the Middle East are particularly fortunate to have at their disposal the extensive and varied source base provided by the Cairo Genizah. In Jewish tradition, a genizah is a repository for waste paper that is inscribed with the name of God. For example, a **Torah** scroll or prayerbook that has worn out and is no longer usable would be placed in the genizah rather than simply thrown away or repurposed. The Cairo Genizah is of particular interest because that community placed in the genizah seemingly any scrap of paper that contained Hebrew letters. Many are not even written in Hebrew, but in Judeo-Arabic—Arabic transliterated into Hebrew characters. Thanks to the Cairo Genizah, we have a wide range of personal and business letters, marriage and economic contracts, inventories, and more, along with literary, biblical, and philosophical manuscripts.

For scholars working on Christendom, whether in the north or the Mediterranean, personal letters are relatively rare, but a wide array of documentary sources is available. Many of the sources employed by scholars of Jewish women in Christian Europe were produced by institutions associated with the Christian majority: court records and contracts drawn up in Latin by Christian officials and scribes. Although they do not always tell us much about women's inner lives, they offer a great deal of insight into specific details of women's lived experiences. Quantitative studies of these sources, made possible in some areas due to the substantial number of surviving documents, allow for assessment of what was normal and what was exceptional for Jewish women.

Chronicles and narrative sources—Jewish, Christian, and Muslim—sometimes portray Jewish women, as do visual sources. While these cannot necessarily be taken as accurately reflecting women's lived experiences, they do tell us about perceptions of gender roles and assumptions—Jewish and non-Jewish—about what Jewish women were or should be like.

Scholars interested in Jewish women's experiences face particular challenges in that the vast majority of the sources at our disposal were created by men. They must be assessed carefully to avoid making assumptions about whether men's perceptions or descriptions of women accurately represented their lived reality.

PART II
Analysis

2 Jewish life in the medieval world

Between the fourth and the seventh centuries of the Common Era, the vast majority of the world's Jewish population came under the rule of one of two other faiths: Christianity and Islam. These three faiths had a great deal in common. All were **monotheistic**, meaning that they believed in only a single deity. Judaism and Christianity shared many sacred scriptural texts, while Islamic scripture retold and, in some cases, reimagined narratives and central figures from Jewish and Christian scriptures. All three claimed biological or spiritual descent from Abraham, who was represented as the first monotheist in the Hebrew Bible. As a result, the term **Abrahamic faiths** is sometimes used to refer to the three faiths as a group. Finally, all three resembled one another in that they were exclusive monotheistic faiths—in other words, many Jews, Christians, and Muslims believed that practitioners of their own faith were right, and those who followed other religious paths were wrong.

The Jewish minority communities that lived under Christian and Muslim rule in the Middle Ages experienced many challenges. They were a not only a minority, but also a subordinated group. They were subjected to specific legal disabilities designed to emphasize religious hierarchies that placed the ruling faith at the top and others below. The people who ruled over them often believed that the Jews had once been God's chosen ones but had been supplanted by the faith that now ruled. The laws imposed on Jews also sought to create and reinforce boundaries, with the aim of discouraging certain kinds of interactions between people of different faiths.

At the same time, however, to tell the story of Jewish life in the medieval world as a series of tragedies would not be true to the lived experiences of most medieval Jewish men and women. Jews were never completely isolated, and they often formed an integral part of the communities in which they lived. Jews lived side-by-side with their Christian and Muslim neighbors and had frequent contact with them through a wide array of social, economic, and political interactions. Jews usually dressed, ate, and thought about the world in similar ways to the people around them.

DOI: 10.4324/9781003104964-4

Even Jewish faith, ritual, and law—seemingly obvious points of difference—were irrevocably transformed by medieval Jews' encounter with the Christian and Muslim people around them. Over the course of the Middle Ages, Jewish communities developed specific local customs, shaped by both local necessities and by cultural norms shared with the surrounding communities. By the year 1500, the world Jewish community was extremely diverse—and Jews often had much more in common with the Christians and Muslims living down the street than with Jews living hundreds or thousands of miles away.

Judaism and the Jewish people: beliefs and practices

By the beginning of the Middle Ages, Jews were both a quasi-ethnic group and the practitioners of a shared faith. Until the first century of the common era, most Jewish worship had been centered on a single sacred location— the Temple in Jerusalem—and revolved largely around the ritual act of animal sacrifice. In 70 CE, the Jewish revolt against Roman rule culminated in a cataclysmic event: the Roman destruction of the Temple. Even before the destruction of the Temple, Jewish ritual and faith had already become increasingly diverse and multifaceted. Jews who were critical of the Temple priesthood and ritual, or who lived too far from Jerusalem to make regular pilgrimage to the Temple, had already begun to develop rituals and practices separate from Temple worship. The loss of the Temple, however, required a broader reevaluation of what it meant to be Jewish.

Increasingly, Judaism became a text-centered faith, rooted in the reading and interpretation of sacred scripture and the effort to live one's life in accordance with the commandments expressed in scriptural texts. Jews referred to the Bible using the Hebrew acronym **TaNaKH: Torah** (the Five Books of Moses), *Nevi'im* (Prophets), and *Ketuvim* (Writings, a broad category that includes such biblical books as Esther, the Psalms, and Song of Songs). The Jewish TaNaKH, often also referred to as the Hebrew Bible, includes most of the texts found in what Christians call the Old Testament. However, some books of the Christian Old Testament—for example, the book of Judith—are not traditionally accepted by Jews as part of the scriptural canon. Moreover, Jews never use the term Old Testament because the idea of an *Old* Testament presumes the existence of a *New* Testament. The Christian New Testament is not part of Jewish scripture, and the figure of Jesus has no status whatsoever within Judaism.

However, Jews did develop sacred texts beyond the TaNaKH. As Judaism increasingly emphasized the importance of scripture, religious authority gradually came to be located with the **rabbis**, professionals in the reading and interpretation of sacred texts. The word "rabbi" literally means "my teacher," and the first rabbis were primarily teachers and scholars. Although they remained known as learned teachers, starting in the third century the rabbis increasingly also took on new roles as communal leaders and authoritative interpreters of Jewish ritual and law. The rabbis were an exclusively male group and would remain so until the twentieth century.

As rabbinic interpretations of texts became more authoritative, most Jews began to accept the idea of an Oral Law with an authority equivalent to the biblical Written Law. The **Mishnah,** the first written codification of the Oral Law (c. 200 CE), even claimed that the oral tradition of reading and interpretation was handed down from Moses on Mount Sinai along with the written Torah. Of course, there is no direct evidence that the text of the Mishnah really represents an unbroken chain of transmission going back centuries. But the representation of the Oral Law as not only passed down across generations, but also ultimately stemming from God Himself, played an important role in legitimizing the authority of rabbinic interpretations of texts.

The Mishnah in turn became a subject of study and interpretation, which would be written down in two interpretive commentaries on the Mishnah: the **Palestinian Talmud** (c. 400 CE), produced by rabbinic circles based in the Roman-ruled Galilee, and the **Babylonian Talmud** (c. 500–700 CE), produced by the rabbis based in the Persian Sassanian Empire, who had developed centers of rabbinic learning in what is now Iraq.

However, not all Jews accepted the authority of the Oral Law. Beginning around the seventh century, a group known as the **Karaites** rejected the validity of the Oral Law and developed their own alternative readings of the biblical text. Most famously, while rabbinic Jews or **Rabbanites** allowed for households to keep a fire burning on the Sabbath—as long as it was lit before the Sabbath began—the Karaites interpreted the biblical prohibition to require that all fires be extinguished as part of Sabbath observance. While the Karaites are sometimes seen as biblical literalists, neither the Karaites nor the Rabbanites approached the Hebrew Bible purely literally. The two groups simply developed distinct strategies and traditions of scriptural interpretation (Rustow 2008: 24–27).

Unlike some other faiths, Judaism does not have a single, universally agreed upon list of principal tenets or beliefs. However, on the most basic level, medieval Jewish belief was characterized by a few shared elements of faith: strict monotheism centered on a deity who had created the world, and who had given the Torah to his prophet Moses on Mount Sinai. The people—almost exclusively men—who wrote the texts that today shape our understanding of medieval Judaism often chose to emphasize practices rather than doctrines. Core Jewish practices shaped everyday Jewish life and distinguished Jews from the people around them. Some of the most important commandments included the circumcision of infant boys (performed on their eighth day of life); the avoidance of all work on the Sabbath, which was observed on Saturday; compliance with Jewish dietary laws (*kashrut*), which include bans on pork, shellfish, and the consumption of milk and meat together; and adherence to laws of ritual purity, which in the post-Temple period centered primarily on menstruation and childbirth.

These aspects of Jewish life can be considered relatively standard in medieval Jewish communities, but Jewish belief and practice were never monolithic. Debates over both faith and practice were far from uncommon, and different communities shaped distinct traditions, which were rooted in local circumstances and often intertwined with the faith traditions of their Christian and Muslim neighbors.

Jewish life in medieval Christendom

Jews had already resided in the Roman Empire for centuries when the empire began its transformation into a Christian polity under **Emperor Constantine I**. After a decisive military victory, which he attributed to the intervention of Jesus Christ, Constantine made Christianity into a legal religion with the Edict of Milan (313). He clearly found the faith attractive and promoted himself as its defender. Constantine's interest in Christianity shaped a new relationship between the Christian faith and the Roman state. He founded elaborate new churches and even presided over the Council of Nicaea (325), which made major decisions about which beliefs and practices constituted Christian orthodoxy—and which should be tarred as heresy. In the late fourth century, subsequent Roman emperors would increasingly position Nicene Christianity as the sole valid imperial religion. The laws passed by Emperor Theodosius I, in particular, dealt a serious blow to both rival forms of Christianity and to the polytheistic Roman religious traditions that for centuries had enjoyed imperial support.

The new bond between Roman imperial authority and Christian faith transformed the status of Jews within the Roman Empire. Even after the unsuccessful rebellion that ended in the destruction of the Temple, Judaism had remained a legally recognized religion. For the most part, Jews were not treated differently from other subjects of the empire. Within the wider context of the polytheistic Roman imperial state, Jews were not important enough to require much in the way of distinct treatment.

But Jews and Judaism mattered a great deal to early Christians. Christianity had begun as a Jewish sect, and Jesus and many of the earliest Christian leaders were Jewish. It took over a century for Christianity to definitively separate itself from Judaism. The effort to establish Christianity as a distinct faith inspired some early Christians to highlight contrasts between Christianity and Judaism, and even contributed to the development of Christian **anti-Judaism**. Jews were condemned as Christ-killers—meaning that Christians not only blamed Jews living at the time of Jesus for his crucifixion, but also portrayed subsequent generations of Jews for bearing responsibility for the alleged sins of their ancestors. Christian rhetoric also ridiculed Jews for interpreting the Law of their shared scripture (what Christians referred to as the Old Testament) in a material, literal sense. The Christian doctrine of **supersession** asserted that Christians had replaced Jews as God's Chosen People.

In the fifth century, after the rise of Roman imperial Christianity, the theologian **Augustine** developed his doctrine of witness, which justified the continued presence of Jews in Christian-ruled lands on the grounds that, dispersed throughout the world, they and their scriptures could testify to the truth of Christianity. On the one hand, this doctrine made an argument against the massacre, forced conversion, or expulsion of Jews. On the other hand, it made Jews' continued security subject to a Christian perception of their theological usefulness.

As Christianity and imperial power became increasingly intertwined, Christian emperors sought to enforce this understanding of Jews and Judaism through laws designed to create boundaries and assert new religious hierarchies, with Christians on top and Jews on the bottom. By the time of the fall of the Western Roman Empire in the late fifth century, Jews could not hinder conversion to Christianity, attack or otherwise harm converts, nor seek converts to their own faith. They were also forbidden from intermarrying with Christians, owning Christian slaves, holding public office, or building new synagogues, although they could repair preexisting structures. Gender and religious identity were closely interlinked in ideas about hierarchy. Although all interfaith marriage and sex was frowned upon, relationships between Jewish men and Christian women caused greater concern, as the perceived gender hierarchy within a marital or sexual relationship threatened to subvert religious hierarchies.

Anti-Jewish legislation did not disappear with the fall of the Western Roman Empire. Some of the kingdoms that arose in a newly fragmented Western Europe preserved laws much like the ones developed under Christian Roman rule. In the Eastern Roman Empire based around the city of Constantinople, imperial legislation continued to mandate anti-Jewish restrictions. The Visigothic rulers of the Iberian Peninsula—today the countries of Spain and Portugal—even attempted to forcibly convert the kingdom's Jewish inhabitants to Christianity in the seventh century.

However, the fragmentation of Western Europe left the choice of how to deal with Jews and Jewish communities in the hands of many different rulers, some of whom embraced more generous policies toward their Jewish subjects. Christian anti-Judaism was never the only force that shaped Jews' lives and legal status in Christian Europe. Individual rulers often made deeply pragmatic choices, linked to political and economic considerations, about how to treat the Jews who lived under their authority. In 1084, Rudiger, Bishop of the town of Speyer—acting in his capacity as a secular ruler, not just a spiritual one—actively sought to encourage Jewish settlement in the town with an array of privileges designed to attract Jewish residents. Jews could govern their own community, change money and trade freely, and even hire Christian servants. But Rudiger was pragmatic, not altruistic. The charter he gave to the Jews opened with the claim that "When I wanted to make the village of Speyer into a city, I thought it would increase the honor of our place a thousand-fold if I were to bring in Jews"

(Rader Marcus and Saperstein 2015: 64). Rudiger associated Jews with urbanization and economic growth and therefore thought the city of Speyer would benefit from their presence.

This claim, while seemingly beneficial to Jews in that it promoted pragmatic toleration, was nevertheless inextricably linked to developing ideologies of economic anti-Judaism. Christians associated Jews with money, materiality, and **usury**—the lending of money at interest. The idea that Jews worked near-exclusively as moneylenders is a myth. In reality, Jews practiced a wide array of occupations, working as artisans and farmers as well as merchants and moneylenders. Nor did Jews dominate local credit markets: Christians worked as moneylenders as well. In addition to the fact that it was a myth, the perception of Jews as being particularly good with money also had its downsides. Anti-Jewish visual and verbal rhetoric portrayed Jews as greedy and unscrupulous. The massacre of the Jews of the city of York, England (1190) was motivated at least partly by Christians' sense of indignation at being indebted to Jewish creditors.

Over the course of the thirteenth through fifteenth centuries, Jewish communities in Christian Europe found that pragmatic toleration only went so far. Their security depended on Christian rulers continuing to believe that Jews' economic utility outweighed the perceived downsides of having Jewish subjects, including both their own anti-Jewish sentiments and those of their Christian subjects. New developments in Christian anti-Judaism also undermined the Augustinian doctrine of witness. Educated Jewish men who converted to Christianity and became high-profile spokesmen in anti-Jewish rhetoric claimed that Jews no longer successfully bore witness to the truth of scriptures, because they lived not according to the Torah, but rather according to the Oral Law—the Talmud.

The thirteenth and fourteenth centuries saw a series of expulsions: England (1290); France (1306); and individual cities and towns in the Holy Roman Empire over the course of the fourteenth century. In the wake of the Black Death, Jewish communities were accused of causing the plague and slaughtered in response. In the Iberian Peninsula, a wave of massacres and forced conversions in 1391 irrevocably transformed the religious landscape. Alongside Christians, Jews, and (in some regions) Muslims, there were now New Christians, who occupied an uncomfortable position between Judaism and Christianity. Their conversions, often made under duress, remained of questionable sincerity even generations later. Some converts attempted to integrate into Christian religion and society, while others secretly held to their Jewish faith and practice. Even sincere converts might retain close connections with Jewish friends or relatives. When **Ferdinand II of Aragon** and **Isabella I of Castile**—whose marriage brought two substantial Christian Iberian kingdoms under shared rulership— expelled the Jews from their lands in 1492, they claimed that the expulsion was necessary to allow converts to fully embrace Christianity, without the bad influence of neighboring Jewish communities. In the late Middle Ages, many longstanding Jewish communities shifted eastward, as Jewish residents were welcomed into places like Poland and the Ottoman Empire.

These last few paragraphs present a seemingly bleak picture of Jewish life in medieval Christendom. But the events and ideologies described here, although important as part of our understanding of the pre-modern Jewish past, give an incomplete picture of Jewish society and culture in the medieval European context. Attacks and expulsions were traumatic, but rare. It is easy for historical narratives to emphasize dramatic turning points and moments of crisis, rather than everyday lived experience. Moreover, efforts to exclude Jews from Christian society stemmed from the fact that Jews were in reality very much a part of the Christian cities, towns, and kingdoms that they had made their homes. Many cities and towns with substantial Jewish communities had designated Jewish quarters, and Jews often chose to live there in order to have easy access to amenities like synagogues and kosher butchers. However, Jews were not typically legally required to live within the Jewish quarter, and Christians were not forbidden to do so. Nor were Jewish quarters isolated; they were often located in the center of the city, frequently mere steps from urban cathedrals.

Jews and Christians therefore lived side-by-side as neighbors and developed shared cultures. They spoke the same language. Hebrew was used in Jewish intellectual circles and as the language of prayer and ritual, much like Christians used Latin. But ordinary Jews did not use Hebrew as their everyday language, and some might only have known a few prayers in Hebrew. The Jewish languages of Ladino and Yiddish are written in the same characters as Hebrew, but they began as Castilian Spanish and High German, respectively, and are much more closely related to those vernacular languages than they are to Hebrew. Jews and Christians communicated freely in the shared vernacular languages of the places where they lived.

Apart from the limitations posed by faith-based dietary restrictions, Jews and Christians ate similar foods. They developed similar governing institutions and visual cultures. They dressed in similar ways, a phenomenon that inspired both Church and royal authorities to attempt to visually distinguish Jews from Christians. The Fourth Lateran Council (1215), a gathering of Church authorities from throughout Europe, demanded that Jews and Muslims be obligated to wear some kind of distinguishing garb or marking. Some local rulers, in response, enacted laws that imposed upon Jews a distinctive cloak or badge. However, these legal efforts to enforce difference and strengthen boundaries never fully masked similarities between Christians and Jews, nor prevented regular interaction between people of different faiths.

The Middle Ages can also be considered a period of Jewish cultural efflorescence. Rabbinic Judaism in Western Europe produced a number of religious and intellectual luminaries, whose commentaries on the Bible and Talmud remain influential today. Jews commissioned stunning illustrated **haggadot**, textual guides for the ritual meal of the Passover seder.

Jewish literary and philosophical texts blended Jewish ideas and traditions with local trends. The Jewish mystical tradition of **kabbalah** shaped new ideas about how to connect with God that remain compelling today. Jewish women were often at the margins of such developments in Jewish high culture, as we shall see in subsequent chapters. Nevertheless, it is important to acknowledge that the wider context of Jewish life in Christian Europe was complicated. Being Jewish shaped people's everyday lives, due to both their chosen religious observances and the anti-Jewish legislation imposed upon them. However, Jews nevertheless should be understood as part of the wider communities of the cities and kingdoms in which they lived. Many Jews would go their entire lives without experiencing extreme persecution.

Jewish life in the Dar-al-Islam before 1500

Jewish presence in the Eastern Mediterranean and beyond long predated the rise of Islam. At the dawn of the seventh century, thriving Jewish communities could be found in the Eastern Roman Empire, in the Persian Sassanian Empire, and in the Arabian Peninsula. Both the Palestinian and the Babylonian Talmud were produced by rabbinic centers located in what is today referred to as the Middle East. Over the course of the seventh and eighth centuries, many of these lands would come under Muslim rule. From their origins, Islamic-ruled polities had to grapple with the presence and define the status of Christians and Jews, people whose faith in some ways resembled their own but nevertheless remained very much distinct.

Muhammad, a merchant residing in the city of Mecca, experienced his first divine revelation in 610. In 622, he would relocate to the city of Medina, where he began to spread his religious message—as well as consolidate political control, first in the city and then in the region more broadly. Initially, he may have hoped that the Jews of Medina would accept his monotheistic divine revelations. The **Qur'an**, Islam's sacred scriptures based on the revelations of Muhammad, clearly identifies Allah as the God of Abraham—and in theory, therefore, as the God of the Jews. If Muhammed had such hopes, however, they were largely disappointed. At least some of the Jews of Medina belonged to factions that opposed the growing power of Muhammad and his followers. He expelled two of the largest Jewish clans from the city, and in 627 accused the Jewish Banu Qurayza clan of conspiring with his enemies; many were killed.

Despite these inauspicious beginnings, however, Jews living under Islam on average enjoyed a greater degree of security than they usually found in Christendom. The Qur'an distinguished Muslims from non-Muslims, but also distinguished between groups of non-Muslims. Christians and Jews—the practitioners of other monotheistic Abrahamic faiths with sacred scriptures—were described as believers in a shared God and eligible for reward in the world to come. The Qur'an also emphasized the principle that "there is no compulsion in matters of faith."

Islam, like Christianity and Judaism, was an exclusive monotheistic faith, and the Qur'an also included passages critical of Christians and Jews. However, the Qur'anic idea that Jews and Christians were inferior to Muslims but superior to polytheists justified the legal category of *dhimmi*. The word *dhimmi* literally meant "protected people," and those included in this category had the right to live under Islam insofar as they accepted certain conditions that highlighted their inferior status. Many of these rules are outlined in a text called the Pact of 'Umar. Jews and Christians were forbidden to hold public religious ceremonies and processions, proselytize, dress in certain items of clothing characteristic of Muslims, hold positions that gave them authority over Muslims, or build homes or houses of worship taller than those of Muslims.

These restrictions represented meaningful limitations on the everyday lives of Jews and Christians, just as similar restrictions shaped the options available to Jews living in Christendom. However, the clear scriptural justification for the toleration of religious minorities helps to explain why massacres, forced conversions, and expulsions of Jews happened less often under Islamic rule than under Christian rule (although they did still happen occasionally under Islam). Religiously motivated anti-Judaism and anti-Christianity undoubtedly existed. For example, medieval Muslim religious polemics denigrated Jews for respecting Jesus (whom Muslims recognized as a prophet) too little and Christians for respecting him too much. However, the fact that Jesus was a prophet, not a deity, meant that the perception of Jews as Christ-killers was far less theologically significant for Muslims than for Christians. Moreover, economic anti-Judaism was seemingly non-existent in the Islamic world. Islam had a less negative attitude than Christianity toward money and materiality, and hence Muslims did not need to divorce themselves from the realities of credit and business by mentally associating them with Jews and Judaism.

The Islamic world was wide and diverse. Muhammad's followers and their descendants accomplished a series of conquests that would ultimately bring the entire Sassanian Empire under Muslim rule and dramatically shrink the territorial base of the Eastern Roman Empire. Muslim forces under the ruling Umayyad dynasty would also establish control in North Africa and in the Iberian Peninsula. Muslim rule over some portions of what is now Spain lasted until the end of the fifteenth century. The territory under Muslim authority was referred to collectively as the **dar-al-Islam** ("abode of Islam"), in contrast with lands not under Muslim rule, which were referred to as the **dar-al-harb** ("abode of war"). These lands, and the people who lived in them, were subject to different rules; for example, *dhimmi* in the dar-al-Islam were protected, but *dhimmi* in the dar-al-harb could be enslaved if captured. By the middle of the eighth century, the majority of the world's Jewish population lived within the dar-al-Islam.

Initially, all Islamic-ruled lands were under the authority of a figure known as the **caliph**. The word literally means "successor," reflecting the fact that the caliph was understood as the successor to Muhammad. However, in such a far-flung empire, daily affairs were often left in the hands of local governors. Moreover, from the tenth century onward, the Islamic world became increasingly fragmented. The caliphs of the Abbasid dynasty faced myriad challenges in their attempts to maintain meaningful control over their lands. The survivors of the Umayyad dynasty, who had established a new base in the Iberian Peninsula, and the Shi'ite Fatimid dynasty, based in north Africa, even declared independent caliphates.

Different Muslim rulers, like their Christian counterparts, made different choices about how to treat protected yet subordinated *dhimmi* populations. In some places, enforcement of even the traditional restrictions proved lax. In al-Andalus, the areas of the Iberian Peninsula under Muslim rule, Jews and Christians rose to administrative and military positions that in practice gave them power over Muslims. Under both the Abbasid caliphate centered on Baghdad and the Fatimid caliphate with its capital in Cairo, the leader of the caliphate's Jewish community received formal authority from the caliph. Although he did not officially exert power over Muslims, contemporary sources indicate that Muslims treated these Jewish leaders with respect in recognition of their status as elites with close ties to the caliph.

Jews were also deeply integrated into local cultures in the Islamic world. The most obvious examples of this integration can be found in high culture. Jewish poets in al-Andalus created Hebrew poetic forms and meters that drew on the traditions of Arabic poetry and wrote poems on the same popular themes, including seemingly transgressive topics like sex and drinking. Jewish philosophers adapted Arabic terminology and shared an interest in Aristotelian philosophy. The philosopher and rabbi **Maimonides** even wrote his most famous philosophical work, *The Guide for the Perplexed*, in Arabic. Synagogues built and manuscripts illuminated in Muslim lands reveal that Jews and Muslims in Islamic lands shared a distinctly local visual culture. Only male elites could fully benefit from the political, social, and cultural opportunities afforded to them. Lower-status Jewish men, and Jewish women of all social strata, rarely participated directly in high culture, at least not in ways visible to us in our sources. However, cultural integration also shaped the lives of women. Jewish women often had Arabic rather than Hebrew names, felt comfortable turning to Islamic courts to pursue justice, and communicated with members of their community in Arabic vernaculars.

However, integration and opportunity were far from the whole story of Jewish life in the Islamic world—just as a narrative of persecution fails to tell the whole story of the lives of Jews in Christian Europe. Simmering tensions could potentially devolve into catastrophe. A Jewish advisor to an eleventh-century sultan of Granada was murdered, allegedly due to his lack of humility about his elevated position. The assassination devolved into a massacre of the Jewish community of Granada. The Almohads of North Africa, who also annexed al-Andalus, made the unusual choice to rescind toleration of the *dhimmi* population. Maimonides, the philosopher and rabbi mentioned above, left al-Andalus as a child after the Almohads arrived; he would eventually resettle in Egypt. Religious polemics also highlight the tensions between Jews and Muslims.

Despite the very real challenges and restrictions experienced by Jews living in the dar-al-Islam, the surviving documentation suggests that medieval Jewish communities in Islamic lands benefited from a greater degree of continuity and security than under Christian rule. Jewish life was characterized by fewer disruptions; expulsions and massacres occurred less frequently. The expulsions of the late Middle Ages in Christian Europe would also contribute to the growth of the Jewish population in Islamic lands. Jewish refugees from the Iberian Peninsula scattered widely in the wake of the 1492 expulsion, but the Ottoman Empire became a major destination. Iberian Jews settled in places like Constantinople, Salonika, and Ottoman Palestine. In the early modern period, the city of Safed would become a major center of Jewish mysticism.

Conclusion

Jewish life in the medieval world was complex and multifaceted. On the one hand, Jews occupied a subordinate legal position under the authority of both Christian and Muslim rulers, and at times confronted persecution. On the other hand, Jewish communities were deeply integrated into the surrounding societies. We can see medieval Jews as in many ways sharing a common culture with the people around them. Differences between Jewish communities reflect both divergent responses to local circumstances and the cultural norms they shared with their Christian and Muslim neighbors.

This chapter has mostly referred in very general terms to the Jewish community as a whole. However, it was not only local and regional differences that shaped Jewish lives. Elite Jews had a very different experience from those living on the margins of their community or in poverty. The daily lives of Jewish artisans, rabbis, farmers, and moneylenders could vary substantially. However, as will be the focus of the remainder of this book, one of the most central factors that shaped the lives of medieval people was gender. Jewish women shared in many of the trials and tribulations of their community, as well as its triumphs and comforts. Yet they also had fundamentally distinct experiences of Jewish faith, family, and community life. It is to those experiences that this work will now turn.

3   Gender roles in medieval Jewish cultures

When his wife **Dolce** was murdered in 1196, **Rabbi Eleazar of Worms** eulogized her as an exemplar of what a Jewish wife should be like [*Doc. 1, pp. 118–119*]. He described how her work supported their family, enabled him and his students to study Torah, and contributed to charity. Dolce was clearly religiously knowledgeable, but she also played a distinct role from that of her learned husband. Eleazar praised his wife for activities like religious observance, support for education, and financially profitable labor—qualities and activities that could be considered admirable for men and women alike. However, throughout the text Eleazar tacitly distinguished between one major aspect of the religious observance of men and women. Men like Eleazar and his students engaged in intense study of the Hebrew Bible and Jewish learning. Women like Dolce did not participate directly in such intellectual exploration. Dolce only facilitated it through her performance of tasks like binding books and cooking for scholars. Even more strikingly, Eleazar also concluded his lament by praising his late wife for her obedience and docility: "She was happy to do the will of her husband and never angered him" (Baskin 2001: 432, 436).

Eleazar's idea of what made an ideal wife was not necessarily shared by all medieval Jews, especially those who lived far from his home city of Worms. In the prose version of his lament for Dolce, for example, Eleazar specifically praised his wife for her profitable moneylending (Baskin 2001: 434). However, as will be discussed in Chapter 7, such work might not have been considered normal—and certainly not the ideal—for most Jewish women in other regions. Nor was Eleazar's idea of what made a woman an ideal wife necessarily exclusively Jewish. Medieval Christian and Muslim men also praised the women of their faiths for piety, charity, effective household management, and obedience.

Jewish ideas about gender were shaped both by their own legal and religious traditions and by their local contexts. As a result, medieval Jewish communities in some ways resembled one another but in other ways differed substantially. Jewish communities might share many ideas about gender with the Christians and Muslims around them, but they also developed distinct

DOI: 10.4324/9781003104964-5

legal and cultural norms, which served to emphasize their Jewish identity. This chapter will explore how different Jewish communities in the medieval world constructed gender roles, for men as well as for women. What made someone an ideal husband or wife? How did Jewish communities respond to men and women who failed to meet social expectations for their gender? How did Jewish men and women maneuver within gendered norms?

Religious roles and expectations for Jewish men

Most of our textual evidence for medieval Jewish life, especially in the realm of religious practice, was authored by rabbis, all of whom were highly educated men. Rabbis belonged to the intellectual and sometimes also economic elite of their communities. Given that rabbis wrote most medieval Jewish texts, it is hardly surprising that the ideal Jew envisioned in these texts was someone very much like the rabbis themselves.

The rabbis introduced a distinction between free, adult men, who were obligated to fulfill all commandments or **mitzvot,** and those who were not subject to all such obligations: women, enslaved people, and children. The choice to group free, adult Jewish women with unfree non-Jews and children could certainly be considered insulting. Regardless, it undoubtedly left Jewish women with a fundamentally different religious role from that expected of Jewish men. As I will discuss in more detail in the following section, women were exempted from a wide range of commandments. Only Jewish men were required to observe all 613 of the commandments traditionally considered to be prescribed in the Torah. As a result, only men could participate in Jewish religious life to the fullest extent. Often, Jewish men appear in pre-modern religious texts as what some scholars call an "unmarked category"—one that is designated as the default. In other words, adult Jewish men were treated as the default for Jewish religious observance, whereas women were exceptional and, arguably, less fully integrated into Jewish religious life.

Although undoubtedly some Jewish boys and men from poor families lacked the opportunity to pursue an education, rabbinic authorities considered the study of Torah to be a crucial part of Jewish men's religious role. The Mishnah obligated fathers to either teach their sons Torah themselves or to find someone to teach their sons on their behalf (Marcus 1996: 41). Although the rabbis understood that praiseworthy Jewish men could and did pursue other careers, they considered men like themselves who were invested full-time in studying Torah and teaching it to others to be particularly meritorious.

The emphasis on Torah study as the highest obligation for Jewish men allowed some rabbis to explicitly prioritize it over other social obligations. Unlike their Christian contemporaries, Jewish intellectuals considered marriage, not celibacy, to be the norm, and read the biblical injunction to "be fruitful and multiply" (Genesis 1:28) as a commandment to procreate. The vast majority of rabbis were married and had children. However, the Talmud also portrayed an alternative path by including the story of Ben-Azzai, a rabbi who used the language of lust and desire to claim that his devotion to Torah study made it impossible for him to marry (Boyarin 1993: 135). While the text presented Ben-Azzai as an outlier, it also reflected a real tension between the religious ideal of complete devotion to Torah study, on the one hand, and Jewish men's obligation to marry and have a family, on the other hand.

Maimonides still expected Torah scholars to marry but stated that they were only required to have sex with their wives once per week, because the study of Torah "exhausts their strength" [*Doc. 11, pp. 128–129*]. In contrast, healthy men engaged in less onerous labor were expected to fulfill their conjugal duty nightly. Maimonides considered work like weaving and construction to be less demanding than Torah study; men who practiced such professions should have sex with their wives twice per week. Especially in northern Europe, men's dedication to Torah study may have created expanded economic roles for women, who served as the breadwinners of the household while their husbands studied Torah full-time (Baskin 1998b: 114).

Jewish texts also constructed the ideal Jewish body as a male one, as only men could fulfill in their bodies the command of circumcision. According to the biblical book of Genesis, God commanded Abraham to circumcise himself and all the men of his household, and to subsequently circumcise all males at the age of eight days (Genesis 17:10–14). The biblical text portrayed circumcision as a crucial symbol of the Israelites' covenant with God. In the Middle Ages, circumcision was an important symbol of Jewish identity. Only the bodies of Jewish men, however, were transformed with a physical marker of Jews' special relationship with God.

Medieval rabbis interpreted the non-circumcision of Jewish women in a variety of ways. Some, for example, claimed that Jewish women did not need to be circumcised because they were subject to the authority of their circumcised husbands and fathers (Cohen 2005: 112–114). On the one hand, rabbis still typically considered women to be part of the covenant despite not being marked by circumcision. On the other hand, as the scholar Shaye Cohen has argued, the lack of a physical marker on the bodies of Jewish women could signify that "the Jewishness of women is of a lesser kind than the Jewishness of men" (Cohen 2005: 111). Regardless of interpretation, only Jewish men carried in their bodies a permanent symbol of their relationship with God and their identity as Jews.

Religious roles and expectations for Jewish women

Rabbis perceived the scope of Jewish women's religious observance as narrower than that of Jewish men. Women were exempted from those commandments designated both as "positive," meaning that they were expressed in the language of what one *should* do rather than what one *should not* do, and as "time-bound," meaning that they were meant to be performed at a specific time. The category of positive, time-bound commandments included an array of *mitzvot* crucial to Jewish life, including hearing the blowing of the ram's horn (*shofar*) on the Jewish New Year (Rosh Hashanah) and putting on phylacteries (*tefillin*) when praying. On the one hand, exemption does not necessarily mean the same thing as exclusion. In Ashkenaz, rabbis increasingly praised women who chose to perform and recite blessings when they performed positive time-bound commandments. In other regions, however, women sometimes were discouraged from performing commandments from which they were exempted. Some rabbis in Sepharad, in contrast to their colleagues in Ashkenaz, criticized women for reciting blessings when they performed positive time-bound commandments. Women were also actively excluded in all regions from public reading from the Torah and from leading men or mixed groups in prayer, although they could lead groups of women in prayer (Grossman 2004: 175–180).

Women's exemptions from certain commandments might have been intended to reflect the fact that their domestic responsibilities, especially childcare, could make it difficult for them to prioritize the active performance of commandments at a particular time. Negative commandments did not raise the same issues. While it might be difficult for women to participate in communal rituals held at specific times, they could certainly both care for children and refrain from consuming leavened bread on Passover, for example.

However, women's exemption from many forms of religious observance undoubtedly affected how both men and women perceived women's Jewishness. Some medieval rabbis debated whether women were truly part of Israel, due to these exemptions. Jewish men daily recited a prayer in which they thanked God for not making them a non-Jew, a slave, or a woman (Cohen 2005: 124–125). The religious role of women was certainly distinct from that of men, and many people—perhaps women as well as men—almost certainly perceived it as less than a full ideal expression of Jewishness.

The very first depiction of a woman in the Hebrew Bible—Eve—both reflected and contributed to misogynist ideas about women that played an important role in both Judaism and Christianity, and to some extent in Islam as well. The book of Genesis contains two different stories about the creation of humankind. In the first version, God simultaneously created a man and a woman: "male and female He created them" (Genesis 1:27). In the second version, God first created man, Adam, and then subsequently created a woman, Eve, out of Adam's rib (Genesis 2:21–24). The rabbis reading the Hebrew Bible in Late Antiquity and the Middle Ages saw these two stories as carrying divinely imparted meanings about the intended role of women. According to one interpretation, first found in a

midrash written sometime between 700 and 1000 CE, the two versions tell two different stories [*Doc. 2, pp. 119–120*]. God first created both a man and woman out of the earth, but this woman, who was named Lilith, immediately began to fight with Adam about who would lie on top during sex. Lilith then fled and became a baby-killing demon, in what is perhaps an overly literal demonization of women with sexual agency. Even before the Lilith midrash became popularized, rabbis understood Eve's creation from Adam's rib as a sign of both women's fundamental difference from men and their subordinate status, as beings created to fulfill men's needs (Baskin 2002: 1–2).

Eve, according to the narrative in Genesis, succumbed to temptation from the snake, consumed the fruit forbidden by God, and then convinced Adam to do the same (Genesis 3:1–7). Rabbinic interpretations of the Bible typically blamed Eve for bringing sin and pain into the world. Both the account in Genesis and later rabbinic interpretations justified the subordination of women to men as part of the punishment imposed on Eve: "Yet your desire shall be for your husband, and he shall rule over you" (Genesis 3:16).

Even the special commandments associated particularly with women, according to a midrash that appeared in a text called *Genesis Rabbah* (c. 300–500 CE), were sometimes interpreted as designed to atone for the sin of Eve. The three commandments specially designated as women's commandments were the observance of the menstrual purity laws, the separation of a piece of dough when baking, and the lighting of candles on the eve of the Sabbath. The midrash explained that women had to shed blood and observe the laws of menstruation because Eve had shed the blood of Adam, making it possible for him to die. Women had to separate the dough, because Eve had corrupted Adam, who was the "dough of the world." Women had to light candles because Eve had extinguished the light of Adam's soul (Baskin 2002: 66).

Even if Jewish men and women did not all accept the interpretation linking women's commandments to the sin of Eve, these three commandments offer other important insights into the perceived religious role of women. Two were clearly domestic, highlighting the fact that the religious role of women was largely centered on the creation and maintenance of a Jewish domestic space rather than on public ritual engagement with the wider Jewish community. The third commandment—the laws of *niddah*, the purification from menstrual impurity—focused on women's bodies and their sexuality. The Hebrew Bible discusses various forms of ritual impurity, all of which required purification before a person could go to the Temple. However, most such practices surrounding ritual purity lost their importance after the destruction of the Temple in 70 CE. Women's impurity, incurred by both menstruation and childbirth, remained important because it determined whether they were sexually available to men. Sex with a menstruating woman was strictly forbidden; women were therefore required to purify themselves before they could have sex with their husbands. Unmarried women were not expected to purify themselves after menstruation, as they were assumed not to be sexually active. The laws of *niddah* therefore mattered mostly for women's relationship with men; impurity did not necessarily have practical religious implications. This commandment, too, was therefore closely linked to women's domestic, wifely role.

Despite the distinct and arguably lesser religious role envisioned for Jewish women, rabbinic sources nonetheless indicate that male religious elites acknowledged and praised women's piety. Biblical narratives offered myriad examples of illustrious pious women, some of whom, medieval rabbis suggested, could serve as models for real-life Jewish women. As will be discussed in future chapters, medieval Jewish women demonstrated their own adherence to their faith and their people through prayer, charity, support of their households, and even the embrace of martyrdom.

The social and familial role of Jewish men

Rabbi Moses ben Maimon, otherwise known as Maimonides, was a Jewish communal leader, rabbinic scholar, and philosopher active in Egypt in the late twelfth and early thirteenth centuries. In one particularly intriguing case, Maimonides authored two separate responsa related to a single marital dispute [*Docs. 3–4, pp. 120–123*]. His two answers are very brief; what is especially fascinating, as is sometimes the case with responsa, is not the rulings Maimonides made, but the two different questions he received. One query appears to represent the husband's perspective; the other presents the wife's perspective. The questions that open responsa often at least briefly identify the positions taken by both sides, so that the rabbinic addressee, and the reader, have a clear sense of the nature of the dispute. Yet responsa very rarely offer such deep insight into both perspectives in a family conflict. The two perspectives offer slightly divergent interpretations of the events that precipitated the decline of their marriage and the reasons behind their current conflict (Melammed 1997: 27–28).

This pair of responsa still obscure some details; for example, we do not know the names of either the husband or the wife. However, they provide a valuable source for how ordinary people perceived the appropriate social and familial roles of Jewish men and women in medieval Egypt. Both the husband and the wife carefully crafted queries in which they worked to portray their spouse as failing to live up to a set of gendered expectations and responsibilities toward their household and family. This strategy was not unique. Scholars have found examples from across the medieval world of Jewish, Christian, and Muslim women who attempted to use ideas about gender to their advantage in order to secure favorable legal outcomes. Social and legal structures, including court systems, were rooted in gender inequality. Women could not count on support from the men dispensing justice, especially when they fought in court against their own husbands. Many women therefore sought to garner sympathy with narratives of events that upheld men's assumptions about women's vulnerability, while casting their husbands or male relatives as having failed to adequately support them. The stories that this husband and wife told about one another's gendered failings offer insight into how medieval Jews thought husbands and wives should behave. Maimonides' responses show us how a medieval rabbi might attempt to intervene in family conflicts to promote solutions that accorded with both *halakhah* (Jewish law) and his own understanding of gender roles.

The two questions allow us to ascertain a few facts on which the couple agreed. The couple had been married for many years, and the wife at least had been quite young at the time of their marriage. The husband traveled regularly, on some combination of personal and business reasons, with the result that he was away from home for long periods of time. In his absence, the wife began to teach Torah to children, first assisting her brother and then maintaining the school independently. The husband, upon his return, resented the fact that his wife's trade required her to spend a significant amount of time away from home, and was uncomfortable with the ways in which her work required her to interact with other men, namely her students' fathers. He asked for her to stop teaching; she refused. Divorce might have been an easy solution, but he was reluctant to divorce his wife for economic reasons. The husband would have been satisfied with marrying a second wife, whom he presumed would prove more obedient, but his wife refused to grant permission.

The version sent on the wife's behalf emphasized a major failing on the part of her husband: he was unable or unwilling to support her and their children financially. The letter at multiple points emphasized the depth of her poverty. The woman and her children appear to have lived for years on the brink of starvation. She even alleged that her husband deliberately abandoned his family and left them with no support because he was aware of his own inability to provide for them appropriately. These details highlighted the general importance of men's social and familial obligation to provide for their wife and children, and the failure of this specific man to do so effectively (Melammed 1997: 30–31). We should note that the wife did not justify her work as a teacher on the grounds that it was a fulfilling or meaningful activity, or a service to the children of her community. Instead, she argued that her work was the only way she could ensure her own and her children's security and survival, due to her husband's failure to live up to his gendered role.

These responsa tell us what ordinary people thought gender roles should look like. In his legal code, the *Mishneh Torah*, Maimonides outlined his understanding of what *halakhah* dictated about the obligations a man owed to his wife and children [*Doc. 5, pp. 123–124*]. He was particularly concerned with husbands' economic responsibilities. The woman teacher, or someone who worked with her to craft the letter, was probably very much aware of *halakhic* expectations in this area. Biblical and rabbinic texts together specified ten obligations that men incurred toward their wives. All but one required some amount of financial support. Men had to provide their wives with basic needs: food, drink, clothing. They also had to provide medical treatment in case of illness, redeem her if she was taken captive, and bury her if she predeceased him. All these forms of care cost money, although families could seek charitable assistance.

A husband needed to use his own financial resources to support his wife not only during his lifetime, but even after death, if he predeceased her. Widows had the right to remain in their husbands' homes and receive maintenance from their estates unless they remarried. When a man got married, he also committed to support any children that he and his wife might have. Daughters were entitled to maintenance from their fathers' estates until they married, and sons were entitled to receive an inheritance from both parents. If a man proved unable or unwilling to support his wife financially, he was even obligated to divorce her. The only non-financially based obligation Maimonides identified in this list was the requirement that a husband have sexual intercourse with his wife.

Together, these two texts suggest that Maimonides ascribed a great deal of importance to a man's obligation to support his family. Many other medieval rabbis would have agreed that this was a crucial part of the role of a husband and father, and at least the bare minimum he owed his wife and children. However, there were also social and even emotional aspects to a man's gendered role within the family. Men were obligated to have sex with their wives; a man who refused to do so could be compelled to divorce his wife. Rabbinic texts also encouraged men to consider their wives' sexual pleasure. Fathers not only bore the responsibility to support their children financially, but also to sustain them intellectually and prepare them for adulthood by teaching them Torah and a trade.

The social and familial role of Jewish women

Jewish families and communities varied in the particulars of how they constructed the social and familial role envisioned for Jewish women. Much like their Christian and Muslim counterparts, Jewish male elites tended to assume that women should ideally be subservient to their husbands or fathers. They also usually prized traits like modesty and devotion to family. However, ideas about what constituted modest behavior and how best women should serve their households and families varied, not only across regions but also even between families.

The responsa discussed above offer an intriguing starting point for our discussion of the role of the wife as well as that of the husband. Just as the wife attempted to secure a favorable ruling by describing her husband as failing to live up to his gendered role as a husband and father, so her husband claimed that her behavior did not conform to gendered expectations for wives. First, he complained that her conduct was inappropriate. During her work teaching children, she could come into contact with their fathers, adult men from outside her family. He described such contact as putting her in an "embarrassing position" [*Doc. 4, pp. 122–123*]. Although Maimonides did not explicitly agree with the husband on this point, he did confirm that as her husband he had the right to prevent her from teaching and that the courts should support him in this endeavor.

Based on the efforts made by this husband to portray his wife's work as at least bordering on immodest, we might assume that Jewish men preferred the women of their families to avoid participating in work that involved frequent contact with men, especially without a husband or male relative present. However, although Maimonides upheld the husband's right to keep his wife from teaching, he did not overtly characterize her work as inappropriate—only her failure to obey her husband's wishes presented a problem. His response to the wife, moreover, suggests that if she were divorced, he would have no objection to her continuing to work as a teacher (Melammed 1997: 32–34). The much more significant problem, from Maimonides' perspective, was the wife's disobedience.

Most Jewish men and women, along with the Muslims and Christians among whom they lived, would have taken for granted the assumption that women were subordinate to their husbands and obligated to obey their wishes. Maimonides' response to the husband's query demonstrates his concern about the wife's inappropriate unwillingness to acquiesce to her husband's wishes. He states that "all doors are locked before her and all paths are to be obstructed, and her affairs will be delayed for as long as it takes until she withdraws and agrees to behave properly toward her husband" [*Doc. 4, p. 123*]. This ruling certainly demonstrates that he had little sympathy for women who refused to obey their husbands—although his response to the wife was rather more sympathetic, probably because she made it clear that her disobedience was a matter of financial necessity.

Overall, proper wifely behavior, for Maimonides, did not necessarily constitute a specific or universal set of actions, but merely obedience to the husband. Plenty of Jewish men expressed no concern about women working outside the home in fields that required contact with men outside their family. Eleazar of Worms even praised his wife Dolce for work in moneylending, which almost certainly would require contact with Christian men. Some rabbis in Ashkenaz indicated that it was normal for women to enter business partnerships with non-related men and to travel on business (Grossman 2004: 118–119). Women in Catalonia and southern France were less economically active than their counterparts in Ashkenaz, but there are enough examples of Jewish women working in fields like credit and real estate that clearly some families considered it acceptable for women to perform work that brought them into contact with men, including men from outside not only their family but also their community. Husband and wives also operated joint businesses in fields like silk weaving (Ifft Decker 2015: 62).

Although women could work outside the home and some families might even have encouraged them to do so, wives' obligations to their husbands reflected the assumption that the husband would manage his wife's wealth and provide for her financially in return [*Doc. 5, pp. 123–124*]. The wife was expected to give her husband her earnings from any work she performed, as well as any object of value she found. He also had the right to benefit from all her property during his lifetime—even including wealth inherited beyond what she brought as **dowry**—and to inherit from her if she predeceased him. In contrast, wives did not have any formal right to inherit from their husbands. Even if women worked, they were expected to hand over their earnings to their husband.

The husband's query also highlights another aspect of women's social and familial role: the performance of expected household duties. He referred to various specific activities, including kneading bread; cooking; making the bed; otherwise cleaning the house; doing laundry; and caring for their children. Women of all faiths who belonged to poorer households could expect to perform this litany of housework. Wealthier families, in contrast, might have delegated many of these tasks to servants. Indeed, since his wife would not permit him to take a second wife, the husband's first solution was to hire a servant. However, given what we know from both letters about this couple's finances, hiring household labor might have represented a significant drain on their household resources.

It is unclear precisely what work the husband portrayed in these letters did outside the home, given that he does not seem to have earned much of an income. Despite his apparent lack of consistent employment, neither the husband, his wife, nor Maimonides raise the possibility that he might perform these household tasks himself. Work like this was expected only of women, or perhaps of enslaved people. Even in wealthy households, women were praised for voluntarily engaging in such domestic tasks. Eleazar of Worms and his family almost certainly could have afforded to hire servants. However, he described his wife as cooking and sewing. In Dolce's case, these domestic responsibilities functioned as an aspect of her piety. Her cooking fed Torah scholars and fueled communal feasts. Her sewing repaired not only clothing, but also books, Torah scrolls, and phylacteries. Christian writers similarly praised women from wealthy families who still chose to perform household duties like cooking, sewing, spinning, and childcare.

Non-Jewish perceptions of Jewish women

As we have already seen, and will see in future chapters, Jewish women played a somewhat marginal role in religious life and at least theoretically a subordinate one in Jewish families. Yet the men of their community nevertheless praised Jewish women for their piety and devotion to their people. In contrast, medieval Christian and Muslim perceptions of Jewish women often suggested that they were less deeply invested in their faith than were Jewish men.

The *Cantigas de Santa Maria*, a richly illustrated set of poems about miracles of the Virgin Mary from thirteenth-century Castile, are populated with imagined Jews and Muslims. Many of the non-Christians in the *Cantigas* are foiled by the Virgin Mary in their plots to harm Christians and Christianity. Some, in contrast, are rescued from danger and converted to Christianity, assuring their salvation. The visual and textual representations of Jewish men and women in the *Cantigas* offer a striking contrast. Jewish men were normally cast as villains, who cheated Christian merchants, desecrated images of the Virgin, and even slaughtered their own children rather than risk losing them to Christianity. Jewish women, in contrast, typically play a far more passive role in the *Cantigas*. Many demonstrate an openness to Christianity and ultimately convert.

The story of the Jewish woman in childbirth (Figure 3.1) offers an excellent example of how medieval Christians imagined Jewish women's supposed religious flexibility. During a difficult childbirth, the Jewish woman—portrayed in the first few panels as heavily pregnant—prayed to the Virgin Mary while in pain. She then safely delivered a healthy infant, which the *cantiga* portrays as a miracle of the Virgin. In the last panel, the Jewish mother and her two children appear together in the baptismal font. Thanks to the intervention of the Virgin, she is brought into the fold of Christianity. The fate envisioned for Jewish women in the *Cantigas* is frequently conversion and salvation; in contrast, the fate most often envisioned for Jewish men is suffering and death.

Their ultimate fates are not the only difference between Jewish men and women in the *Cantigas*. An array of visual signs physically distinguished Jewish men from Christian men: prominent noses, slightly darkened skin color, pointed hats. In contrast, only context clues differentiated Jewish women from Christian women. The pregnant Jewish woman has the same skin tone as the Christian women featured in the manuscript, along with similar facial features and indistinctive clothing and headgear. Historian Sara Lipton argues that the manuscript portrayed Jewish women as physically similar to Christian women and as ideal candidates for conversion because of prevalent gender ideologies. Contemporary rhetoric often described women as weak, vulnerable, and inconstant—in other words, the kind of people who might convert (Lipton 2008: 156–157). Additionally, Christians represented Jewish men as the quintessential Jewish enemy, as contrasts to their own male intellectuals. At least in fiction, Christians could imagine Jewish women as people who might be more easily integrated into the fabric of Christian society if they chose to convert. The character of Jessica in William Shakespeare's *The Merchant of Venice* exemplified similar attitudes. Jessica was the daughter of the Jewish moneylender

Figure 3.1 Cantigas de Santa Maria, Castile, 13th century, Cantiga 89, Jewish
Woman in Labor © Heritage Image Partnership Ltd/Alamy Stock Photo.

Shylock but is consistently described as thoroughly unlike her father. Her
pliable femininity made her voluntary embrace of Christianity (and of her
Christian lover Lorenzo) more plausible.

Islamic law also presumed that Jewish and Christian women were
more tractable than the men of their faith. On the grounds that women,
by nature, would be subject to and influenced by their husbands, Muslim
men could marry *dhimmi* women. The reverse, however, was forbidden: a
Muslim woman could never marry a Jewish or Christian man. However,
Muslim jurists were nevertheless aware that, in practice, such marriages
created important personal and social connections, and *dhimmi* women
could prove influential (Safran 2013: 132–133).

Outside of rhetoric and representation and on real medieval city streets, neither Jewish men nor women were so easy to distinguish from members of the ruling faith. Jews usually dressed much like the Christians or Muslims around them. The Pact of 'Umar banned Jews and Christians from wearing certain items of clothing associated with Arab Muslim elites in an effort to create visual boundaries between Muslims and non-Muslims. In 1215, the Fourth Lateran Council, a Church council presided over by Pope **Innocent III**, mandated that Jews and Muslims wear a distinguishing item of clothing or badge to differentiate them from Christians. Allegedly, this rule was necessary because Christians were "accidentally" having sex with Jews and Muslims, because they assumed they were Christian.

The Church did not actually have the power to impose this requirement on Jews directly, but Innocent and some of his successors encouraged local rulers to pass laws that would inflict a distinguishing marker on Jews. Jewish women, like Jewish men, were in some places required to wear distinctive cloaks, overskirts, or badges, often a yellow or red circle or a representation of the tablets of the Ten Commandments. In some cities in Italy, a specific regulation was passed for Jewish women: both Jewish women and prostitutes were required to wear earrings (Hughes 1986: 22).

The connection to prostitutes might have served to link Jews with the sin of lust (Hughes 1986: 24–25). Medieval Christians also imagined Jewish women as dangerously seductive figures. Several Castilian chronicles claimed that King Alfonso VIII of Castile was seduced through a combination of beauty and magic by a "Jewess of Toledo." The story may in part have served to criticize kings who showed too much favor to Jews (Nirenberg 2007: 16–17, 25). Polish legends claimed that King Casimir the Great issued generous privileges to the Jews out of love for his Jewish mistress Estherke. These stories used sexualized representations of Jewish women to explain why some rulers showed favor to Jews. Many of these women might have been more legendary than real, but they reveal another facet of how Jewish women might be perceived by non-Jews.

Conclusion

Medieval Jews, Christians, and Muslims all shared a few fundamental gendered assumptions about women. Intellectual elites of all three faiths promoted the obedience and subordination of women to their fathers and husbands. They often saw women as intellectually and spiritually inferior to men. They might not oppose women working outside the home, but they nevertheless emphasized women's dedication to domestic work and childcare.

However, some aspects of gendered roles differed across faiths and between regions. Jewish men in Ashkenaz praised women who earned money outside the home; Jewish men in Sepharad and in the Islamic East were more ambivalent about such work. All three faith communities had few formal religious roles for women and used the example of the sin of Eve to justify misogynistic assumptions. Judaism and Islam, however, never developed anything quite like Christian nunneries, which opened some opportunities for women to embrace spiritual life professionally. On the other hand, neither Judaism nor Islam promoted celibacy, an ideology which could easily devolve into misogyny. Gendered roles and expectations affected men as well as women. Jewish men were expected to provide financially for their families. If they failed to do so, they could receive communal censure and even be forced to divorce their wives.

4 Marriage, divorce, and widowhood

On August 20, 1325, Reina, daughter of Bonjueu Cresques of Girona, and her new husband Saltell Gracià, son of Bonjueu Saltell of Barcelona, participated in a set of agreements designed to supplement the marriage contract they had signed back in the beginning of July [*Doc. 6, pp. 124–126*]. Their marriage tied together two elite Jewish families from two different cities in the same kingdom, located about 100 kilometers apart. The references to money and property throughout the documents indicate that both families were wealthy; additional documentary evidence corroborates this impression. Saltell received from his father a grant of a large urban estate. Reina brought to her marriage a **dowry** valued at 1,000 gold maravedis, over three times the size of the average dowry brought by the Christian women of her city (Ifft Decker 2019a: 492). Both cities were part of the region of Catalonia, in the northeastern Iberian Peninsula, and the political entity known as the Crown of Aragon, a federative monarchy that brought together much of the eastern Iberian Peninsula as well as parts of what are now southern France, Italy, and Greece. Although the young couple might not have known one another very long before they got married, they would have shared a common language and grown up under the same legal and political structures.

The group of contracts signed by Reina, Saltell, and their families tells us a great deal about how elite Jewish families negotiated the marriages that created important social, economic, and political alliances between families and communities. This specific set of contracts is also significant because it highlights the nature of Jewish marriage as both distinctively Jewish and as shaped by the norms of the people around them. Reina and Saltell first married with a *ketubah*, a contract written in a combination of Hebrew and Aramaic in accordance with Jewish law and custom. While the *ketubah* has not survived, Reina and Saltell referred to it when they signed these additional contracts, written in Latin and drawn up by a local Christian **notary**, an urban public official. Reina, Saltell, and their families did not make any choices incompatible with Jewish law when they signed these contracts. They appear to have merely confirmed arrangements already

DOI: 10.4324/9781003104964-6

made in contracts drawn up in accordance with the norms of *halakhah*. However, the choice to secure their financial arrangements in Latin as well as Hebrew, in accordance with the legal norms of the Christian majority as well as that of their own community, reflects the ways in which even something as personal and as intra-faith as marriage can reveal the relationship of Jews in general, and Jewish women in particular, with the non-Jewish communities around them.

Marriage mattered deeply in the everyday lives of Jewish women across the medieval world. Getting married irrevocably transformed a woman's status. Unmarried daughters, wives, divorcées, and widows had distinct communal, economic, familial, and religious roles. As we have already seen in the previous chapter, much of a woman's expected social role centered around her relationship with her husband, and virtually all Jewish women expected to marry.

Some Jewish marriage customs had their origins in the sacred texts of the Bible and Talmud. But medieval Jewish marriage also reflected an array of local circumstances, including cultural exchange and engagement with Christians and Muslims, and therefore differed from place to place. This chapter will explore how and under what circumstances Jewish couples married, and some of the ways in which marriage shaped women's lives. It will also address how the dissolution of marriages—through divorce or widowhood—affected Jewish women. This chapter is not meant to be exhaustive. Marriage was a fundamental part of women's lives and of medieval Jewish understandings of gender roles; as such, discussion of marriage, married life, and marital status will be interwoven throughout the book. However, this chapter will provide a crucial basis for the reader to understand some of the basics about what made a marriage and what, at least in theory, a Jewish woman in the medieval world might expect married life to look like.

Age at first marriage

Scholars of the medieval world very rarely have the demographic data that we would need to answer questions that to students seem very basic. For example: the average age at first marriage for Jewish girls is a matter of debate, not a question answered by clear statistics. How old were Jewish girls when they got married? How does the average age at marriage for Jewish girls compare with that for Christian or Muslim girls? A wide array of anecdotal evidence allows us to identify a spectrum of what was legally and socially possible but leaves open to argument the question of what was "average" or "normal."

The Talmud distinguished between minor girls and girls who had reached puberty, and many passages actively discouraged marriage to prepubescent girls. According to some rabbis, fathers were forbidden from formally betrothing their daughters before they had reached puberty [*Doc. 7, p. 126*]. If fathers could not even enter their daughters into a formal engagement when they were still prepubescent, they certainly could not have them married at such a young age. Other Talmudic passages employed vitriolic language to insult men who entered marriages with very young girls and fathers who found husbands for their prepubescent daughters. However, many passages in the Talmud suggest that child marriage was permitted even if it was not promoted. Even the passages insulting men who entered child marriages and fathers who married off very young girls imply that such marriages were not outside the realm of possibility. Many rabbis agreed that fathers had the legal right to marry off their daughters, even to adult men, when they were only three years of age. Husbands of toddlers also legally had the right to consummate those marriages (Krakowski 2018: 117–118).

The ambiguity about the subject of child marriage stems in part from the fact that the Talmud is not a legal code, with clear rulings on different subjects. It is a collection of debates, interpretations, and narratives. The text incorporates both majority and minority opinions and sometimes includes seemingly contradictory statements. Passages that praise very early marriage coexist alongside passages that condemn it. Some medieval rabbis interpreted this apparent contradiction as a distinction between the marriage of prepubescent girls and the marriage of girls who fell into the category of *bogeret*, which applied to young women over the age of twelve and a half. The *Sefer Hasidim*, composed in central Europe in the thirteenth century, proposed thirteen as an ideal age for a girl to get married (Grossman 2004: 42). Today, of course, most people would still consider these preteen and teen girls to be children, legally as well as emotionally.

Despite the consistent presence of rabbinic voices that criticized child marriage, rabbinic responsa nevertheless indicate that, throughout the medieval world, some Jewish girls got married before they had reached the age of twelve. In other words, disagreement over child marriage left open the possibility for it to happen at least occasionally, and perhaps even regularly, in some communities. The woman Bible teacher discussed in the previous chapter got married when she was nine years old [*Doc. 3, p. 120*]. In another responsum, Maimonides stated that it was the "custom of the Jews in Damascus" to marry off their daughters when they were around eight or nine years old. A case from the Iberian Peninsula dating from the late tenth or early eleventh century, when the region was under Muslim rule, referred to a girl of six married to a man of forty (Grossman 2004: 38–41). The marriage contract from Catalonia, with which this chapter began, suggested that the bride was around thirteen and the groom around fourteen years old when they married [*Doc. 6, pp. 124–125*].

Anecdotal evidence suggests that child marriages might have been especially common for orphaned girls, whose families or legal guardians may have perceived them as a burden. The term "orphan" often referred to children who had lost their fathers but still had living mothers. Widowed mothers who wished to remarry may have preferred or felt obligated to marry off their daughters rather than bringing them into their new households. The woman Bible teacher made no mention of her parents, although the text referred regularly to her siblings. She might have married so young, and her mother-in-law might have agreed to support her financially, because she no longer had parents to help her [*Doc. 3, p. 120*].

Child marriage was certainly not universal. Evidence from the city of Perpignan, in southern France, suggests that most Jewish boys and girls there married around the age of eighteen (Winer 2006: 91). The elegy that Eleazar of Worms composed for his daughters, murdered along with their mothers, described his thirteen-year-old daughter Bellette as "modest as a bride" but did not indicate that she was married or even formally betrothed (Baskin 2001: 436–437). Jewish communities might have shared similar marriage practices with the people around them. Many scholars agree that child marriage was rare, though not unheard of, in medieval Christian Europe, and more common, albeit not universal, in Islamic contexts. However, medieval Jews did not completely follow the example of the people around them: some Jews in Christian northern Europe, for example, appear to have encouraged the marriage of girls in their early teens. Overall, while we can definitively say that child marriage happened in Jewish communities across the medieval world, we cannot determine how normal such marriages were nor definitively identify an average age at marriage. Undoubtedly, however, many medieval Jewish brides married younger than people would consider acceptable today.

Finding a marriage partner

In most communities in the medieval world, for people of all social strata, marriage was a family matter with political, social, and economic implications. It was not an expression of a personal connection of romantic love between two individuals, nor an equal partnership of loving companions. At the time, Jews, Christians, and Muslims would have only recognized the validity of certain kinds of marital relationships. Marriage could only occur between a person socially considered a man and a person socially considered a woman. Additionally, with few exceptions, legally valid marriages united two people who belonged to the same faith. Islamic law permitted marriages between Muslim men and Jewish or Christian women but forbade Muslim women from marrying outside the faith. Church law forbade all marriages between Christians and Jews, although legal authorities took different positions on the thorny question of whether a convert should remain married to a spouse who had stayed Jewish (Brundage 1988: 28–29). The vast majority of Jewish girls and young women therefore expected to marry men of their own faith.

As in Christian and Muslim communities, Jewish girls who embarked on their first marriage rarely had much say in whom they married. Jewish law did require brides to give their formal legal consent. The Talmudic sage Rav even stated that men were forbidden to betroth their daughters while they were still minors, on the grounds that they should wait "until she grows up and says, 'I want so-and-so'" [*Doc. 7, p. 126*]. Taken by itself, Rav's statement could be read as a robust defense of young women's right to give or withhold consent. It could even imply that parents should allow their daughters to play an active role in choosing a marriage partner. In practice, however, while the consent of the bride remained a legal requirement, social expectations throughout the medieval world dictated that a girl's parents or legal guardians would choose a husband for her. Very few young women found themselves in a position to insist on a particular husband or refuse one that her family had chosen for her.

One particularly intriguing responsum provides a rare example of a Jewish bride who refused to give her consent to an arranged marriage. The question was sent to **Rabbi Solomon ibn Adret**, who was active in and around Barcelona in the late thirteenth and early fourteenth centuries. The query describes the situation confronted by two families when the bride-to-be refused to marry the prospective husband selected for her by her grandfather, who was her legal guardian [*Doc. 8, pp. 126–127*]. This case demonstrates that it was legally and socially possible for girls to refuse to marry the men selected by their fathers or guardians and demands that we take Jewish girls' agency seriously. This girl upset the arrangements of two families by making her wishes known and refusing to bow to the will of her family.

On the other hand, ibn Adret's response claimed that very few Jewish girls exercised their right of refusal. The debate that required the intervention of a well-respected rabbi was not about whether the young woman had the right to refuse her marriage. All those involved seem to have accepted without question the fact that her unusual refusal made the marriage impossible. The conflict instead focused on money. The two families had agreed on a financial penalty in the event that either party cancelled the marriage agreement—a common safeguard designed to protect against cancelled engagements (Grossman 2004: 51). Did the girl's grandfather, who allegedly at least still supported the marriage, have to pay the fine when the engagement was cancelled in accordance with his granddaughter's wishes? Ibn Adret ruled that the grandfather did *not* have to pay. Her refusal was so unusual that no one could have anticipated it. It therefore represented a legal exception to the usual penalties. Ibn Adret might have slightly exaggerated for effect when he claimed that "all girls are willing [to marry] whoever their father or relatives wish." Nevertheless, his ruling demonstrates that he could convincingly justify a claim that a bride's refusal was rare enough to be impossible to anticipate. Most young women probably succumbed to their parents' wishes, regardless of their personal opinions.

Families' reluctance to allow young women to choose their husbands stemmed from medieval concepts of marriage, which differed substantially from modern understandings of marriage. Neither personal compatibility nor romantic interest would have been considered crucial to pre-modern marriages. Instead, marriages created or cemented social, political, and economic alliances, which would prove valuable to the families of both bride and groom. Family negotiations over marriages sometimes included discussion of conditions that would shape the couple's married life, but the biggest consideration in most negotiations was the money that would change hands.

Young men marrying for the first time probably had little more choice in the matter than young women. Adult men, whether longtime bachelors or those embarking on a second marriage, would have had more of a say in selecting their brides. Previously married adult women also had the right to choose new husbands for themselves. In practice, however, widows and divorcées might confront continued social and familial pressures to marry (or not marry) specific men.

Jewish families and communities adopted a wide range of strategies when selecting marriage partners for their daughters. Some young women married close to home. Local elites in urban Jewish communities could use marriage ties to reinforce other political and economic relationships (Klein 2006a: 179–180). In both the Eastern and Western Mediterranean, marriages between first cousins or between uncle and niece could strengthen bonds of kinship within a family. Such marriages also might have helped to keep wealth within the family, especially when daughters without brothers stood to inherit.

Other families pursued marriages over longer distances. Mercantile families in medieval Cairo and Fustat established connections in other economic centers through marriage alliances (Goitein 1978: 57). These practices continued in early modern Jewish communities; exiled Sephardic Jews used marriages to both establish international partnerships and exchange capital via the dowry (Trivellato 2009: 139–146). Long-distance marriages could prove difficult for Jewish brides. In both the Eastern Mediterranean and Ashkenaz, some Jewish women preferred to divorce their husbands than to move with them to places far away from their families (Baskin 2008: 230, 236). Distance also made it more difficult for families to support their married daughters and safeguard their assets (Winer 2011: 251–253).

Creating a Jewish marriage

Once an appropriate partner had been selected and the families had agreed upon an engagement, marriage required two ceremonies: the betrothal (referred to in Hebrew as *erusin* or *kiddushin*) and the marriage itself (*nissuin*). The betrothal itself was legally binding and could only be dissolved by a formal divorce. In the Middle Ages, the two ceremonies were united, such that they were performed one immediately after the other. By celebrating the two ceremonies at once, families and communities could avoid leaving girls trapped in a marriage that had never even begun—a real possibility if the groom-to-be absconded between the betrothal and marriage and refused to grant the bride a divorce. As men could marry a second wife, but women could not marry a second husband, the groom would not be trapped in the same way as his bride. A communal edict from eleventh-century Spain offered an alternative solution to this potential problem by mandating that betrothals be made conditional; they would be nullified automatically if the groom were absent for over a year (Grossman 2004: 49–51).

Engagements without *kiddushin* were not legally binding, but families were still concerned about cancellations that could upset their plans. Families and communities therefore often introduced verbal or written financial penalties for cancelled engagements. The man whose granddaughter refused to wed the man he had chosen for her was hoping that he could avoid paying the fine, given the unusual and unexpected nature of the situation. Ibn Adret's response indicates that the death or serious illness of the bride or the groom could also permit the cancellation of an engagement without paying a fine [*Doc. 8, p. 126*].

In the *Mishneh Torah*, Maimonides identified three ways to create a valid Jewish marriage: through the transfer of a contract, through an exchange of money, or through sexual intercourse (Maimonides, *Misnneh Torah*, Ishut 1.1–2). Both an exchange of money and sexual intercourse required an oral expression of intent. In other words, a man could not make a woman his wife simply by having sex with her; he had to state explicitly that he was acquiring her as a wife through the act of intercourse. In practice, many medieval Jewish marriages were created by a combination of all three methods. The couple would have intercourse, but only after they and their families had first drawn up a *ketubah*, or marriage contract, which recorded a financial exchange.

The *ketubah* specified the names of the bride and groom, the date and place on which the marriage took place, and the marital gifts exchanged between the two parties. Traditionally, the *ketubah* was written in a combination of Hebrew and Aramaic. This contract not only constituted a legal marriage but also delineated the financial arrangements and conditions negotiated by the couple and their families. The husband committed to give his wife a sum of money, also referred to by the term *ketubah*, which referenced the practice of acquiring a wife by giving her money. In practice, the *ketubah* was often a small and symbolic sum in the Middle Ages. In places where custom dictated that husbands should offer a more significant financial gift to their wives, the groom could supplement the *ketubah* with additional funds. This supplementary gift was referred to as the **tosefet ketubah**, or literally "addition to the *ketubah*."

In many Jewish communities, the most significant financial exchange associated with marriage was the wife's grant of the dowry, referred to in Aramaic as the **nedunya**. The dowry could include cash, household goods, clothing and other textiles, and even real estate. Fathers were responsible for providing appropriate dowries for their daughters. Although the dowry did not necessarily represent a share of the family estate equal to that bequeathed to sons, it represented the only form of inheritance daughters could claim. The custom of providing a dowry can already be found in the Talmud and might reflect Roman influence (Hezser 2007). The transition from brideprice to dowry as the dominant marital gift can also be seen among medieval Christians, especially in the Western Mediterranean (Hughes 1978: 276). Although Islamic law focused on the importance of the husband's gift, in practice many medieval Muslim societies also emphasized the dowry (Rapoport 2005: 13).

Jewish communal leaders, much like their Christian counterparts, expressed concern about the phenomenon of dowry inflation. In some places, the Italian Peninsula in particular, dowries grew larger and larger as girls' families sought to attract the sort of husbands who would be most valuable as social or political allies and economic partners. The phenomenon of dowry inflation may have undermined some families' inclinations to effectively disinherit their daughters (Chojnacki 2000: 142). However, if the dowry had to be returned to the bride or her family in the event of death or divorce, the substantial dowries that had sustained families could now bring them to financial ruin. As a result, the rabbis of Padua in 1507 passed ordinances specifying the maximum value of the dowry (Toaff 1998: 15).

Jewish law included few provisions for daughters' inheritance. Parents were expected to provide for their daughters until marriage and then give them a dowry appropriate to their station, but they did not have the right to inherit equally with their brothers. Dowry inflation may have helped Jewish girls claim a more substantial share of their family estate, but still did not necessarily guarantee that a woman with brothers would inherit as much as they did. When Reina, daughter of Bonjueu Cresques got married, one of the contracts her family concluded with the Christian notary was one in which she relinquished all claims beyond her dowry on her father's estate [*Doc. 6d, pp. 125–126*]. Reina clearly was not disinherited: the dowry she brought to her groom was a substantial one. But given that her father was a wealthy man who apparently had no other children, it seems likely that she should have inherited more than her dowry alone. Her father, who had remarried, may have requested this contract in the hope that he might have sons at a later date (Ifft Decker 2019a: 492).

Because marriage was in many ways an economic relationship, financial arrangements are a crucial part of the text of *ketubot*. However, couples could also use the *ketubah* to dictate conditions that would shape their married lives. These conditions included living arrangements: would the couple live with the bride's parents, the groom's parents, or neither? Could the husband require his wife to move away from her family? Especially in the Islamic East, where polygyny was freely permitted, *ketubah* conditions tackled the complicated topic of whether a husband could take a second wife (Goitein 1978: 147–150). The woman Bible teacher and her husband appear to have included such a condition in their ketubah [*Doc. 4, p. 190*].

Marriage contracts are valuable sources for understanding how Jewish families and communities understood marriage and constructed expectations for husbands and wives, as well as how marriages were constituted both legally and socially. However, these contracts also have their limits. The formulaic language of *ketubot* and other types of marriage contracts means that they do not always yield insight into family particularities, although they sometimes describe local customs. Moreover, *ketubot* identify the financial and social arrangements couples made, but do not usually tell us how families came to the decisions we see inscribed in marriage contracts, nor what the marriages they created looked like in practice. The question of how Jewish women in the medieval world experienced married life in practice demands an answer too broad and varied to be addressed in a single section. However, in this and in subsequent chapters, thematic discussions will allow us to explore some of the spectrum of possibility.

Ceremony and celebration were also an important part of creating a Jewish marriage, which was often a major familial and even communal affair. After the ceremony itself, in which the groom committed to fulfill his legal obligations to his wife, they would hold a wedding feast. According to Jewish tradition, seven blessings were recited in celebration of the marriage. Especially in wealthy families, the marriage and feast were occasions for conspicuous display. The clothing of the bride and groom, the food served, the home in which the ceremony was held, and the number of guests could all serve as spectacular demonstrations of wealth. Some communities even passed laws attempting to limit wedding expenses: a number of Jewish communities in central Italy, for example, in 1418 undertook to limit the number of wedding guests in order to cut costs (Toaff 1998: 17).

Polygyny in medieval Jewish communities

The practice of **polygyny** was legal under Jewish law and presented as normal in the Hebrew Bible. This text employs the word "polygyny," rather than the more familiar "polygamy," deliberately. The word "polygamy" refers to the practice of having multiple spouses. The term "polygyny" is more specific: it means that a person has multiple *wives*. As with many other aspects of marriage, a person's ability to practice polygamy was dictated by gender. A man could legally have multiple wives, but a woman could never have multiple husbands, and same-sex marriages were not legal options. The legality of polygyny, with no comparable permission extended to women, contributed to the inequality of husbands and wives in a variety of ways. A man unhappy in his marriage not only had the right to initiate divorce, as will be discussed in the next section, but also, if he preferred, to take an additional wife who might better suit his needs. In contrast, a woman unhappy in her marriage had few legal options to separate from her husband without his consent, and no legally permissible option to find another spouse. A man without children could, and according to Jewish law should, try again with a different woman. A childless woman could not try to have children with another man unless the courts agreed to pressure her husband to divorce her. Childless men could try an indefinite number of times to have children with multiple or successive wives, but a childless woman was presumed barren if she attempted and failed to conceive with two successive husbands. She could only marry a third time if the prospective husband already had children (Baskin 2002: 127).

Once again, we lack the demographic data to determine definitively how common polygyny was in medieval Jewish communities. However, anecdotal evidence and legal sources indicate that polygyny was more common in some Jewish communities than others. The norms and legal expectations of the majority faith appear to have played a crucial role in shaping how Jewish communities thought about polygyny.

Christianity strictly banned polygamy of all varieties. Neither men nor women could take a second spouse while the first still lived. This stringent approach to the marriage of multiple spouses might explain why the Jews of medieval Ashkenaz banned polygyny outright. **Rabbenu Gershom**, a respected communal leader based in the city of Mainz (today in Germany), issued a series of ordinances, called *takkanot*, which legislated new norms for the Jewish community. Often, local understandings of Jewish law were rooted, at least in theory, in the interpretation of the Bible and Talmud. *Takkanot*, in contrast, had no overt basis in the written or oral law, and sometimes even contradicted biblical and Talmudic legal norms. One of the most famous *takkanot* of Rabbenu Gershom was his prohibition of polygyny. Men could not take a second wife, except with the support of a hundred men from three different provinces. Moreover, they had to justify their choice with a good reason, such as a wife's infertility; sexual desire for another woman was not licit grounds for polygyny under the ban.

Prior to the acceptance of the ban, it is unclear how the Jews of Ashkenaz thought about polygyny. The ban could indicate that polygyny had once been common in the region, but that communal leaders wished to put a stop to it, out of concern over the wellbeing of Jewish wives or the potential negative opinions of local Christians. On the other hand, the ban could represent a mere affirmation of the fact that local communities already for the most part eschewed polygyny. Regardless of what was the norm before the eleventh century, we can say definitively that, due to local respect for Rabbenu Gershom, the Jews of Ashkenaz came to treat the ban as law and subsequently refrained from practicing polygyny. The reputation of Rabbenu Gershom probably explains why the ban was considered authoritative beyond the bounds of his home city of Mainz.

However, not all Jewish communities in the medieval world considered Rabbenu Gershom's ban binding. The Jews of Sepharad, whether they lived under Muslim or Christian rule, understood polygyny as legal according to

Jewish law. For Jews living in the Christian-ruled kingdoms of Castile and Aragon, restrictions on polygyny came not from rabbinic authorities but from royal ones. The Christian kings in the Iberian Peninsula only allowed Jewish men to practice polygyny if they formally applied for and obtained a license. Increasingly, kings only granted such licenses in cases where the first wife was infertile (Assis 1997: 262–264). In Crete, as well, the Jewish community adhered to Rabbenu Gershom's ban on polygyny, although some Jewish men argued before Christian courts that Jewish law permitted them to marry a second wife in cases of infertility (Lauer 2019: 143–146). Restrictions imposed by both Jewish communal leaders and Christian rulers tended to ensure that even though polygyny remained legal for Jews living in some of the Christian-ruled regions of the Mediterranean, it was probably relatively rare. Some Jews may have come to share Christians' discomfort with polygyny; others may have feared that the practice could inspire anti-Jewish hostility.

In regions under Muslim rule, Jewish laws permitting polygyny were compatible with the law of the land. Islam permitted men to marry up to four wives, in accordance with the example set by the Prophet Muhammad. Both Jewish and Muslim jurists worked to regulate the financial and sexual obligations of men with multiple wives. Men should not marry more women than they could afford to appropriately maintain. They were also cautioned to ensure that they met their obligation to engage regularly in sexual relations with each wife [*Doc. 11, p. 128*]. Some men simply desired more than one wife, but Jewish law also mandated that men take a second wife if their first went ten years without bearing children. These circumstances made polygyny permissible, but not universal. Evidence from Eastern Mediterranean Jewish communities also indicates that some women disliked the idea of their husband marrying a second wife—and that this was something that families could negotiate. *Ketubot* sometimes included conditions requiring that a husband divorce his wife if he wanted to marry another.

Divorce in medieval Jewish communities

Jewish law about divorce had its roots in the Hebrew Bible, and rabbinic authorities consistently permitted divorce. However, men and women did not have equal legal ability to end an unhappy marriage. Husbands could unilaterally divorce their wives; wives could not unilaterally divorce their husbands. A valid divorce required a husband to give his wife a *get*, or bill of divorce: a physical document that not only recorded but also created a divorce. The unilateral nature of divorce left some women trapped in unhappy or even abusive marriages; a woman in this position was referred to as an *agunah*: a "chained woman." Some *agunot* had recalcitrant husbands who refused to divorce them; others were married to men who had disappeared. Absentee husbands sometimes could be found in other cities with other wives, but some had been taken captive or even died. However, Jewish courts would not permit an *agunah* to remarry without witness testimony that her husband was in fact dead. Courts sometimes showed more flexibility than usual in such cases about what and who constituted a valid witness, but an entirely unwitnessed death could still leave a widow chained to her dead husband.

Despite the legal requirement that only husbands could formally initiate divorce, Jewish communal leaders made some efforts to protect women from being either divorced against their will or chained to unhappy marriages. Rabbenu Gershom prohibited husbands from divorcing wives without their consent; some Jewish communities in Provence instituted similar ordinances (Grossman 2004: 88). Women who wanted to divorce recalcitrant husbands had a few legal loopholes at their disposal. Courts might pressure men to divorce their wives if they failed to fulfill their duties as a husband. Impotence, inability to support a family, and violent mistreatment could all serve as grounds for courts to compel men to divorce their wives. Intriguingly, a man could also be pressured to divorce his wife if she insisted that she found her husband repugnant, although rabbis became increasingly reluctant to accept this justification after the thirteenth century (Grossman 2004: 239). If a couple did not have children after ten years, the husband was expected to try to reproduce with another partner, either by taking a second wife or divorcing his first and remarrying. The commandment to reproduce was only incumbent upon men. However, childless wives had some success in convincing courts to compel their husbands to divorce them on the grounds that they desired children.

Some unhappy wives attempted to pressure their husbands into granting a divorce by refusing to fulfill their wifely duties. A woman who refused to have sexual intercourse with her husband or to perform household tasks was termed a *moredet*, or "rebellious wife." Perhaps as early as the seventh century, rabbis in the Islamic East began to compel husbands to divorce "rebellious wives." One figure, Rav Sherira Gaon, explained the reason behind this ruling: communal leaders feared that Jewish women with no legal recourse under Jewish law would turn to Muslim courts to force their husbands to divorce them. Some rabbis may have worried that women in this position would not only turn to non-Jewish courts, but even convert to Islam (Grossman 2004: 240–241). Flexibility around divorce allowed rabbis to avoid the bigger problem of Jews pursuing justice in non-Jewish courts, as well as the specter of conversion. However, rebellion usually required sacrifice: a woman divorced as a *moredet* would lose the money promised to her in the *ketubah*. For some women, the financial loss was worth it to escape an unwanted marriage. But for all but the wealthiest women, pursuing divorce as a *moredet* posed a real risk: it could jeopardize their economic stability (Ifft Decker 2017: 39).

It is difficult to determine how common divorce was in medieval Jewish communities. In the Middle East, divorced women remarried without stigma: divorced brides appeared in 20 percent of Genizah marriage contracts (Goitein 1978: 274). The lack of stigma around divorce in this region could reflect the norms of the surrounding society. Divorce was also permitted in Islam, and as many as 30 percent of Muslim marriages in fifteenth-century Cairo may have ended in divorce (Rapoport 2005: 83).

In northern Europe, rabbis regularly railed against the prevalence of divorce (Grossman 2004: 244–246). However, it is difficult to tell whether these protests genuinely reflected a high divorce rate. Even if rabbis were responding to a rising divorce rate, divorce still might have remained relatively uncommon. Alternatively, the rabbis' complaints could indicate a growing discomfort with divorce rather than a growing normalization of divorce. The rabbis' hesitation about divorce—like their hesitation about polygyny—could even indicate some amount of Christian influence. Although Church law allowed for annulment of marriages under certain circumstances, and sometimes permitted couples to live separately, Christians could not divorce one another and then remarry freely in the same manner as Jews and Muslims.

Rabbinic responsa, appeals to the royal court, and some Latin contracts demonstrate that divorce undoubtedly happened in the Jewish communities of the Iberian Peninsula. A notarial contract from the Catalan town of Vic offers an example of how Jewish couples ending their marriages might turn to both Jewish law and the law of the land [*Doc. 9, p. 127*]. In this Latin contract, a Jew named Astrug Bonjuses confirmed to his ex-wife Tolsana that he had delivered to her a *get*, here termed *libellum repudii*—a Latin word for a divorce writ found in both the Latin Vulgate and in Roman legal codes. He also confirmed that, with the divorce, he had returned his wife's dowry. Contracts like this one demonstrate that even though Christian legal professionals did not regularly handle divorce, they nevertheless provided their services and authority to Jewish divorcing couples.

Tolsana apparently acted alone, but many Jewish women seeking divorce relied on support from their parents and siblings. Fathers, mothers, and brothers helped women pursue divorce cases in both Jewish and non-Jewish courts. These kinship ties may have meant the difference between success and failure for some would-be divorcées who had difficulty navigating unfamiliar court systems.

Widowhood

For many Jewish women, widowhood was the first time they would independently control financial resources. Widows were entitled to either receive maintenance from their husbands' estates, if they refrained from remarrying, or to collect their dowry and *ketubah* money. Although Jewish law did not formally permit widows to control their late husbands' estates, some nevertheless did so in practice. Especially in southern France, Jewish widows also established control over family property in their capacity as the legal guardians of their minor children. Due to these economic circumstances, scholars have emphasized the role of widows as the most "commercially effective" of Jewish women (Winer 2006: 99).

Some Jewish widows embraced the opportunity to independently manage households and raise their children. Others instead sought to remarry, whether because they missed personal or sexual companionship, or because marriage provided women with greater financial security. Age disparities in marriages meant that many women were widowed young, perhaps even before bearing children, and may have wished to remarry at least once.

Some rabbis exhibited anxiety about widows' remarriage; a mystical text called the *Zohar*, composed in thirteenth-century Castile, discouraged widows from remarrying on the grounds that the spirit of the first husband remained attached to his living widow. The Talmud classified a widow who had lost two husbands as a "murderous wife," and forbade her from remarrying (Grossman 2004: 258–262). In some situations, however, widows were actively encouraged or even required to remarry. Childless widows were expected to bear a child on behalf of their late husband by entering into a **Levirate marriage** with her husband's brother. In practice, however, many such prospective couples underwent a formal ceremony called *chalitzah* in which they ritually rejected the Levirate marriage. However, the requirement that childless widows either enter Levirate marriages or perform the *chalitzah* ritual could leave them trapped in certain circumstances—if the brother had disappeared, for example, or converted to another faith [*Doc. 24, pp. 139–140*].

Conclusion

Marriage was the norm for men and women in all medieval Jewish communities, and an important part of their lives. However, marriage did not necessarily represent a dramatic change in men's status. For women, in contrast, marriage, divorce, and widowhood wrought major transformations. Marital status was one of the most important factors in shaping women's everyday lived experiences and legal status—not only in the Jewish communities of the medieval world, but in the surrounding Muslim and Christian communities as well.

As we have already discussed briefly in this chapter, sex was an important part of marriage for Jewish couples. However, sex did not only occur within the confines of marriage. The next chapter will explore the wider role sex and sexuality played in Jewish women's lives.

5   Sex and sexuality

Jewish communal leaders often turned to illustrious rabbis outside their own communities when they needed help grappling with particularly difficult problems. In the Jewish community of Toledo, sometime in the late thirteenth or early fourteenth century, the sexual history of a Jewish couple from Seville had become one such problem. Toledo's communal leaders wrote to Rabbi Solomon ibn Adret of Barcelona to ask what they should do about a man and woman who initially appeared to be a Jewish married couple, but had a checkered past [*Doc. 10, pp. 127–128*]. Their relationship had begun, it turned out, as an adulterous affair. The two had then converted to Christianity, after which the woman's husband divorced her. Even though the woman was now legally free of her husband, she was not free to marry whoever she wished. Jewish law forbade marriage between a couple whose relationship had begun in adultery. Under Jewish law, this couple could never have a valid marriage. Despite this clear legal impediment, however, the pair turned up in another city, living as Jews despite their conversion to Christianity and as a married couple despite their forbidden relationship under Jewish law. They may have used conversion strategically, rather than sincerely, as a means of pressuring the woman's husband into divorce and perhaps even sanctioning their marriage among Christians (Ifft Decker 2014: 44–46).

The rabbinic responsum that tells this woman's story does not share her perspective directly, nor does it even give her name. Yet it offers a glimpse into the life of a medieval Jewish woman who made difficult choices, broke laws, and took risks in order to pursue her romantic and sexual desires. It also offers insight into some of the challenges for scholars studying medieval Jewish women's sex and sexuality. Many of women's sexual experiences and desires are only visible through texts written by men, who often saw women's sexuality as dangerous. This chapter will address both how elite Jewish men thought about women's sexuality and how we can use the sources at our disposal to understand Jewish women's own experiences.

DOI: 10.4324/9781003104964-7

Virginity, sex, and adolescence

The Mishnah used the term "ripened fig" to describe a young woman who had reached sexual maturity (Mishnah Niddah 5:7). This category was used to describe girls in their early teens. However, both the chosen terminology and the legal expectations associated with it implied that girls of this age had reached full sexual maturity and now were unambiguously suited for marriage and sexual intercourse. The assumption that girls in their early teens could enter into and sexually consummate marital relationships—sometimes with older men—went essentially unquestioned. Although some rabbis criticized marriage and sex with underage girls, and in practice many Jewish girls remained unmarried until their late teens, sex with girls in their early teens remained legal as long as it was within the confines of a valid marriage. This assumption of teenage girls' sexual maturity was far from unique among ancient and medieval Jewish communities: their Roman, Christian, and Muslim counterparts similarly would have had few qualms about a thirteen-year-old girl marrying and having sex with a man in his late teens or early twenties.

Jewish law was unusual in one respect: Jewish young women were considered legally free of their father's authority once they reached physical and sexual maturity. In contrast, many other legal systems—including both Roman law and Islamic law—presumed that daughters would remain under the legal authority of their father at least until their first marriage, regardless of age (Krakowski 2018: 115–116). The legal category of the *bogeret*, a girl who had reached physical and sexual maturity, therefore links young women's development with their legal standing and capacity to make major life decisions. The rabbinic discourse suggesting that girls should be allowed to choose whom they wanted to marry—that they could grow up and say "I want so-and-so" [*Doc. 7, p. 126*]—could be a tacit acknowledgment of girls' sexual desires as well as their affections.

These texts appear to suggest that elite Jewish men took the sexual desires and agency of young woman seriously. However, the legal category of the *bogeret* sexualizes women young enough that, in many places today, they would not be legally able to consent to sexual intercourse. The sexualization of pre-teen girls justified entering them into marriages in which they would be expected to have sex at a young age. Boys as well as girls were presumed sexually mature when in their early teens. The Sefer Hasidim urged fathers to find wives for their minor sons out of the concern that they might already be overwhelmed by sexual urges, and could pursue sexual relationships with inappropriate partners, like other men's wives or non-Jewish women (Grossman 2004: 43).

The presumption of teen girls' sexual maturity left some rabbis anxious about what might happen if fathers allowed their daughters to remain unmarried too long. The respected sage **Rabbi Akiva** interpreted the biblical verse "Do not profane your daughter to make her a whore" (Leviticus 19:29) as referring to parents who kept their adolescent daughters from marrying (Krakowski 2018: 117). In other words, some rabbis assumed that unmarried adolescent girls would engage in illicit sexual intercourse. While it is intriguing that the rabbis fully acknowledged that teen girls as well as boys experienced sexual desire, they tended to exhibit more anxiety than celebration about young women's sexual maturity. Moreover, while some rabbis expressed concern about unmarried adolescent boys as well as girls engaging in premarital sex, the word "whore" only applied to sexually active girls.

Jewish religious rhetoric did not idealize virginity or celibacy in quite the same way as medieval Christian rhetoric, and Jewish law that delineated girls' legal and social maturity emphasized puberty rather than marriage and non-virginity. Nevertheless, Jewish girls were presumed to enter their first marriage as virgins, and virginity had some legal significance. The presumption of virginity determined the brideprice that women received from their husbands in the *ketubah*. Virgins, or those embarking on their first marriage, would receive 200 *zuzim*, whereas widows and divorcées entering a second (or subsequent) marriage would receive 100 *zuzim*. In practice these sums quickly became symbolic and had little financial impact. The husband's supplementary contribution and the wife's dowry would have mattered far more for securing her financial future. Nevertheless, the legal distinction between virgins and non-virgins, or at least first-time brides and remarrying brides, implied that virginal women were literally more valuable than women who had previously engaged in sexual relations.

Jewish marriage practices increasingly incorporated celebrations of virginity. The *Halakhot Gedolot*, an eighth-century Jewish law code, described a tradition according to which, after the consummation of the marriage, the husband should bring out and display a stained sheet in order to visually demonstrate the virginity of his bride. After he did so, the wedding guests were then expected to recite a blessing celebrating the bride's virginity and fertility. This practice appears to have originated among Jews living in the Islamic world and may have stemmed from similar Muslim rituals that publicly acknowledged the bride's virginity. However, the ritual also spread to Christian Europe (Langer 1995: 77).

Some amount of respect for the virginal status of unmarried women is also implicit in Jewish polemics insulting the Virgin Mary. Medieval Christianity considered virginity as the ideal state for women. Christian women venerated as saints usually either remained lifelong virgins or at least embraced celibacy later in life. It was a central tenet of Christian doctrine that Mary, the mother of Jesus Christ, had conceived and born a child without the sin of sexual intercourse. The ***Toledot Yeshu***, a polemical retelling of the Gospels that circulated among medieval Jewish communities, insulted Mary by claiming that her virginal status was a lie. According to these narratives, Mary conceived Jesus during adulterous sex with a man who fraudulently claimed to be her husband, while she was menstruating. These stories undermined Christian claims about Mary's virginity while also linking her with other sexual taboos: adultery and sex during menstruation (Cuffel 2007: 120).

Sex and marriage

Medieval Jews understood sex as a normal part of married life, and Jewish elites treated marriage as the expected path for virtually all men and women. Jews resembled their Muslim contemporaries more than their Christian contemporaries in this regard. Plenty of Christian couples pursued procreation and sexual fulfillment within the bonds of marriage and the consummation of a marriage through sexual intercourse was a crucial part of its legal validity. However, the idealization of celibacy in Christian religious culture nevertheless shaped how many Christians thought about sex and marriage. A few particularly pious Christian couples even pursued celibate marriages, in which they remained legally and socially tied to their spouses but mutually agreed to live together chastely (Elliott 1993: 196–205). In Jewish tradition, in contrast, husbands were required both to procreate and to provide sex to their wives. Muslim men, similarly, were expected to have children and engage in sexual intercourse.

Jewish law presented sex as a duty that a husband owed his wife, rather than the other way around. Rabbinic authorities even went so far as to specify how often men of different professions owed their wives intercourse. According to Maimonides, for example, an indulged and wealthy man who does not work should have sex with his wife every night, whereas men who perform manual labor like weaving or construction should have sex with their wives once a week. Maimonides further specified how men with multiple wives should divide their sexual attentions between wives [*Doc. 11, p. 128*]. Jewish courts could compel a man to divorce his wife if he withheld sex from her or if he was physically unable to have intercourse (Grossman 2004: 236–238). Maimonides includes a few examples of such situations: for example, if a man vowed not to have sex with his wife, or if he became too ill [*Doc. 11, pp. 128–129*].

Despite the fact that most rabbinic texts constructed sex as a duty a husband owed his wife, wives were nevertheless expected to consent to their husbands' sexual advances. Consent was largely presumed in the context of marriage: a married woman who did not actively refuse to have sex with her husband was assumed to have consented. This concept of consent does not mean that rabbinic authorities entirely ignored women's pleasure, wishes, or sexual needs. In fact, rabbis instructed husbands to try to make the experience pleasurable for their wives. Maimonides, for example, encouraged couples to engage in sex only when both were "willing and happy" (Maimonides, *Mishneh Torah*, De'ot 5.4). But rabbis' understanding of consent differed substantially from twenty-first-century discussions about active consent. Once given, consent was assumed unless explicitly withdrawn; silence could also imply consent. In other words, ancient and medieval rabbis had some concept of marital rape and valued a wife's consent—but their idea of what consent entailed differed from our own.

Nor should the promotion of consent in marital sexual relations be equated with the celebration of women's sexual agency. Even though rabbis understood sex as a duty husbands owed their wives, textual depictions of marital sex still tended to present the husband as initiating sex with his wife. The Lilith midrash claimed that the conflict between Adam and his first wife Lilith originated in an argument over who would be on top during sex [*Doc. 2, pp. 119–120*]. Lilith's insistence on having sex the way she wanted, according to the text, started her on a slippery slope that ended in her transformation into a baby-killing demon.

Women could withhold sex from their husbands in order to pressure them to grant a divorce. Maimonides explained that if a woman claimed she was too revolted by her husband to have intercourse with him, she should be granted a divorce, as "she is not like a captive who must engage in sexual relations with someone she hates" [*Doc. 11, p. 129*]. On the one hand, the emphasis placed on a wife's right to withhold consent from intercourse with her husband acknowledges that she was a person free to make her own decisions. On the other hand, she was financially penalized for her agency: a woman who refused to have sex with her husband was declared a *moredet*. Her husband was forced to divorce her, but in return she had to forfeit the *ketubah* money that her husband had committed to give her. The legal concept of the *moredet* suggests that withholding sex was a choice that women had to take seriously. It is unclear whether in practice all women would have felt able to rebuff their husbands' sexual advances, especially if they only wished to refuse sex on certain occasions rather than "rebelling" and ending the marriage.

At least in theory, a Jewish married couple's sex life was structured around the wife's menstrual cycle. Sex with a menstruating woman was taboo; couples were supposed to not only refrain from sexual intercourse, but also from other kinds of intimate and physical contact, lest it arouse them to have sex. The laws surrounding menstrual impurity kept couples physically apart for perhaps as much as half of each month: after her menstrual period ended, the wife was supposed to count seven "white days," on which she did not see blood. Only then could she ritually bathe in the **mikveh** and once again become sexually available to her husband (see Figure 5.1). The rabbis, at least, took this prohibition very seriously. The Babylonian Talmud even relates a cautionary tale of a scholar who died young because he ate, drank, and slept next to his wife (albeit without sexual contact) during her "white days" (Baskin 2002: 25).

Figure 5.1 Mikveh of Besalú, Catalonia, Spain, 13th century (photo by author).

Sex and mysticism

During a Talmudic discussion between rabbinic sages about the value of procreation, one rabbi, El'azar ben Azariah, criticized another, Ben-Azzai, for failing to practice what he preached. Ben-Azzai spoke strongly in favor of the mandate that Jewish men "be fruitful and multiply"—but he had failed to marry and father children himself. In other words, as El'azar put it, "You interpret well, but do not behave well." In his defense, Ben-Azzai responded: "What shall I do? My soul desires Torah. Let the world continue by the efforts of others!" (Boyarin 1993: 134). In this conversation, Ben-Azzai presents the desire for Torah as conflicting with the obligation to engage in sexual intercourse and procreate with a wife.

Regardless of whether faiths promoted celibacy, sexual desire and desire for God often intertwined in medieval mystical traditions. The experience of desire for God, or Torah, raised questions for medieval Jewish men about how that could be reconciled with their desire for their wives. Ben-Azzai presented these two desires as fundamentally incompatible: his desire for Torah rendered marriage impossible. But some of the practitioners of the Jewish mystical tradition known as *kabbalah* understood human sexuality, and its link to God, very differently. A mystical text called the Zohar, which claimed to be written in the second century CE but was in reality composed in thirteenth-century Castile, linked the real-life Jewish wives of kabbalist husbands with the **Shekhinah**, a feminine manifestation of God's presence in the world [*Doc. 12, pp. 129–131*]. Men could ensure continued spiritual closeness to the Shekhinah through the physical presence of their wives (Biale 1992: 110).

When kabbalists went on a journey, they believed that through prayer they could bring the Shekhinah with them—but that this figure remained closely tied to the wife they had left at home. Upon their return home, men were ordered to have sexual intercourse with their wives. Sex both renewed men's connection with the Shekhinah and allowed them to thank their wives for giving them access to the female Divine Presence. Concentration on the Shekhinah during the physical act of sex also ensured that if the wife became pregnant, the Shekhinah would give to the child a "holy soul."

The Kabbalist discourse about sex emphasized the importance of the wife's physical pleasure. Attention to the wife's pleasure provided her with appropriate thanks for her role in bringing her husband closer to the Shekhinah, while also helping to ensure the excellence of the children produced by their union (Biale 1992: 103). However, although the Zohar encouraged kabbalist men to take seriously their wife's consent and enjoyment of sexual intercourse, this text demonstrates that male Jewish mystics saw women's religious and spiritual role as fundamentally different from that open to men. Mystics' wives played an intermediary role in the sexualized relationship between their husbands and the divine presence. Women therefore served as vehicles for their husbands' mystical experiences, without being expected to have their own.

The link between sex and mysticism as seen in the kabbalistic tradition points to a significant difference between how Jews and Christians envisioned the possibilities for men's and women's ecstatic mystical experiences. Some Christian women mystics in medieval Europe described their union with Christ in intensely sexual terms. If Jewish women experienced sexual pleasure and mystical connection with the divine while having sex with their husbands (or at other times), their experiences are not revealed in our written records. The Zohar presents Jewish women as central in bringing the Shekhinah into Jewish homes, but does not overtly portray women as experiencing a personal connection to the Shekhinah like the one their husbands obtain through their bodies. In medieval Jewish mysticism, such religious and carnal pleasures were reserved for men.

Sex outside marriage

Extramarital sex was treated very differently depending on whether the husband or the wife pursued a sexual relationship outside of marriage. Hebrew poetry from Muslim-ruled al-Andalus describes men's desire, at least, for sexual relationships with young men and women (Scheindlin 1986: 88). Although poetry cannot be equated to lived experiences, it is likely that some elite married men may have engaged in sexual relationships with young men and women, including those outside their own faith community. Sources from Ashkenaz indicate that a husband's adultery, although not subject to legal penalties, could serve as grounds for courts to force the man to divorce his wife if she wished it (Grossman 2004: 144). Some Jewish men, especially those who married only one wife, kept concubines, in part because they were cheaper to maintain (Assis 1988: 36). Concubinage also may have functioned as an alternative for men who wanted an at least semi-legitimate relationship but lived in places where they could not legally marry a second wife. Concubines sometimes came from outside the Jewish community.

In contrast, Jewish married women who consensually had sexual relationships with men other than their husbands could be subject to harsh punishments. Biblical death sentences were not typically carried out, but Jewish communities could potentially inflict fines and even corporal punishment. The men who had sex with married women could be punished as well. Husbands were required to divorce their wives for adultery, and a couple who had been guilty of adultery could not subsequently marry, even if the woman received a divorce from her husband. The couple from Seville aroused such ire in Toledo at least in part because they had remained together in a pseudo-marital relationship. In his response to the query, ibn Adret emphasized that the couple should be physically separated and exiled in different places if they insisted upon continuing to live together and, presumably, continuing their sexual relationship [*Doc. 10, p. 127–128*].

Adultery also had potentially tragic legal consequences for any children born of an adulterous union. These children were designated as belonging to the category of **mamzer**. According to Jewish law, *mamzer* does not simply mean "bastard" or "illegitimate." It carried real legal implications, which could not simply be ignored. A child born of an adulterous union could not licitly marry non-*mamzerim* and often had difficulties claiming their share of inheritance from their family members.

Jewish women did not, as far as we know, typically write poetry glorifying extramarital relationships, like some of the men of their community. Most did not write poetry at all; the extensive canon of surviving Hebrew poetry from al-Andalus includes only a single example of a poem written by

a woman [*Doc. 13, pp. 131–132*]. The poem is attributed to the wife of
Dunash ben Labrat, who was also a poet; her first name is not known. Like
many of the poems written by men, it is a love poem, written on the occasion
of her husband leaving the country, perhaps due to a falling-out with his
patron (Cole 2007: 27). Unlike most of the love poems written by men, however, the relationship depicted in this poem appears to be within the confines
of marriage. It is also worth mentioning that the poem includes no overt
sexual imagery, a common feature of love poetry written by Jewish men.

Sex with non-Jews

Extramarital sex—especially when it involved a married woman—always
raised a host of social and legal issues. However, sex between Jews and
non-Jews sparked additional anxieties in Jewish, Christian, and Muslim
communities. Among the ruling faiths of Christianity and Islam, attitudes
toward interfaith sex were deeply gendered. As a result, Jewish women who
had sex with non-Jews often would not be subject to the same sort of legal
penalties as Jewish men who had sex with women of the ruling faith.

Christian religious rhetoric took a dim view on interfaith sex in general, and the Church forbade interfaith marriage. However, when secular
rulers passed legislation banning interfaith sex, they tended to emphasize
the problem of sex between Christian women and Jewish or Muslim men.
Jewish men found guilty of sex with Christian women were in some places
technically subject to the death penalty, although often pardoned in practice
(Assis 1988: 44). Similarly, Islam formally permitted marriages between
Muslim men and Jewish or Christian women but forbade the reverse. This
legislation relied on the assumption, shared by all three faiths, that women
were subject to the authority or influence of their husband or male sexual
partner. As a result, sex between a woman of the ruling faith and a man
of the subordinate faith threatened to subvert religious hierarchies. Sex
between men of the ruling faith and women of the subordinate faith did
not inspire quite as much anxiety on the part of rulers.

Some Jewish communities fought for the privilege to penalize Jewish
women who had sex with Muslim or Christian men, as well as to fine the
men in question. Even when they could not punish such behavior, Jewish
communities often demonstrated anxiety about the possibility of sex
between Jewish women and non-Jewish men. The bodies of Jewish women,
for some rabbis, took on a symbolic function: their hoped-for purity and
inviolability represented the strength of the Jewish community's boundaries, while the penetration of their bodies by outsiders symbolized a threat
to the community and its boundaries. Such anxieties are on full display in
the rabbinic responses to a case in thirteenth-century Ashkenaz, in which
a Jewish woman was forcibly converted to Christianity and then held captive by Christians. Their debate over whether or not they should assume
she had sex with Christian men during her captivity reveals some of their

fears about the stability of the community in the wake of attacks and mass conversions (Furst 2008: 180).

The Middle Ages also saw the development of the Christian trope of the beautiful and seductive "Jewess," whose ability to influence rulers through seduction brought benefit to Jews and danger to Christians. Rahel, the "Jewess of Toledo," Esther, the supposed Jewish mistress of Casimir the Great of Poland, and, according to some scholars, Pulcellina of Blois all represent examples of this phenomenon.

Queer sex and sexuality

Scholars continue to debate whether and how to talk about gay, lesbian, bisexual, or trans people in the Middle Ages and other eras of the distant past. On the one hand, incontrovertible evidence indicates that some medieval people experienced same-sex desire and, in some cases, acted on that desire. Textual evidence also indicates that medieval people knew of the existence of individuals whose bodies did not fit neatly into the category of "male" or "female," as well as individuals assigned one gender at birth who then lived as another gender. However, it is important to acknowledge that terms like "gay" or "trans" represent modern identity categories, which did not necessarily map onto how people in the Middle Ages understood their lived experiences.

While the choice of terminology might be complicated, it is very clear that neither same-sex attraction nor gender fluidity are new or specifically modern phenomena. The written evidence for sexual activity and romance between men is more extensive than the evidence for sexual activity between women. However, this disparity certainly should not be treated as proof that men were more likely than women to pursue same-sex erotic intimacy. Rather, the near-invisibility of women's same-sex desire in the past once again highlights the reality that the vast majority of medieval texts were authored by men. We therefore have far more written examples of men talking about their desire for other men than women talking about their desire for other women. Legal texts, including responsa, also devote more attention to sex between men than sex between women; male legal authorities might have been less concerned about, or less aware of, women acting on same-sex attraction.

Yet at least some elite male rabbis realized that sex between women happened. Even more interestingly, while they clearly considered sexual activity of this kind to be in some way sinful, they treated it as a minor offense. A passage in the Babylonian Talmud referred to "women who rub with one another" [*Doc. 14, p. 132*]. The passage indicates that some rabbis, at least, argued that women who had sex with other women should not be permitted to marry men of priestly lineage—who were also forbidden from marrying divorcées. However, the text detailed no other apparent punishment that women who had sex with other women might incur. Nor is it clear that all rabbis agreed on the prohibition against women marrying a priest if they had participated in sexual relationships with women. Maimonides banned sex between women, but prescribed no penalty whatsoever: such women should not receive corporal punishment, because the act was not specifically prohibited in the Torah. He also permitted them to marry men of priestly lineage. Married women who had sex with women could be lashed—but the act was not considered adultery, so they could remain married to their husbands (Sienna 2019: 70).

Rabbinic texts also referred to gender fluidity. A midrash in the Talmud suggests that the reason Sarah and Abraham were barren was that they belonged to the category of *tumtum*, a person who cannot be clearly identified as either male or female, or that Sarah was an *aylonit*, a term used for a person assigned female at birth who did not develop female secondary sex characteristics during puberty (Sienna 2019: 40–41). Maimonides' son Avraham condemned people who wore clothing associated with the sex not assigned to them at birth. However, his condemnation points to prevalent customs in which women dressed like men and men dressed like women in certain playful, celebratory settings (Sienna 2019: 76). In some settings, gender fluidity might have occurred without comment.

Altogether, the textual evidence indicates that rabbis had some discomfort with queer sex and with gender nonconformity. However, they fully accepted the existence of people who did not fit neatly into the categories of male or female, if only in cases where their physical bodies defied such categorization. Moreover, despite occasional condemnations of certain behaviors, it is clear that neither gender fluidity nor same-sex desire represented major concerns for the rabbis.

Women's sexual health

Christian, Jewish, and Muslim women all played a role in healthcare in the medieval world—sometimes as professional doctors (see Chapter 7), but often simply as part of their domestic responsibilities and their care for their own bodies. Medieval medical texts recorded remedies, sometimes explicitly attributed to women, associated with their sexual and reproductive health. Women clearly had and shared knowledge around conception, the prevention of miscarriages, the health of the uterus, postpartum pain, and other ailments associated particularly with women (Caballero-Navas 2008: 151).

Some of these remedies hint at interfaith women's networks, within which women shared medical knowledge specific to their own bodies. One medieval Jewish recipe, for example, instructed women to stop menstruation by inserting into the womb a combination of pig dung and eggshells; the text attributed this recipe to "the Ishmaelites" (Caballero-Navas 2008: 152). Evidence also indicates that Jewish women turned to Christian midwives, and vice versa. Although the evidence at our disposal for Jewish women's healthcare is rather scanty, it nevertheless suggests that women took their sexual and reproductive health seriously, and that remedies for women's healthcare circulated between faith communities in the medieval world.

Many Jewish families only had two or three children; it therefore seems likely that they practiced some form of birth control. Medieval medical literature includes numerous examples of contraceptives, albeit not necessarily all effective ones. For example, if a woman had children and did not wish to have more, she should place in her afterbirth as many grains of barley as the number of years for which she hoped to avoid pregnancy (Green 1996: 131). Women also had medical remedies designed to encourage conception. Ibn Adret ruled in favor of a woman who wanted to drink a syrup that would help her conceive, counter to her husband's objections that pregnancy would ruin her appearance (Assis 1988: 32).

Sexual assault

People in the Middle Ages had a different conception about what constituted consent from that of many people today, but they did take consent seriously. In contrast to film depictions of the Middle Ages, in which sexual assault often occurs with abandon and goes unpunished, medieval people were genuinely concerned about sexual assault.

Jewish legal discourse in late antiquity and the Middle Ages even encompassed discussions about the possibility of what today might be termed marital rape. The Babylonian Talmud cited one authority as saying that it was unequivocally forbidden to force one's wife to have sex against her will. As an added incentive to avoid marital rape, another rabbi is said to have claimed that the children born of such a union would be in some way "unworthy" (Babylonian Talmud, *Eruvin* 100b). In contrast, a woman who demanded that her husband fulfill his sexual obligation was promised exemplary children. However, the language of prohibition is not accompanied by any kind of specific penalty. It is not clear that, in practice, a man would be in any way formally punished for raping his wife.

Maimonides also included overt discussion about sex and consent in the context of marriage in his *Mishneh Torah*. At first glance, Maimonides can be read as a firm critic of marital rape. He compares a woman forced to have sex with a husband she finds hateful to a captive forced into sex with her captors [*Doc. 11, p. 129*]. The language of captivity—a situation in which, under Jewish law, any sexual relationship is legally presumed to be non-consensual—emphasizes the fact that, in a situation like this, a woman has withheld consent and her wishes should be respected. However, he still does not question the financial penalty imposed on a woman divorced under these circumstances.

An additional passage in the *Mishneh Torah* raises important questions about how much a wife's consent really mattered in medieval rabbinic culture. Although Maimonides might have been aware that women could and did withhold consent to sex during marriage, he also stated that "a man's wife is permitted to him at all times" (Maimonides, *Mishneh Torah*, De'ot 5:4). He went on to frame non-consensual marital sex not as forbidden—but simply as less than ideal. A man who had sex with his wife without her consent—either because she explicitly refused or because she was asleep or very drunk—was paralleled to a man who simply had sex too frequently. The choice to treat obtaining a wife's consent as praiseworthy rather than mandatory left a great deal of space for husbands to ignore their wives' wishes.

The patriarchal social and legal culture inhabited by Jews, Christians, and Muslims in the medieval world gave rise to deeply complicated and fraught understandings of women's consent, and when—or whether—it mattered. Even if women *could* withhold consent in the context of marriage, and their husbands were at least encouraged to respect their wishes, how much freedom did women really have to withhold consent? Given the reality that women were often socially and economically dependent on their husbands, we must take seriously the possibility that the very real power relationship in medieval marriages made it very difficult for a woman to withhold consent. Nor is there evidence of men being formally penalized for marital rape. The limited ability of women to make choices about getting or staying married should also raise additional concerns about just how meaningful women's consent was in practice.

Outside of marriage, rape was undoubtedly taken seriously; however, there is relatively little textual evidence of rape in medieval Jewish communities. Especially within the source material from Ashkenaz, nearly all references to rape involve Jewish women held captive, and at least presumed to have been raped, by non-Jews (Grossman 2004: 144). In the Iberian Peninsula, all the references to Jewish men raping Jewish women appear in Latin legal documentation, created in the context of Christian courts (Assis 1988: 49). As is the case today, however, we should assume that rape, and in particular rape within the Jewish community, was both underreported at the time and under-documented in the surviving source material.

Conclusion

Sex was a part of everyday life for most adult Jewish women, but it remains particularly difficult for modern scholars to access how Jewish women thought about and experienced sex and sexuality. Many sources remained silent on the topic entirely, while others focused primarily on men's perspective. The evidence available to us tells us a few details. Sex was intended to be performed within the confines of marriage, but various kinds of illicit sex—including sex outside marriage, sex with non-Jews, and sex between women—undoubtedly occurred. We also know that sex was only one part of married life. The next chapter will turn to other aspects of women's family life: in particular, the birthing and raising of children.

6 Family, childbirth, and child-rearing

According to an anecdote in the Babylonian Talmud, Rabbi Joseph bar Hiyya, who was blind, would stand up whenever he heard his mother's footsteps and announce, "Let me rise up before the approaching Shekhinah!" (Romney Wegner 1998: 73). This idealized vision of the maternal, in which a rabbi showed so much respect to his mother as to equate her with the divine presence, reflects the fact that most rabbinic authorities thought the greatest accomplishment women could aspire to was motherhood and caring for a family. Even though the commandment to "be fruitful and multiply" only applied to men, male Jewish writers tended to assume that women desired children and found much of their joy and fulfillment in motherhood.

Despite the rabbinic assumption that marriage and childbearing were the destiny and goal of most women, not all families—happy or otherwise—were alike. Most Jewish women married, but some did not; others were widowed or divorced young and never remarried. Some newly married couples established a new household, into which they hoped to eventually bring their own children. Others lived with parents, grandparents, and siblings. Although motherhood was considered the ideal, and infertility provided grounds for divorce or bigamy, not all women had children. Wealthier families might build households that encompassed waged or enslaved laborers, including non-Jews. Family also extended beyond the household; even when they did not live together, adults maintained close social and economic ties with their parents and siblings.

Many of the sources available to historians of medieval Jewish families are prescriptive texts that explain what their authors thought families *should* be like. But scholars can also consult a wide range of responsa, chronicles, poetic elegies, contracts, and court records, which describe the complex dynamics at work in many families. Medieval Jewish families worked sometimes together and sometimes against one another in the pursuit of their goals. Together, the sources tell us that in the Middle Ages, as today, family meant very different things to different people. This chapter seeks to highlight some of the complicated and varied ways in which women experienced family life.

DOI: 10.4324/9781003104964-8

Family in the medieval Jewish world

Constructions of family and household varied widely across the medieval world and even within Jewish communities. Increasingly, scholars have suggested that many medieval Jews lived in something akin to a small nuclear family: many couples created independent households upon marrying and over the course of a few years had two or three children (Stow 1987: 1086). Evidence from the Cairo Genizah indicates that some couples even wrote this family structure into their marriage contracts. Discussions of living arrangements were common in *ketubot*, including conditions that the couple would not have to live with the parents or extended family of one of the spouses. A scribe named Halfon ben Menashe, active in twelfth-century Egypt, drew up a list of standard conditions in marriage contracts, in both the local Judeo-Arabic vernacular and the formal Aramaic version that would appear in the *ketubah* itself. One condition stated that if the bride did not wish to live with her mother-in-law, he must find her a separate apartment, "as is fitting for her." This phrase could suggest that at least in elite families, who had the means to purchase or rent multiple dwellings, new brides could expect to live alone or with only their husband (Krakowski 2018: 272). Women whose husbands had multiple spouses could also demand the right to live separately from the other wives.

However, the fact that couples felt it necessary to include conditions like these in near Eastern *ketubot* suggests that, without contractual intervention, some families might live in multi-generational households. For one thing, not all families could afford to purchase or rent multiple apartments. Living with in-laws might be a necessary evil, financially speaking, in lower-income families. The couple who disputed over whether the wife should be allowed to teach scripture classes to children lived with the husband's mother for at least part of their marriage. Their financial troubles, which left them constantly on the brink of poverty and even starvation, suggest that, at least before the wife started teaching, the couple would not have had the funds to live separately from her mother-in-law [*Docs. 3–4, pp. 120–123*].

Some marriage contracts specified that the couple would plan to live with, or near, one set of in-laws. Although in theory a bride was expected to leave her parents' home and transition to that of her husband, in practice her family might require that the couple live with them or at least stay nearby. One contract even flatly denied the bride the right to choose to live apart from her mother, even if she wanted to (Krakowski 2018: 272). Other contracts stipulated that the couple would live with members of the husband's family, but sometimes added the condition that a bride could request to relocate if she "hated" living with her in-laws. Court records indicate that relations between a bride and her in-laws could devolve into outright hostility: one woman appears to have claimed that her husband's mother and sister "tormented" her. A letter from thirteenth-century Fustat related the tragic story of a woman whose sister-in-law "took to beating her with a shoe," and whose father-in-law "curses her whenever he comes in" (Krakowski 2018: 273–276). Women in such situations had very good reason to demand a private home, but less dramatic conflicts must have occurred as well.

Privacy for new couples, and separation from parents and siblings, might have been the hallmark of wealthy Jewish households. However, wealthy families also built households that encompassed non-relatives. In his lament for his wife Dolce, Eleazar implied that his students formed a regular part of his household [*Doc. 1, pp. 118–119*]. Waged and enslaved laborers might also live full-time in the households where they worked. While the people who provided labor for wealthy Jewish families belonged to the larger entity of the household, they were not precisely family. Some were not Jewish, which may have created an even greater sense of distance between the householders and the people who worked for them.

Family formed the primary source of social and economic support for women. While men had the ability to form a broad range of relationships with other members of the Jewish community, women more often had no one to rely on other than their close kin. But kinship did not guarantee support: some people were unwilling or unable to support their women relatives. Kinship ties needed to be actively maintained in order to remain meaningful (Krakowski 2018: 58). A letter found in the Cairo Genizah, written by a woman who had fled to Tripoli from Jerusalem after Christian Crusaders conquered the city, highlights both the potential benefits of kinship ties and their limits [*Doc. 15, pp. 132–133*]. The precise relationship between the writer and the addressee is not overtly stated, but the woman may have been writing to her sister's son (Goitein 1975: 82). The woman calls on the addressee to "be mindful of the family bonds and blood," appealing directly to their kinship tie as a reason for him to write back and to provide her with financial support during a difficult time. However, the letter also implies that they are currently not in active contact; moreover, the writer indicates that other kinship ties have failed her as well. Her husband had a falling-out with his brother over an inheritance dispute, and they can no longer count on his support. Kinship could provide a basis for trust, emotional closeness, and economic support if needed—but conflict and lack of contact could weaken those kinship ties.

Pregnancy and childbirth

Pregnancy and childbirth were presumed to be occasions for joy. Men could fulfill the commandment to "be fruitful and multiply." While women were not obligated to fulfill this commandment, most male writers in the medieval world assumed that women wanted to have children and would feel fulfilled by motherhood. However, even if couples were overjoyed by pregnancy and eager to meet their new child, pregnancy and childbirth were also dangerous propositions, which necessitated both medical and ritual expertise. Midwives played a crucial role in providing care for expectant mothers through pregnancy and birth, as well as for newborn infants. Once women suspected pregnancy, they would be examined by a midwife, sometimes at the *mikveh* (ritual bath). Jewish women relied on both Jewish and Christian midwives for care (Baumgarten 2004: 43–45).

In medieval culture, medical care was often intertwined with religious rituals and magical practices. Amulets and charms—for example, red stones or rabbit hearts—combined with prayers and incantations played a crucial role in protecting women during pregnancy and childbirth. Special amulets, including an iron knife placed under the woman's pillow, protected women and their infants from the demonic figure of Lilith during and immediately after childbirth (Baumgarten 2004: 48–49). Families also prayed about the sex of the child: it was presumed that they would usually pray for the birth of a son. Rabbinic texts tended to assume that the birth of a son would occasion celebration, while the birth of a daughter would prove disappointing (Baskin 2002: 15). However, due to the belief that the child's sex had been determined 40 days after conception, expectant parents were forbidden to pray for a son after this period (Baumgarten 2004: 41).

An illustrated narrative from the Castilian *Cantigas de Santa Maria* (see Figure 3.1) offers some insight into how women might have experienced the dangers of childbirth, a difficulty shared by Christian and Jewish women alike. In her panic over a difficult childbirth, the fictional Jewish woman called out to the Virgin Mary while giving birth. After she received the divine assistance that she had requested, the new mother converted to Christianity, along with her infant child. Like all the representations of Jews in the *Cantigas de Santa Maria*, this story tells us more about Christian perceptions of Jews than it does about Jews' lived experiences. However, this particular story might reflect some truth: terror in the face of childbirth might have inspired some Jewish women, in desperation, to call out to a wider range of supernatural beings than would have been considered strictly acceptable under Jewish law. The popularity of stories that describe conversion miracles during childbirth might have concerned some rabbis, who feared Christian midwives might persuade Jewish mothers to convert (Baumgarten 2004: 51).

Medical care also blended with magical and religious rituals in the care of new mothers and their newborn infants. Mothers received strengthening foods; babies were washed, sprinkled with salt, and then swaddled. They were never left alone, in an effort to safeguard them from evil spirits (Baumgarten 2004: 52). Infancy and early childhood were indeed dangerous times. Popular representations of the medieval period often misrepresent the low average lifespan in the medieval world as an indication that most people died in their forties or fifties. The real reason for the low average lifespan is that high rates of infant and early childhood mortality brought down the average. The Lilith *midrash*, which claimed that Lilith could harm male infants up to their eighth day of life and female infants up to their twelfth day of life, could reflect the writer's awareness that the first few weeks of an infant's life were an especially dangerous time [*Doc. 2, pp. 119–120*].

Childbirth also brought about ritual impurity for the mother, even if the infant was stillborn. The length of ritual impurity differed based on the sex of the child: new mothers were ritually impure for seven days after the birth of a son and fourteen days after the birth of a daughter (Meacham 1999: 259–260). This disparity could reflect the fact that girls and women were more often linked with impurity in ancient and medieval culture.

Infertility

For men, parenthood was a commandment: the biblical injunction to "be fruitful and multiply" was understood as an obligation to produce children, ideally at least one son and one daughter. Even though women were formally exempted from this commandment, the bearing of children was nevertheless understood to be a fundamental part of women's role. Scholars have debated why women were not obligated to bear children; some have suggested it reflected the belief that men played a more important role in the conception of children, while others have argued it stemmed from the view that women had a natural desire to bear children and thus did not need to be commanded (Baskin 2002: 124–125).

Rabbis were very much aware of the reality of infertility. The Hebrew Bible features so many barren matriarchs that it can be considered a motif. Sarah, Rebecca, and Rachel all struggled to conceive and bear children, and only eventually managed to do so through divine intervention. Infertility also had legal consequences for medieval Jewish women: it could serve as grounds for divorce. After ten years, men without children were expected to attempt to fulfill their reproductive obligation with another wife. They could divorce their first wives, or take a second alongside her. In places where polygyny was considered acceptable, childless men could marry a second wife without question. In contexts where polygyny was forbidden or highly discouraged, the wife's infertility was one of few cases in which it might be permitted. Husbands in Ashkenaz could request an exception to the ban of Rabbenu Gershom on the grounds of infertility. In the Christian-ruled Iberian kingdoms, husbands could apply to the king for a special license to marry a second wife; infertility was one of the few cases in which such licenses were often granted (Assis 1997: 262–264).

Women could also appeal for a divorce on the grounds of infertility. Although they were not commanded to bear children, they were assumed to naturally desire children, and to feel sorrow if they proved unable to bear children. It usually was not clear, medically speaking, if the husband or wife was at "fault" for the couple's barrenness, and some women asked for the chance to try again to bear children with another husband. However, women considered infertile were subject to legal restrictions and penalties. Rabbis debated whether a woman divorced on the grounds of infertility was entitled to receive her *ketubah* money; some, including Maimonides, suggested she should forfeit it unless it were clear that the husband, not the wife, was infertile (Grossman 2004: 238). Additionally, a woman who married twice without bearing children over the course of two successive ten-year periods was presumed barren and forbidden to marry a childless man (Baskin 2002: 127).

Rituals of motherhood

The birth of a baby boy required a ritual shortly after birth: the circumcision. Jewish law required that boys be circumcised on their eighth day of life, only to be postponed if the child was ill. Mothers presumably attended their sons' circumcision ceremonies; their period of impurity ended precisely on time for them to be present for the circumcision of their infant sons. However, mothers played very little formal role in the ceremony, and the obligation to circumcise sons was incumbent primarily on fathers. Women were legally permitted to act as circumcisers, based on the biblical precedent of Moses' wife Zipporah, who circumcised their two sons when Moses failed to do so. However, some rabbinic opinions discouraged women from circumcising infants if capable men were available, and they may not have acted as circumcisers regularly (Baumgarten 2004: 65). Some texts from medieval Ashkenaz also refer to a figure called the *ba'alat ha-brit*, who held the child during part of the ceremony, and whose role may have been akin to godmothers in Christian baptismal ceremonies (Baumgarten 2004: 70–71).

Jewish mothers appear to have developed and participated in rituals which allowed them to play a more active role in ceremonially welcoming their children. Some of these rituals, unlike circumcision, were observed regardless of the child's sex; they therefore allowed mothers to celebrate the arrival of infant daughters as well as sons. In Ashkenaz, such rituals included the Hollekreisch ceremony, in which infants received a non-Jewish name; Wachnacht, a meal at the newborn's home the night before circumcision; and a ritual held on the Sabbath on which the mother's ritual impurity had concluded and she went to the synagogue for the first time after giving birth (Baumgarten 2004: 93–105). Such rituals allowed for communal celebrations in honor of both mothers and infants and provided spaces in which families and communities could rejoice at the birth of healthy infant girls as well as boys. Some of these rituals may have been inspired by Christian practices, including baptism, a ceremony of ritual immersion practiced for infant boys and girls, and churching, the ceremony in which the mother attended church for the first time after giving birth.

The naming of children, and in particular daughters, may have had ritual or at least personal significance for mothers. S.D. Goitein argued that the variety of women's names in medieval Egypt, combined with the rarity of biblical and Hebrew names, suggested that mothers named their daughters. Such names, he suggests, reflect mothers' wishes for their daughters: they include frequent references to power and rulership, a variety of personal qualities, and expressions of wishes for health and happiness (Goitein 1978: 314–319). Goitein's theory remains only a theory—we have little clear evidence to determine precisely how medieval Jewish parents selected names for their children. However, in Ashkenaz and Sepharad, as well as the Middle East, Jewish girls were rarely given biblical names. Names in the local vernacular, which might have meanings like "Pleasant" (Dolce) or "Fortunate" (Astruga), were far more popular. The prevalence of vernacular names for Jewish girls across the medieval world could imply that mothers played a more significant role in naming daughters than in naming sons.

Nursing and wetnurses

Nursing of children was taken very seriously, as the breast milk given to infants was thought to impart various qualities to them. In theory, it was considered ideal for children to be breastfed by their own mothers. In practice, however, families who could afford to do so often hired **wetnurses** to nurse infant children in place of birth mothers. The choice to hire a wetnurse was often quite a practical one. Nursing women were not supposed to have sex, as people believed that sexual intercourse would spoil the milk. Hiring a wetnurse thus made a woman sexually available to her husband sooner, and therefore also able to produce additional children.

However, hiring wetnurses raised a host of legal and social concerns for Jewish families. All families, regardless of faith, had to worry about the character of the wetnurse. What characteristic might her milk impart to the infant? Could she be trusted to refrain from intercourse to keep someone else's child healthy? Jewish families had additional concerns, especially if they sought to hire non-Jewish wetnurses. One obstacle was legal: Christian and Muslim rulers regularly forbade Jews to hire servants who belonged to the ruling faith. A relationship between a Jewish master and a Christian or Muslim servant threatened to undermine religious hierarchies. In the Mediterranean, Jewish families would sometimes rely on enslaved wetnurses, many of whom belonged to another subordinate religious group. Enslaved Muslim women often served as wetnurses to Christians in the medieval Crown of Aragon, and could legally act as wetnurses for Jewish families as well (Winer 2008: 166–172).

Rabbinic authorities also expressed fears about whether non-Jewish wetnurses could be counted on to protect the physical and spiritual welfare of Jewish children. The Mishnah cautioned Jewish families to require that care take place within the child's home, rather than allow a non-Jewish wetnurse to care for a Jewish infant at her home. Later sources explain some of the reasons why non-Jewish wetnurses might have sparked so much anxiety. Non-Jewish women could not necessarily be trusted to follow Jewish dietary laws; they might bring non-kosher food and utensils into Jewish homes. The Ashkenazi ethical text *Sefer Hasidim* expressed concern about Christian wetnurses singing infants "idolatrous" lullabies, perhaps quietly educating Jewish children in Christian doctrine. A debate in the Talmud even suggested that families should avoid hiring non-Jewish wetnurses on the grounds that they were likely to deliberately kill Jewish infants (Aranoff 2019: 7–9). Christian wetnurses were also known on occasion to surreptitiously baptize Jewish children. According to Christian doctrine, baptism even without a parent's consent was transformative: the child was now legally Christian and could potentially be taken away from their Jewish parents.

Jewish law understood nursing as an obligation that a wife owed to her husband, not to her son. Husbands were therefore expected to contract wetnurses if needed. If a couple divorced while their child was still in infancy, the father was expected to hire a wetnurse or to pay his ex-wife for nursing their child. A responsum by Rabbi Asher ben Yehiel, who was educated in Ashkenaz but relocated to the Iberian Peninsula, offers surprising insight into the obligations that mothers and wetnurses owed to infant children [*Doc. 16, p. 133*]. According to the text, a woman, referred to with the pseudonym Rachel, conceived a child out of wedlock. The father, "Reuven," then married her, but not long after he abandoned her and married another wife. Since her own child was already with a wetnurse, and her husband had apparently left her with nothing, Rachel hired herself out as a wetnurse. Reuven abandoned his child as well as his wife: the infant had apparently been living with the wetnurse, and he stopped paying her salary. A dispute then arose over whether Rachel's obligation was to nurse her own child, or the child she had contracted to nurse.

Rabbi Asher ben Yehiel ruled in favor of the father who had hired Rachel to nurse his child. In part, his judgment reflects the specific circumstances of the case. The child Rachel had been nursing would no longer nurse from anyone else, while Rachel's son had spent his life being nursed by another woman. However, the response also reveals broader attitudes and expectations around nursing. Since Rachel's marriage was apparently of questionable validity, and since the infant's father did not support her, she was under no obligation to nurse her own son. She was, however, under a contractual obligation as a wetnurse to nurse her employer's son. Rabbi Asher ultimately instructed the court to force the infant's father to pay a wetnurse, with the added provision that the court should pay the wetnurse if the husband could not be forced. Even though women were expected to take on many child-rearing duties, they could not be forced to breastfeed their children.

Child-rearing

The care of children was considered an essential element of women's work. In practice, however, wealth determined what childcare entailed. Affluent families might leave many childcare responsibilities to servants or slaves. In families of moderate or lower socioeconomic status, mothers and older siblings (especially daughters) took on most childcare responsibilities.

Not long after children were weaned, expectations and norms around childcare quickly became gendered. Medieval cultures in general, including Jewish cultures, encouraged families to raise boys and girls differently. Biblical and Talmudic commands that delineated parental duties first and foremost emphasized the obligations a father had toward his son: to circumcise him, to perform the ceremony of redemption of the firstborn (if applicable), to teach him Torah, to find him a wife, to teach him a trade or craft, and to teach him to swim (Babylonian Talmud, Kiddushin 29a). Rabbinic texts had far less to say on either the childcare obligations of mothers or on the obligations either parent owed to their daughters.

The obligation to educate sons, but not daughters, ensured that the childhood experiences of boys and girls diverged when they were still very young. When boys were about five years of age, some aspects of their care would pass to their fathers, or to schools and hired teachers. Rituals celebrated the beginning of boys' education. Eleazar of Worms described a ceremony in which Jewish boys would recite the Hebrew alphabet with their teacher and eat letters formed by honey, then eat a cake and an egg inscribed with biblical verses. Such initiation rites helped young boys associate learning with sweetness (Marcus 1996: 27–28). Rituals like this one highlight the formative nature of education in the upbringing of Jewish boys. Fathers played a prominent role in these rituals, due to their responsibility to either educate their sons or send them to schools. Mothers, in contrast, played no significant role. The invisibility of mothers in Torah study initiation rituals symbolizes the transition of boys from the care of their mothers to their fathers (Aranoff 2019: 4).

Girls, in contrast, remained under their mother's care for a longer period of time. As they grew older, they would have assisted their mothers with the work of the household and with caring for younger children. Eleazar of Worms' lament for his two daughters, murdered alongside their mother, offers some insight into the upbringing of daughters. Both girls—Hannah, age six, and Bellette, age thirteen—could recite at least basic prayers, although Hannah only knew the Sh'ma and Bellette, the older sister, was familiar with a wider array of "prayers and songs." Both girls "spun and sewed and embroidered," suggesting that girls learned these basic skills at a very early age. Bellette also assisted her mother in caring for her father— the lament stated that she "prepared my bed and pulled off my shoes each evening." Interestingly, Bellette also "sat to listen to Torah from [her father's] mouth." The education of girls therefore could also encompass some Torah study as well as prayers. Moreover, the text suggests that fathers and mothers both participated in daughters' religious education (Baskin 2001: 436–437).

Families who wanted their children to learn a trade other than their own might enter them into apprenticeships. Apprentices could be as young as eight or nine years old. Practitioners of trades would commit to feeding and clothing apprentices and teaching them their trade. A few examples of Jewish apprenticeship contracts have survived. In 1389, for example, a boy named Mosse, son of Samuel Mosse, contracted as an apprentice with the veil-weaver Issach de Montblanc of Barcelona (Rich Abad 1999: 157). However, the contract between Mosse and Issach—like all the surviving Jewish apprenticeship contracts—records a case in which a Jewish boy was apprenticed to a Jewish man. Jewish girls apparently did not contract as apprentices, nor did Jewish women agree to supervise apprentices—at least not in the surviving documentation. Jewish women might have had greater difficulty in securing apprentices. Apprenticeships required families to hand over their children not only for teaching, but also for everyday care; some parents might have feared Jewish women were not financially capable of caring for someone else's children. However, Jewish apprenticeships are probably underrepresented in the sources. Jewish women and girls might have concluded Hebrew contracts, which have not survived, or made informal arrangements without written contracts.

The historian Philippe Ariès once claimed that, due to high rates of infant and childhood mortality, medieval parents did not much care for their children. In recent years, scholars have roundly debunked this claim. Jewish sources offer important insight into this—for example, when Eleazar of Worms lamented the death of his wife, he also offered a lament for his daughters, whom he described in loving terms, albeit in less detail than he devoted to his wife. Counterintuitively, Jewish parents' slaughter of their children during the Crusade massacres even indicates love, although it suggests that some parents at least were more concerned about their children's souls than about the survival of their bodies [*Doc. 23, p. 139*].

Some medieval Christian sources created a false dichotomy between Jewish mothers and fathers. Christian stories about Jewish families presented Jewish mothers as loving but portrayed Jewish fathers as violent and uncaring. A narrative from the *Cantigas of Santa Maria*, also found in other sources, told the story of a Jewish child who accidentally took communion and prayed to the Virgin. His father threw him into a furnace in a fury. The image in the *Cantigas* emphasizes the difference between mother and father: the father, unrepentant; the mother, horrified. After the Virgin miraculously rescued the child, he and his mother both converted to Christianity. The father, in contrast, was burned alive in the very same furnace in which he had sought to kill his child. The overt anti-Jewish aspects of this story mean that we should be very careful about taking it as representative in any way of lived experiences. The dichotomy between

Jewish mothers and fathers in the *Cantigas* reflected prevalent ideas about gender and Jewishness, and probably cannot say much about everyday reality. However, the *Cantigas* nevertheless affirmed that most parents cared deeply for their children's safety. The father's lack of concern for his son's wellbeing functioned to villainize him; in contrast, the mother's love for her son made her an acceptable candidate for conversion to Christianity.

Guardianship

Fathers were always presumed to be the legal guardians of their minor children. Mothers, however, were not. The term "orphan," used to define a category of minor children particularly deserving of charity, applied to minors who had lost their father but still had a living mother, as well as children who had lost both parents. Jewish communities, like the Christians and Muslims around them, developed legal and social norms to ensure that fatherless children would receive appropriate care and support.

Orphans without family financial resources to support them could turn to the Jewish community for charity. The Jewish court claimed to serve as "the father of orphans and the judge of widows," meaning that they were supposed to take special care to protect both orphans and their widowed mothers (Cohen 2009: 142). Charitable institutions both provided basic maintenance and helped to shepherd orphaned children to adulthood. The dying might also offer support to orphans and other impoverished children, often in deeply gendered ways. Sara, the widow of Daví de Cabestany of Perpignan, in her 1286 will bequeathed funds to educate poor Jewish boys and to provide dowries for poor Jewish girls (Winer 2006: 78).

Dying fathers made arrangements in their wills for the legal guardianship of their minor children. Guardianship was not necessarily about the everyday care of children; nor did the choice of guardian necessarily revolve around assumptions of who might best ensure their physical and emotional wellbeing. Instead, legal guardianship was first and foremost a financial role. A legal guardian was responsible for providing financial maintenance for a minor child and safeguarding their eventual inheritance.

In the Western Mediterranean, Christian mothers were often selected to serve as the guardians of their minor children. If Jewish mothers served as guardians, however, they typically did so as part of a panel of guardians, which might include male relatives as well as illustrious community members (Winer 2006: 113). These groups jointly took responsibility for safeguarding children's financial futures. On the one hand, these groups of guardians ensured that widowed mothers would have support from their extended family and community. On the other hand, the preference for group guardianship may indicate that many fathers assumed that their wives were not necessarily competent as managers of financial resources. The choice to name an alternative or co-guardian alongside a child's mother also reflected the complicated nature of widows' relationships with their minor children. If they wished to remarry and recover their dowry and *ketubah*, they had to extricate these funds from the estate of their minor children (Klein 1993: 68–69). Mothers who remarried had to relinquish guardianship. The expectation was that the new husband would take control of his wife's finances, and that he would not necessarily be the ideal person to take charge of his stepchildren's financial future.

However, it is important to note that legal guardianship was not necessarily tied to physical custody. Even when mothers did not serve as their children's legal guardians, they very well might have remained responsible for everyday care. In other words, women retained childcare responsibilities, but were not necessarily entrusted with financial responsibilities.

Mothers and adult children

Close relationships between mothers and their adult children could prove socially and economically beneficial to both mother and child, as well as personally fulfilling. However, such relationships could also be fraught with tension. In the Middle Ages, as today, interpersonal conflicts could easily arise in families and emotional closeness was not necessarily the norm. Genizah letters highlight some of the complicated dynamics between mothers and their adult children or sons- and daughters-in-law in medieval Egypt. In one letter, a man wrote to his mother to let her know of his marriage, apologizing profusely for not being able to be with her in person (Goitein 1978: 241). Yet family conflict existed alongside powerful affective ties. One young man sued his mother for his father's estate, to the horror of the judge, who emphasized that the mother had supported her children through her own labor. Widowed mothers might also have to sue their grown sons to recover their dowries (Goitein 1978: 247–248).

In Catalonia, evidence drawn from notarial registers and court records demonstrates the value of connections between Jewish mothers and their adult children. Widowed mothers gained newfound control over financial resources, which brought them new responsibilities as managers of wealth and as supporters of the most vulnerable members of her family. Bonadona, widow of Astrug Caravida of Girona, supported her daughter Ester through a messy divorce (Roth 2017). Support could go both ways: Bonadona also relied on her other son-in-law, Bellshom Scapat, the husband of her daughter Bonafilla, to help manage her late husband's wealth (Ifft Decker forthcoming). However, like in Egypt, mothers sometimes found themselves in the position where they had to sue children or stepchildren to recover their dowry or other assets. Continued economic ties between mothers and adult sons reflect their shared claims over family assets but might also reveal continued personal closeness. Some Jewish men even selected their mothers to serve as the legal guardians for their minor grandchildren.

While rabbis tended to value filial piety and to encourage adult sons to show respect to their mothers and fathers, particularly close relationships between mothers and adult sons could also become a source of anxiety. One passage in the Babylonian Talmud tells the story of a mother who wove oddly revealing priestly garments for their adult sons. Marjorie Lehman has argued that the story illuminates rabbis' concern about the continued power of mother–son relationships and the potential threat they posed to the bond between teacher and disciple (Lehman 2014: 59–60). While the passage points to the preservation of close ties between mothers and adult sons, it also portrays the power of mothers as dangerous.

Conclusion

Family played an especially crucial role for Jewish women. Men could more easily establish wide-ranging networks beyond their own near kin. As a result, Jewish women needed family, not only for personal and emotional connection, but also for very practical economic, legal, and social support. Yet family did not mean the same thing for everyone. Some women had children while others did not. Some relied on their husbands, while others found that their husbands were unreliable or lost them at a young age. Relationships with parents and siblings could be supportive, but they could also be contentious. The vagaries of family belonging and connection, which differed dramatically on an individual basis, had much greater significance for medieval women than for men: kinship ties shaped almost every aspect of their lives. The following chapter, on women's work, will demonstrate how even women who worked outside the home often relied on the men of their family for encouragement and support.

7 Jewish women's work

Licoricia of Winchester cut a powerful figure in thirteenth-century England. She worked professionally as a moneylender, with close ties to the royal court of King Henry III. As part of her work, she traveled regularly on business, gathered pledges, collected on loans, and took possession of landed estates in payment of debts (Bartlet 2009: 67–75). The city of Winchester has even announced plans to erect a statue in her honor—a sign not only of England's renewed interest in their medieval Jewish community, which was expelled in 1290, but also of Licoricia's importance in her own time and of how compelling she remains today. Licoricia was clearly an exceptional figure. There are very few medieval Jewish women about whom scholars could write a book-length biography. However, she also offers an example of what might be possible for working Jewish women in the medieval world. Despite the importance of marriage and family in structuring Jewish women's lives, women regularly also worked outside the home, as moneylenders, silkweavers, butchers, doctors, prostitutes, and more.

Women's work has a long history of being undervalued and dismissed. Today, women are still paid on average less than men for doing the same jobs. Medieval historians have typically portrayed women's work in all faith communities as low-paid and low-status. Much of the work women performed was perceived at the time as unskilled, or not recognized as work at all. Women's labor also tended to be underrepresented in many historical sources. For example, while documents including tax records, business contracts, court records, and wills regularly used profession as a way to identify men, the scribes and notaries who meticulously noted men's trades rarely considered women's professions worth recording.

For Jewish women, this problem is exacerbated by the fact that medieval documents rarely identified the trade or profession of *any* Jews, either men or women, unless it was directly relevant to the contract. The label of "Jew" generally served as the main identifier. Responsa sometimes refer offhandedly to Jewish women who practiced various trades, but do not always clarify whether it was normal for Jewish women to do such work. Increasingly, however, scholars of medieval women in general and Jewish

DOI: 10.4324/9781003104964-9

women in particular are finding ways to identify and analyze the work performed by women in the premodern world, using a wide array of both Jewish and non-Jewish sources.

Jewish women in credit and long-distance trade

Due to a long history of stereotypes, most people assume that medieval Jewish men and women exclusively or predominantly worked in the fields of moneylending and long-distance trade. According to the standard narrative, Jews were banned from practicing other trades and forced into moneylending, in part because Church law forbade Christians from lending at interest. Over the last several decades, excellent scholarship on both anti-Jewish rhetoric and on quotidian Jewish economic life has demonstrated that this narrative is largely a myth. Although some Jewish men and women worked in credit and international trade, Jews as a group also practiced a wide variety of other professions. Moreover, Christians regularly ignored or circumvented ecclesiastical restrictions on interest-bearing loans, and the Church permitted some types of interest under certain circumstances. Even in cases where Jews played a disproportionately large role in the credit market, Christians often still extended the majority of loans.

In some places, only a small minority of the wealthiest Jews worked as creditors; this may have been the case in England (Mell 2017: 199). A wealthy moneylender and royal financier like Licoricia would have belonged to the highest socioeconomic stratum of Jewish society. In other regions, Jews from a wider spectrum of social ranks worked at least part-time as creditors. In some parts of what is now Spain and France, most medieval debtors took out **consumption loans,** loans of small sums of money required to meet immediate needs. Although loan contracts rarely specified why debtors borrowed, the small size of loans makes it unlikely that they would have been used for major purchases or for commercial ventures. They were more like payday loans—or purchases made with a credit card. The small size of these loans meant that Jews of more moderate means could work at least part time as creditors. Long-distance trade, to an even greater extent than credit, would have been a profession open to only a few very wealthy individuals.

Stereotypes associating Jews with credit and finance did not exist in the medieval Islamic world. Thanks to the survival of the Cairo Genizah, Jewish business activities are better documented than those of the Muslim majority. However, hints in Genizah documents, combined with Muslim sources, suggest that Jewish and Muslim business practices and professions might have looked relatively similar. Genizah documentation offers numerous examples of wealthy Jews who worked as merchants, some of whom also extended loans. Women played an important role in creating and strengthening business relationships within and between families—the eleventh-century merchant Nahray ben Nissim, for example, established a web of commercial connections through the influence and intervention of his mother (Goldberg 2012: 33–34). However, the vast majority of Jews working professionally as merchants were men.

Credit was not the sole occupation open to Jews; nor did Jews dominate local credit markets. However, stereotypes are not the only reason that historians have dedicated so much attention to Jewish work in the credit industry. Credit might not have been the main form of Jewish work, but it was the best-documented form of Jewish work. Jewish credit transactions are almost certainly overrepresented in the documentary record, relative to other kinds of economic activity. This is because Jewish credit in Christian Europe was highly regulated. Popular portrayals of Jewish creditors as greedy and unscrupulous left rulers concerned that, without supervision, Jews might cheat their Christian clients—or that Christian debtors might accuse Jews of unsavory business practices, with or without justification. Jews were often legally required to register loans with Christian officials. The Exchequer of the Jews in England was created to keep track of Jewish loans. In the Crown of Aragon, Jews were obligated to register loans to Christians with local notaries.

Credit transactions are also particularly well-represented in the documentary record because credit was the sort of business that generated a high volume of documentation. Debtors might not repay their loans for months or even years. Sometimes, their heirs were left with the responsibility to repay debts. Both borrowers and lenders benefited from clear records of what was owed and what had been repaid. In contrast, the immediate exchange of cash for goods or services usually did not require a written contract. Jewish credit is also documented in court records, as Christians sued their Jewish creditors over claims that Jewish moneylenders had charged immoderate interest or had failed to acknowledge that a debt had already been repaid. Some of this litigation might have arisen from genuine misunderstandings; however, some Christian debtors also attempted to wield anti-Jewish sentiment to avoid repaying their debts.

The rich documentation for Jewish credit means that even if credit was not the most common occupation practiced by Jewish women, it offers a particularly clear arena in which historians can directly compare Jewish women's work with Jewish men's work, as well as Christian women's work. The substantial number of surviving credit contracts from multiple regions also provides an excellent picture of how Jewish women's work in this economic sector varied from place to place. In northern Europe, Jewish women played a highly visible role in the credit market. Their prominence in this industry stemmed in part from the fact that they filled a specific economic niche. Jewish women in northern France often extended loans to Christian women, who either preferred or felt obligated to borrow from women rather than men (Jordan 1978: 50–55).

However, the economic success of Jewish women in Ashkenaz also reflected the fact that wealthy widows, and even some married women, regularly controlled financial resources. A widow had the right to collect her dowry and *ketubah* money after her husband had died. In Ashkenaz it was considered normal for women to use this wealth in business ventures. **Rabbi Meir of Rothenburg**, for example, related the case of a woman who had invested the few resources she managed to recover from her husband's estate, in payment for her *ketubah* and supplement [*Doc. 17, p. 134*]. Through her investments, she became much wealthier than her late husband had been. Conflict only arose because her husband's heirs attempted to claim that she had drawn her wealth from her late husband's estate, and that it therefore now belonged to them. This responsum is one of many from medieval northern and central Europe in which rabbis referred offhandedly to women who worked both in credit and in high-volume, long-distance trade. They apparently considered women's involvement in business to be fairly unremarkable (Tallan 1991: 61). Responsa also indicate that Jewish women regularly traveled on business and encountered non-Jewish men in the course of their work. Rabbis considered these practices standard and refrained from criticizing the businesswomen of their community (Grossman 2004: 118–119).

Even more women in Ashkenaz might have worked behind the scenes, assisting their husbands in trade. **Glückel of Hameln**, who in the early eighteenth century authored the first memoir written by a Jewish woman, stated that her husband relied on her for business advice and described a business partnership in which she drew up the contractual agreement that her husband and his male business partner then signed. Contracts alone probably would have rendered her work invisible; only her memoir demonstrates how important a role she played in the family business. Although Glückel was active in a later period, and it is unclear how representative she was of Jewish women even in her own time, her example raises the possibility that Jewish women also participated in family businesses in ways that are not necessarily evident to modern scholars.

Jewish women's work in credit and trade looked very different in the Western Mediterranean. Quantitative studies indicate that Jewish women extended only a tiny fraction of the loans made by Jews. Lending to Christian women would not have provided much of an economic niche: Christian women rarely borrowed money independently (Ifft Decker 2016: 169–170). Additionally, evidence suggests that women in this region did not typically travel on business or participate directly in long-distance trade, although they did sometimes invest in commercial ventures (Winer 2006: 97–98).

When Jewish women in the Western Mediterranean did work in credit, they sometimes faced challenges that undermined their effectiveness. Bonafilla, wife of Vidal Gracià of Barcelona, collected on a loan owed to her husband—but she had to provide a guarantor [*Doc. 18a, pp. 134–135*]. Guarantors often appeared in loan contracts acting on behalf of debtors; they committed to repay the loan if the debtor proved unable or unwilling to do so. Bonafilla is the sole known example of a creditor providing a guarantor. This unusual feature of the loan contract could indicate that the debtor suspected that Bonafilla, one of very few Jewish wives in Barcelona to collect on loans for an absent husband, did not actually have the authority to collect the debt. This is the only surviving contract that records her involvement in business.

Other Jewish women creditors only achieved success under special circumstances. Reina, daughter of Bonmacip of Vic, had recently gotten divorced, and may have been encouraged by her father to work in moneylending [*Doc. 18b, p. 135*]. Bonadona, widow of Astrug Caravida of Girona, had received from her husband "a grant of his loans and his goods" that effectively made her his heir, even though usually Jewish women were not supposed to inherit from their husbands [*Doc. 18c, pp. 135–136*]. Starona, widow of Salomó Abraham of Barcelona [*Doc. 18d, p. 136*], acted in the wake of the Black Death, when the loss of much of the Jewish community to both plague and massacres left an unusually large number of young widows active in the credit market (Ifft Decker forthcoming).

Even in northern Europe, where scholars have suggested that Jewish men and women played a near-equal role in the credit market, medieval Christian art almost always imagined Jewish moneylenders as men. The only known image of a Jewish woman moneylender comes from a cartoon placed atop an exchequer role in England. The caricature still relies on stereotypes: the three Jews have exaggerated noses and other strange features and are linked in the image with demons. However, this image at least claimed to depict a real woman, who was labeled with the name "Avegaye," or Abigail (Lipton 2016: 8). The visual focus on men in nearly all Christian images of Jewish moneylenders provides another good reminder of the danger of relying on Christian rhetorical and legal sources to understand Jewish moneylending. These visual sources could lead people to assume that no Jewish women worked in credit at all.

Artisanal production and local trade

Jewish men and women both worked in artisanal production and local trade. The textile trade was especially important as a sector that offered opportunities for women across the medieval world to work outside the home. Jewish women worked as weavers, silk weavers, and cloth dyers. The prominence of women working in these industries might reflect the fact that girls and young women learned skills like sewing, spinning, and weaving at home as part of their basic household education. Eleazar of Worms related that his six-year-old daughter already had learned spinning, sewing, and embroidery before her untimely death (Baskin 2001: 437). Some very wealthy Jewish women even worked as cloth merchants. For example, Venguessone Nathan of Arles, in southern France, sold textiles and pottery out of a shop (Iancu-Agou 1987: 43–44). Jewish women also worked as silversmiths, coral cutters, button-makers, and peddlers (Rich Abad 2014: 80).

Many of these professions required practitioners to maintain elaborate workshops with specialized equipment and could only be carried out profitably by hiring a corps of skilled and unskilled laborers. As a result, practitioners of these trades needed access to financial resources. Even people who inherited fully functioning workshops needed to be able to pay workers' wages or support apprentices, purchase raw materials, and occasionally replace equipment. Those without capital resources, or enough other assets to serve as collateral, would have difficulty maintaining successful workshops independently. These barriers to entry meant that fewer women ran workshops independently: Jewish women, especially in the Mediterranean, rarely independently controlled enough wealth to start a workshop. As a result, many of the Jewish women who ran such businesses worked alongside their husbands. Documentation from Barcelona referred to several Jewish married couples in the silk industry who worked together to purchase raw materials on credit (Ifft Decker 2015: 62). Some widows may have taken over family workshops after their husbands' deaths.

Women's work in the artisanal trades could raise legal questions about to whom their wages belonged. Jewish law dictated that husbands had a right to their wives' earnings. However, in Egypt it became increasingly common starting in the twelfth century for marriage contracts to include a clause saying that working wives could keep their earnings. A legal petition from the late twelfth century referred to a woman who sought to keep the wages she made from embroidery (Goitein 1978: 132–133).

Jewish women probably also worked in the food trades. Although less direct evidence has survived for the work of Jewish women specifically, urban regulations, tax records, and offhand remarks in other texts indicate that women in Christian Europe regularly worked as bakers, fishmongers, and brewers. Jewish women might have worked as butchers, a job that required specialized knowledge of how to slaughter animals in accordance with Jewish dietary laws. Regulations passed by the urban government of Perugia referred to both Jewish men and women working as ritual slaughterers (Toaff 1998: 71). *Conversa* women in fifteenth- and sixteenth-century Spain confessed to performing specific tasks associated with Jewish ritual slaughter in their homes, such as removing the sciatic nerve and draining blood from the animal (Melammed 1999: 86–87). While most of these women performed this work in their homes for their own families rather than for profit, the prominence of *conversa* women as ritual slaughterers after the Spanish Expulsion could indicate that Castilian Jewish women had once worked as professional butchers for their communities.

Real estate

Another oft-cited myth about Jewish work in the medieval world is the claim that Jews were never permitted to own land. This claim, however, is demonstrably false. Jews across the medieval world owned both family homes and an array of investment properties. Some Jews worked rural agricultural lands as farmers, while others hired laborers or leased out properties to tenants who undertook to work the land and give a share of its proceeds to the owner. Jews also owned substantial urban properties, which they sometimes leased out to tenants as homes or shops.

Jewish women also owned and managed property. Restrictions over Jewish women's control over financial resources meant that, overall, women owned less landed wealth than men. Daughters inherited only in the absence of sons. In Catalonia, surviving dowry contracts provide no examples of Jewish brides who brought dowries including real estate. However, rabbinic responsa refer occasionally to women whose dowries included real property (Schraer 2019: 129). In Egypt, brides primarily brought household goods, jewelry, and clothing, but sometimes also had dowries including houses or portions of houses (Goitein 1978: 125). Although many wives might have left the management of these real estate holdings to their husbands, women were more likely to manage such wealth in widowhood.

Surviving documentation confirms that Jewish women, especially widows, worked as managers of real property. Dura, widow of Samuel Cap in Barcelona, in 1285 sold a vineyard, which for a number of years she had leased out to a Christian tenant (Ifft Decker 2019b: 15). Families in Egypt presumed that granting their daughters real estate holdings would help to ensure their long-term economic security; widows and divorcées owned property for both residence and revenue (Goitein 1978: 326–327). Occasionally married women managed property as well; one woman in Cairo, Sitt Naba', made special arrangements with a tenant to reflect the fact that he had made improvements on the rental property; although she clearly took on the primary responsibility for managing these properties, her husband confirmed her actions at the end of the document (Goitein 1978: 328).

Although technically married couples were not meant to jointly own property, in practice the debt of the wife's dowry gave wives certain rights over their husbands' real property holdings. As a result, several documents attest to husbands and wives selling property jointly. In some cases, spouses even acted together to purchase property; widows would then at least attempt to claim ownership over these properties, against their husbands' heirs (Ifft Decker 2019b: 27–28).

Medicine and midwives

Medicine was a common profession among the Jewish elite. Jewish women worked both as doctors and as midwives; the latter was an almost exclusively female profession during the Middle Ages. As both women and Jews, Jewish women were barred from certain kinds of formal medical education. Europe saw the rise of universities specializing in medical education, including the medical school established at Salerno in the ninth century.

However, these institutions did not confer degrees on either Jews or on women, regardless of faith. However, men and women in the medieval world often learned a great deal about medicine from apprenticeships; observing and learning from other medical practitioners could be at least as valuable as university study of contemporary medical texts. Many Jewish women probably learned medicine from family members; a woman named Chava, a surgeon active in fourteenth-century Manosque, came from a whole family of doctors (Shatzmiller 1994: 12). In turn, women also taught others; Sara de St. Gilles, based in Marseille, in 1326 contracted to teach a male student medicine (Taitz, Henry, and Tallan 2003: 86). Jewish women may have specialized in eye ailments; four of the seven Jewish women doctors active in Frankfurt in the fifteenth century were designated as eye doctors. Rabbi Yehudah ben Asher stated that a Jewish woman physician, whom he described as a "skilled oculist," rescued his sight (Taitz et al. 2003: 88).

Jewish women doctors could come into contact with the uppermost echelons of Christian society. Na Floreta ça Noga, a Jewish woman physician of Santa Coloma de Queralt, treated the queen of the kingdom of Aragon (Taitz et al. 2003: 79). Yet work in medicine could also get Jewish women into trouble, especially when they treated Christians. A Jewish woman midwife named Floreta d'Ays in 1403 found herself hauled before a court on malpractice charges when a Christian woman she treated died in childbirth (Green and Smail 2008: 192).

Prostitution

Men of all faiths turned on occasion to prostitutes, and in most urban centers sex work was legal and highly regulated. Abundant documentation described Jewish men's encounters with Christian and Muslim prostitutes. However, sex with prostitutes who belonged to the majority faith could be dangerous. Sex with a Christian prostitute sometimes incurred a lesser penalty than sex with other Christian women. However, particularly in the Iberian Peninsula, Christian prostitutes functioned as boundary markers, meant to police interreligious boundaries by refusing to have sex with Jewish or Muslim men. Both the prostitutes and their clients could be subject to execution, although Jewish men were virtually never executed in practice (Nirenberg 1996: 47–48).

Christian authorities licensed Jewish prostitutes in part out of the hope that Jewish men would have sex with them rather than with Christian prostitutes. Jewish communal leaders, meanwhile, were of two minds about Jewish prostitutes. Some thought that Jewish women entering prostitution was a lesser evil than Jewish men having sex with non-Jewish women. Others, however, expressed anxiety about permitting the "immorality" of not only Jewish women working as prostitutes, but also Jewish men working as their agents and intermediaries. Intriguingly, Jewish prostitutes were typically not based in the Jewish quarter. This surprising choice of location could suggest that they catered to non-Jewish clients as well as Jewish ones (Assis 1988: 45).

Scholars have increasingly managed to recover the voices of Christian women prostitutes through court records. However, scholars have not yet successfully done so for those Jewish women who worked as prostitutes. As a result, there is substantial evidence about how Jewish men perceived the women of their community and beyond who engaged in sex work, but very little to be said definitively about how Jewish women prostitutes might have understood their own work and their personal and professional identities. Court records from Marseille described both close personal relationships between prostitutes and acrimonious conflicts that broke out occasionally. These documents also complicate assumptions about women's honor in the Middle Ages: prostitutes went to court to defend their character; their voices demonstrate that there was more to women's honor than sexual purity (McDonough 2021: 8–9).

Domestic labors

Women of all social strata were expected to play some role in the basics of household management. However, wealth dictated what was included in women's domestic labor. Some women were responsible for tasks like childcare, cooking, and cleaning for their own families. Other women did the same work but in the households of others; Jewish women worked as waged servants, and Jewish families both hired servants and purchased slaves to meet their domestic labor needs. The wealthiest women worked to oversee the enslaved and waged laborers who worked in their households.

Medieval Jewish visual culture offers some insight into the kinds of domestic tasks that women might perform. Illustrated haggadot sometimes included visual representations of Jewish families and communities readying themselves for Passover, with tasks like food preparation and cleaning. The Birds' Head Haggadah (see Figure 7.1), produced around 1300 in what is now Germany, depicted a woman working with two men to make matzah, the unleavened bread consumed on Passover (see Figure 7.1). In an effort to avoid depicting human figures, this Haggadah represented both biblical and medieval Jews with the heads of birds (Epstein 2011: 49–51). The head scarf worn by the figure in the center designated her as a woman, whereas the beard on the figure to the left designated him as a man. Jewish men and women worked together, according to this image, on a task that blended domestic labor with ritual.

The Golden Haggadah, produced in Catalonia in the fourteenth century, included a striking image of a woman and a girl cleaning the house before Passover (see Figure 7.2). Ritual observance of the holiday required Jewish families to take care to remove all traces of leavened bread from their household. The two women go over the ceiling and floor with brooms. The image also depicted a man holding a candle and a boy holding a bowl; they

Figure 7.1 Birds' Head Haggadah, Germany, c. 1300, Making Matzah © The Picture Art Collection/Alamy Stock Photo.

appear to be searching for any final traces of leavened bread and preparing to burn a few crumbs, in a ritual that symbolically confirms the absence of leavened bread from the home. While the women's holiday preparations centered on domestic labor, the man and boy focused their attentions on ritual tasks. Some scholars have argued that a woman commissioned this manuscript, which focuses heavily on women's experiences and role in the Passover story (Epstein 2011: 191–192). If so, this image could offer valuable insight into how women thought about their own domestic work, both on its own and in relation to the work men did in the home.

The testimony that crypto-Jewish women gave before the Inquisition incorporated details about the domestic work that women performed. Many Jewish men and women had converted to Christianity under duress in the Iberian Peninsula, during the massacres of 1391 and after the expulsion of the Jews from Spain was ordered in 1492. If convert families wished to continue practicing Judaism, they had to do so in secret; those discovered by the **Inquisition** faced a variety of penalties, including execution for repeat offenders. The need to practice their faith in secret meant that observances centered on the domestic space of the Jewish household became increasingly important. *Conversa* women therefore played a central role in maintaining Jewish households through their domestic labor. Women cooked special meals, including both the traditional challah bread for the Sabbath and matzah for Passover, cleaned the house, and washed clothing in honor of the Sabbath and festivals. They also meticulously slaughtered and cleaned meat in accordance with the Jewish dietary laws (Melammed 1999: 73–88).

Women of moderate wealth still did some amount of domestic labor; Dolce of Worms, for example, was clearly well-off, but still cooked, spun, and sewed for her household [*Doc. 1, pp. 118–119*]. However, Jewish

Figure 7.2 Golden Haggadah, Catalonia, c. 1320–1330, Passover Preparation
© The History Collection/Alamy Stock Photo.

families who could afford to do so also hired servants to perform some household tasks. Jewish families may have exhibited some preference for hiring Jewish girls as servants. In most places, it was technically illegal for Jews to hire servants who belonged to the ruling faith. Such master–servant relationships threatened to undermine religious hierarchies. Rabbinic authorities also expressed concern about the hiring of Christian servants. Men were assumed to have free sexual access to the women servants in their household, and rabbis often disapproved of resulting sexual relationships between Jewish men and non-Jewish women—although they were hardly more pleased about the sexual exploitation of Jewish servant girls (Grossman 2004: 136–138). Some families preferred to hire impoverished and orphaned Jewish girls as servants, as a means of charitably supporting them while still benefiting from their labor (Winer 2006: 135). Jewish women from the lower strata of society often needed to work outside the home to make ends meet, and younger women, in particular, often found domestic service to be a good option.

Wealthy Jewish families also hired or purchased wetnurses to nurse their infant children. Jewish couples hired both Jewish and non-Jewish wetnurses, although the latter occasioned a great deal of concern (Baumgarten 2004: 134–144). Jewish women sometimes played an active role in contracting wetnurses for their own children. In 1349, for example, Astruga, widow of Jucef de Beziers of Barcelona, moved back to her home city of Girona and hired a woman named Clara, wife of Salomó Carnisser, as the wetnurse for her infant daughter Druda (Ifft Decker 2019a: 498–499). Although often men took responsibility for hiring wetnurses or even contracting their wives' services, this contract highlights women's role in both hiring wetnurses and in agreeing to contracts. Clara's husband consented but did not otherwise participate. Astruga was widowed, but had several local male relatives, none of whom were involved at all in the contract.

While domestic servants were considered part of a wider household, they were also subject to exploitation. Enslaved women were especially vulnerable—and Jewish women are documented as buyers and sellers of slaves. Sometimes, these slaves worked in Jewish households for years. In other cases, enslaved men and women only passed briefly through Jewish households, as pledges for debts (Winer 2006: 143). Jewish women also participated in the buying and selling of slaves. Goig, wife of David Canviador of Vic, a successful woman moneylender, in 1276 sold a Muslim slave woman for 100 sous, in a contract which did not even include the enslaved woman's name (Ifft Decker forthcoming).

Conclusion

The work performed by Jewish women was varied and encompassed a variety of fields. It included both high-status and low-status labor tasks. Some of their work is easily recognized as such, both by us and by their contemporaries—for example, weaving and embroidering. Other forms of Jewish women's work tend to be excluded from wider conversations around gender and labor, like the management of money and property. Some are not acknowledged as "real" work at all, like cooking and childcare women performed for their own families. Socioeconomic status and location, as well as their religious status, shaped the work options available to Jewish women. In some ways, their work resembled that of the Christian or Muslim women around them. Yet distinctly Jewish communal attitudes, as well as restrictions on members of the Jewish minority, meant that Jewish women's work could sometimes differ from both that of Jewish men and that of non-Jewish women.

8 Gender, faith, and worship

The texts written by rabbis often say more about how they expected pious Jewish women to behave than they do about how real women behaved, or about how women understood their own faith. One text from twelfth-century Ashkenaz, included in the writings of Rabbi Simcha ben Samuel of Vitry, but sometimes attributed to the great sage **Rashi**, instead described a pious popular practice that women appear to have invented themselves, initially to the surprise of rabbinic authorities [*Doc. 19, p. 136*]. The laws of *niddah* mandated that menstruating women refrain from going to the Temple—but said nothing about the synagogue, a Jewish house of worship and communal center that had replaced the Temple as the primary center of Jewish worship but could never entirely fulfill all of the Temple's functions. Some pious women of medieval Ashkenaz, however, took it upon themselves to avoid attending synagogue while they were menstruating, as an additional stringency.

The author initially seemed rather befuddled by the lack of legal justification for this practice: it only made sense if the synagogue were the same as the Temple, but if that were the case, no one could ever enter the synagogue, as it was no longer possible to enter a state of true ritual purity without Temple sacrifices. Ultimately, however, he decided that since the synagogue was a "place of purity," these women's actions were praiseworthy, albeit not strictly necessary (Baumgarten 2014: 21–22).

At first glance, the idea that women might avoid the synagogue as an act of piety appears paradoxical. Medieval Jewish religious observance was closely tied to the physical space of the synagogue. How, then, could the absence of women from the synagogue be a chosen act of religious observance rather than a sign of their exclusion from the ceremonial life of their faith? It is important to recognize that, based on the evidence at our disposal, Jewish women's pious absence from the synagogue represented a form of agency. The sources suggest it was a choice that women made without male intervention and an act that they performed without male permission. When making this decision about their religious observance, women relied on their expert knowledge of a body of Jewish law centered

DOI: 10.4324/9781003104964-10

on their own bodies—the laws of *niddah*. This case illuminates some of the complexities behind our understanding of medieval women's religious observance. Jewish women's piety and ownership over their own religious lives looked distinct from the observance of medieval Jewish men—but also differed from the ways in which Jewish women today, particularly those who consider themselves Jewish feminists, practice and experience Judaism.

Prayer and ritual

After the destruction of the Temple, prayer and new or adapted forms of religious rituals became central parts of Jewish religious life. The synagogue functioned as a crucial space for communal prayer as well as community life more broadly. Extensive evidence demonstrates that medieval Jewish women regularly attended synagogue, both on the Sabbath and for weekday prayers. The writings of male rabbinic authorities referred in passing to women's synagogue attendance, criticized women who left the synagogue before prayers had ended and praised those who arrived early and left late, and suggested that anyone who wanted to make sure to impart information to women could do so by an announcement in synagogue (Grossman 2004: 180–182). Women's practice of absenting themselves from the synagogue while menstruating implies that, when not in a state of ritual impurity, women would attend synagogue regularly; their absence was notable. Rabbinic sources also attest that women would deliberately interrupt the synagogue service in order to pressure the community into addressing their grievances (Klein 2006b: 50). The normalcy of this practice also points to women's regular synagogue attendance.

In practice, women were usually not permitted to perform certain public functions in mixed-gender communal prayer. Women did not normally lead the entire community in prayer or recite passages from the Torah. However, Rabbi Meir of Rothenburg imagined at least a theoretical exception to this norm: a town in which every single inhabitant was a *cohen*, a person of priestly lineage [*Doc. 20, pp. 136–137*]. *Cohanim* were believed to be descended from people who had been priests in the Temple. Although being a *cohen* no longer carried with it much in the way of particular ritual or communal obligations, a few laws still differentiated between *cohanim* and other Jews, referred to as Israelites. One custom specially honored *cohanim* by giving them the right to be the first person called up to read from the Torah during synagogue services. This custom meant that a *cohen* should not be called to read from the Torah after the first portion, lest someone think that the choice to call upon a second *cohen* implied that the status of the first was somehow defective.

In a town of all *cohanim*, Rabbi Meir suggested, it would be preferable to ask women to read from the Torah than to risk dishonoring the local *cohanim*. He pointed out that, technically, women were not forbidden from reading from the Torah, although they were not obligated to perform this commandment. Rather, custom (not law) dictated that women should not read from the Torah because of the "honor of the community." In other words, if someone saw a woman read from the Torah, they might assume that none of the local men knew how to do so; the men would thus be dishonored, along with the community as a whole. However, for Rabbi Meir, that form of dishonor to the community mattered less than the potential dishonor to the *cohanim*. This text suggests that Rabbi Meir assumed that women were competent to read from the Torah and technically permitted to do so. However, he only encouraged communities to call on women to perform this ritual obligation in a bizarre hypothetical situation; it is not clear if there really were any such towns composed entirely of *cohanim*.

Although women did not normally lead the full community in prayer, some women led other women in prayer, in spaces separated fully or partly from the men of the community. Dolce of Worms taught women to recite prayers with music [*Doc. 1, p. 119*]. The epitaph of Urania of Worms, who died in 1275, stated that she "sang the *piyyutim* for the women with musical voice" (Grossman 2004: 181). Often, medieval Jewish women prayed in a special women's section within the synagogue, often on an upper level of the building, or even in an entirely separate adjacent building, under the leadership of a woman prayer-leader. Such women prayer leaders are not overtly attested in Sepharad, but several rabbis in the Iberian Peninsula noted the practice of women reciting their synagogue prayers in the vernacular (Grossman 2004: 182). It is therefore likely that there, too, they prayed at least partly separately. The Golden Haggadah, from Catalonia, incorporated a panel that specially highlighted Miriam, Moses' sister, leading other women in prayer (see Figure 8.1). The emphasis on Miriam as prayer leader, in a haggadah possibly commissioned by and for a Jewish woman, could imply that the woman prayer leader was a familiar figure to Catalan Jewish women.

Women also prayed privately, whether as part of silent devotions within the synagogue or in their homes. In early modern Ashkenaz, printers published collections of women's prayers in Yiddish, known as **tkhines**. Some prayers marked special occasions, whether the Sabbath or Yom Kippur; others were associated with specific devotional acts, such as emerging from the ritual bath or attending synagogue; some expressed wishes for women themselves or their husbands and children (Weissler 1998: 6–7). At least some of these early modern *tkhines* could reflect earlier oral traditions associated with women's private prayer and spirituality.

Although women participated in many of the wider rituals of the Jewish community, they also developed their own rituals, for example those that celebrated newborn infants (Baumgarten 2004: 92–116). They also participated in ritual observances rooted in the home. An image from the Sarajevo Haggadah, produced in Barcelona around 1350, placed a man at the head

Figure 8.1 Golden Haggadah, Catalonia, c. 1320–1330, Miriam Leading Women in Prayer © The History Collection/Alamy Stock Photo.

of the table in an implicit position of leadership (see Figure 8.2). But it prominently featured several Jewish women as active participants in the ritual meal of the Passover seder.

Education and Torah study

The women prayer-leaders of Ashkenaz offer clear proof that at least some Jewish women in that region had sufficient education to read Hebrew and develop familiarity with the liturgy. In general, rabbis agreed that women needed at least a basic religious education. In order to fulfill their duties as wives, mothers, and mistresses of households, they needed to know the

Figure 8.2 Sarajevo Haggadah, Barcelona, 1350, Passover Seder © Album/Alamy
Stock Photo.

halakhah associated with the performance of the commandments, particularly things like the laws associated with menstrual purity, dietary laws,
and Sabbath observance.

Women's in-depth study of Torah, however, proved somewhat more
complicated and fraught. Educated women certainly existed, in both the
Middle East and in Ashkenaz. The woman Bible teacher of Egypt first
learned Torah from her husband, then continued her studies with her
brother [*Doc. 4, p. 122*]. She progressed far enough in her studies that she
was considered capable of teaching children. While this standard might not
mean that she was as well-educated as elite male rabbis, she was clearly

sufficiently knowledgeable that both men and women respected her and trusted her to educate their children.

It is intriguing that she began her education by learning from her husband. Since she was only nine years old when they married, she probably would not have had much chance to study before her marriage. But it is not clear why her husband chose to educate his wife; he may simply have considered it valuable for women to have a basic education, whether for her own betterment or to teach their own sons. He certainly did not approve of her teaching as a profession; nor does he otherwise appear unusually concerned with women's welfare in general or that of his wife in particular. This case suggests that such basic education might have been commonplace for women. Moreover, the fact that she could successfully attract students suggests that there was no particular stigma against women learning or teaching Torah. She even took pains to emphasize that, although her older son assisted her, "People do not bring their sons to our older son, who is only a boy, but to me."

In Ashkenaz, several sages based in northern France, including Rashi, are reputed to have educated their daughters. However, while rabbinic authorities encouraged fathers to teach the basics of *halakhah* to their daughters, most did not consider girls and women to have the same obligation to study Torah as boys and men (Grossman 2004: 169–170). One strand of rabbinic thought even suggested that teaching girls Torah could be dangerous. In the Babylonian Talmud, rabbis debated whether teaching a girl Torah "taught her lasciviousness"—in other words, whether educating a girl could inspire her to engage in promiscuous behavior (Boyarin 1993: 176–178). Even though Rashi apparently educated his own daughters, he also cited, and perhaps even originated, an expanded tradition that illustrated the link between women's Torah study and promiscuity. According to this tradition, **Beruriah**—a woman sage mentioned in the Talmud—was seduced by a student of her husband and, as a result, committed suicide (Baskin 2002: 82–83).

In Sepharad, the evidence suggests that Jewish women were unlikely to receive more than a very basic religious education. In Muslim-ruled al-Andalus, where a substantial corpus of Hebrew poetry has survived, there is only one extant example of a poem written in Hebrew by a Jewish woman [*Doc. 13, pp. 131–132*]. Women like the wife of Dunash ben Labrat, who were learned enough to write complicated Hebrew poetry, might also have studied Torah. However, rabbinic discourse from Christian Spain tended to presume not only that most Jewish women did not study Torah, but also that they should recite prayers in the vernacular because they were not necessarily literate in Hebrew (Grossman 2004: 171). In the Crown of Aragon, Jewish women had men sign contracts in Hebrew on their behalf; even if they could read Hebrew, they might not have learned how to write, since reading and writing were taught as separate skills in the Middle Ages (Ifft Decker 2019b: 18). In this region in particular, the evidence suggests that

Jewish women may have been largely excluded from the intellectual and religious culture centered on Torah study.

Menstruation and ritual purity

Once Jewish women married, regulating their ritual purity in the context of menstruation became a crucial part of their religious observance. According to Jewish law, women entered a state of menstrual impurity when they first saw blood. The rabbis added an additional stringency to the laws surrounding impurity: women also had to count seven "white" days after they finished menstruating—in other words, seven days in which they did not see blood (Baskin 2002: 25). Only after these seven clean days should they go to the *mikveh* to ritually immerse, and only after this ritual immersion did they again become sexually available to their husbands. Some medieval *mikvaot*, like the one in the town of Besalú, can still be seen today (see Figure 5.1). The term *niddah* is used to describe both the menstruating, ritually impure woman and the constellation of laws and rituals surrounding menstruation and purification.

For some modern Jewish feminists, the history of the laws of *niddah* can seem troubling. The Hebrew Bible describes multiple sources of ritual impurity, which apply to both men and women, yet only the impurities associated with menstruation and childbirth—impurities considered exclusive to female bodies—remained meaningful parts of Jewish life after the destruction of the Temple. Moreover, the laws of *niddah* often imply an equation between womanhood and menstruation, which many today see as excluding the experiences of trans, non-binary, and genderqueer people. In the medieval world, however, it is important to acknowledge that at least some Jewish women took ownership over the laws of *niddah* and participated in their own prayers and rituals surrounding it.

Women's pious avoidance of the synagogue during their period of impurity apparently began as the innovation of a few particularly pious women in the eleventh and twelfth centuries. However, during the later Middle Ages and the early modern period, rabbinic authorities in Ashkenaz increasingly presented this practice as a legal norm for all women—although they typically stated that women should return to synagogue during the period of their seven "clean" days (Baumgarten 2014: 32–33). Without the voices of women themselves, it is impossible to know whether all women accepted this stringency as an expression of their personal piety. Once this practice became imposed on women rather than adopted by them, some women may have felt saddened by this exclusion from the communal space of the synagogue.

Women also recited popular prayers developed around *niddah*, some of which may have been created by women, for women. Intriguingly, while male rabbinic literature regularly associated menstrual impurity with the sin of Eve, women's prayers usually did not. They instead focused more broadly on themes of purity and impurity or wishes for fertility and the piety of their future children. The *tkhines* that did refer to the sin of Eve at times even appear to question the idea of menstruation as a punishment for Eve's sin, now inflicted upon all women (Weissler 1998: 71–74).

The laws of *niddah* required women to keep track of their own ritual purity. Ideas about women's modesty forestalled in practice any regular rabbinic intervention to determine when women began and ceased their menstrual cycles. As a result, women functioned as ritual experts when it came to their own bodies and even the bodies of other women. Under normal circumstances, women determined independently when their cycles began and ended, as well as if a particular discharge was menstrual blood or not. Women also might be called upon to examine other girls and women (Fonrobert 2000: 138–141). However, the Mishnah and Talmud also worked to position male rabbis as the most authoritative experts on women's blood (Fonrobert 2000: 113–115). By promoting themselves as the authorities, rabbis introduced additional questions about whether women should be believed and trusted in their assessments of their own blood and that of other women (Fonrobert 2000: 118–127).

Fasting

All Jews are mandated to fast on a few occasions each year, most famously on the holiday of Yom Kippur, the Day of Atonement. As the commandment to fast is typically framed as a negative commandment—do not eat—rather than a positive one, Jewish women were consistently obligated to fast along with their community. Only pregnant and nursing women were exempted, as were men and women suffering from certain other illnesses. Along with the various annual fasts on the Jewish calendar, medieval Jewish communities sometimes prescribed fasts in times of grave danger, as when under attack during the Crusades, in the hopes of incurring divine favor. Jewish men and women also fasted for personal reasons and on the occasion of certain life-cycle events. For example, brides and grooms typically fasted on the day leading up to their wedding (Baumgarten 2004: 63–65).

Fasting featured prominently in the piety of medieval Christian women. Caroline Walker Bynum's book on the subject, *Holy Feast and Holy Fast*, has become a must-read for scholars and students on topics including women, food, and religious culture in the medieval world. Christian women's pious fasting was deeply intertwined with Eucharistic piety—rituals and pious practices associated with contemplation and consumption of the **Eucharist,** the consecrated wafer that according to medieval Christian doctrine was physically transformed into the body of Christ through a process called **transubstantiation**. Some holy women, for example, attempted to subsist exclusively on the Eucharist. However, Christian women's pious practices associated with food and fasting were also linked to their role as providers of food for themselves and their households, including their provision of food out of their own bodies for their infant children (Bynum 1987).

Jewish women played a similar role in providing food for their households. Dolce of Worms took responsibility for providing food not only for her immediate family, but also for her husband's students, and may have even understood such food-giving as a pious practice in itself [*Doc. 1, pp. 118–119*]. Although Jewish and Christian theology and practice surrounding fasting differed, and the extreme fasting particular to women mystics does not have a parallel in medieval Jewish culture, the fasts of Jewish laywomen may have shared some elements with the fasting practices of the Christian laity (Baumgarten 2014: 91–94).

Donations and pious works

Jews, Christians, and Muslims in the medieval world understood donations to religious institutions and houses of worship as pious acts. Donations could include not only financial resources, such as cash, landed property, and high-value goods, but also the volunteer contribution of physical labor and objects made with their own hands. Jewish women engaged frequently in charitable giving. The Nürnberg Memorbuch, a register of charitable donations given to the local synagogue in Nürnberg, indicates that women donated as often as men and gave similar or even larger sums. Women's giving supported the construction of new synagogues and maintenance of old ones, the upkeep of communal cemeteries, the purchase of oil and candles to light the synagogue, the provision of education, and the care of the poor and sick. Some women gave ritual objects, such as books, Torah scrolls, silver cups, and cloth coverings for Torah scrolls and tables (Baumgarten 2004: 121–126). Women also labored to make ritual objects for their communities. Dolce of Worms sewed Torah scrolls, bound books, and made the thread for phylacteries [*Doc. 1, pp. 118–119*]. In the Iberian Peninsula, Rabbi Jonah Gerondi encouraged women to not only give to charity but also play an active role in collecting funds and providing care to the poor (Grossman 2004: 184–185).

Women gave during their lifetimes, but also made charitable donations in their wills (Burns 1996: 114). Regina, wife of Bondia Coras of Puigcerdà, a town in Catalonia, distributed some of her property to her family, but also took care to support her community when she had a Christian notary draw up her will [*Doc. 21, pp. 137–138*]. She donated her bed to the *scola* of the town; while the word is often used to mean synagogue, here it might refer to a school for Jewish children. Some of the students, especially those from poor families, might have slept at the school. Regina also specified that 100 sous be given as charity "for my soul" on the day of her death, although she left it up to her executor to determine how that charity should be distributed. Nevertheless, the text suggests that Jewish women thought of charitable giving as an important way to demonstrate their piety, both to their community and to God.

Affluent women might give extremely generously. Jewish women's wills from fifteenth- and sixteenth-century Italy recorded posthumous gifts of books, embroidered silk cloths, and silver objects, as well as directed donations to the poor and for the restoration of the community synagogue. The 1457 will of Ora di Giuseppe, of Perugia, described the objects she gave in sumptuous detail—for example, "a cloth of taffeta and blue silk, with gold brocade embroidery with images of birds and faces, with letters of silver and fringes of various colors" (Toaff 1998: 45). The description makes it clear that this was not only a beautiful object, but a very expensive one, due to both the materials involved and the craftsmanship put into the embroidery.

Where are the Jewish women mystics?

Medieval Christendom saw the flourishing of women's mysticism, especially in the thirteenth and fourteenth centuries. Women like Catherine of Siena, Julian of Norwich, Angela of Foligno, and Mechtild of Magdeburg developed a reputation for sanctity, often linked with extreme fasting and intense visions, some of which imagined an intense sexual or maternal relationship with Christ. Some were even canonized, meaning that the Church formally recognized them as saints after their death. In contrast, there are no known examples of Jewish women mystics active in the medieval world, either in Christendom or beyond.

Why did Jewish women never develop a significant mystical tradition akin to that seen among their Christian neighbors? The disparity certainly does not stem from the absence of mysticism within Jewish religious culture. The tradition known as Kabbalah, which arose in southern France and the Iberian Peninsula in the twelfth and thirteenth centuries, allowed its adherents to achieve a mystical union with the divine. Yet all the luminaries of the Kabbalistic tradition were men.

However, Kabbalah looked very different from the mystical culture found in Western Christianity. Christian mysticism involved forms of piety to which anyone, in theory, could aspire. Mystics, and even some among the laity, sought to imitate Christ and experience his suffering; the height of devotion was to live in a manner akin to that of Christ, the Virgin Mary, and the apostles. No education, beyond a basic knowledge of the Gospels, was required. Indeed, while some women mystics wrote down their own visions, others relied on male confessors to put their visionary experiences into writing. In contrast, Kabbalah was deeply text-based; it was closely linked to the intense study of Torah and presumed that union with God was reserved for educated men. Few Jewish women had the educational background required to fully participate in Kabbalah.

Conclusion

Jewish tradition understood the fullest form of Jewish observance as reserved for men. A range of practices, from circumcision to the wearing of *tefillin* to hearing the blowing of the *shofar* on Rosh Hashanah, were only commanded for men—and medieval rabbis differed as to whether women could or should fulfill such commandments. Nevertheless, Jewish women sought out avenues to express their piety and their identity as Jews. Special prayers and rituals, the laws of *niddah*, fasting, and donations allowed Jewish women to experience connections with God and with their people. Women attended synagogue regularly, and in some regions even taught Torah or led other women in prayer. The story of medieval Jewish women's religious observance on the one hand involves restriction: Jewish women simply could not participate in certain avenues of Jewish religious life. Yet the story also tells us about Jewish women's perseverance and agency as they crafted prayers, rituals, and social expectations for themselves.

9 Jewish women between communities

In 1368, a Jewish woman named Elea Mavristiri turned to a Christian court for support in her ongoing battle against her ex-husband, Solomon Astrug. Elea lived in Candia, the capital city of Crete, which at that time was under Venetian rule; it was therefore a Venetian ducal court in which she demanded that her former husband pay the sums owed to her according to her *ketubah* (Lauer 2019: 139). Elea's case is one of many examples of Jewish men and women pursuing justice in non-Jewish courts across the medieval Mediterranean. Elea did not exactly seek to circumvent Jewish law: she claimed before the court that her demands were in accordance with Jewish practice, and she genuinely might have believed that her interpretation was valid. Going to a non-Jewish court, however, enabled her to shape a debate in which the interpretation of Jewish law became a matter of her word against her ex-husband's, whereas in a Jewish court rabbis would have served as interpretive professionals.

Elea had a long and complicated journey as a marginal member of the Jewish community who, eventually, would convert to Christianity (Lauer 2019: 126). Although in many respects she was an unusual figure, she is also emblematic of the complex position of Jews as both members of a self-governing minority community and participants in wider social and legal structures, governed by representatives of a faith not their own. In many areas, especially family law, Jews could govern themselves in accordance with their own laws. Given the importance of religious identity in the medieval world, practicing a different faith also meant that many aspects of their everyday life centered on their minority community. Anti-Jewish attitudes also might have made some Jews feel that they could rely more on other Jews than on their non-Jewish neighbors.

Despite all these factors, however, Jews were never fully isolated. As has been noted throughout this book, Jewish women and men had non-Jewish neighbors, servants, and even friends. They did business with people of other faiths. They passed through and spent time in religiously mixed spaces when they went to the markets, to the courts, to notaries, and to homes of Christian clients. Sometimes, the interstitial position of Jews, between their

DOI: 10.4324/9781003104964-11

own community and that of the dominant faith, offered benefits for Jewish women. Both women and men employed non-Jewish courts to maneuver between different legal cultures and use the varying norms of Jewish, Christian, and Islamic law to their advantage. Yet the position of Jews as a minority community also brought dangers. Anti-Judaism was a very real threat, particularly in Christian Europe but occasionally in the Islamic world as well. Jewish communities were targeted in massacres, forcibly converted to other faiths, blamed for epidemics, and even expelled from their homes. Jewish women underwent these traumatic moments as part of the wider Jewish community, but their lived experiences were also shaped by gendered norms and in some ways distinct from the experiences of Jewish men.

Women in Jewish courts

Medieval Jewish communities typically functioned as self-governing institutions within a particular polity. In other words, Jews could govern themselves in accordance with Jewish law, along with whatever other regulations they saw fit to pass. However, they remained ultimately subject to the authority of the king or other ruler of the region. Disputes between Jews and non-Jews would automatically go to a non-Jewish court. The breadth of Jewish communal jurisdiction varied by region. Organized Jewish communities almost always had the right to exercise civil jurisdiction in most cases between Jews—a category that included intra-Jewish business disputes, real estate purchases, loans, inheritance cases, marriages, and divorces. Yet only some Jewish communities were granted the right to exercise criminal jurisdiction, and even fewer had the right to enact capital punishment.

Jewish women regularly pursued disputes in Jewish courts—although, as discussed in the next section, some Jewish women instead sought the intervention of local Christian or Muslim courts. The women who turned to non-Jewish courts probably did so because they expected a more favorable verdict from those courts, but they risked incurring the displeasure of Jewish communal leaders. Rabbis and other communal authorities were on guard to protect their jurisdictional authority and criticized those Jews who turned to non-Jewish courts. Jewish women therefore were expected, at least in theory, to handle much of their legal business in Jewish courts. Issues related to marriage and divorce, in particular, fell firmly within the boundaries of *halakhah* and under the jurisdictional authority of the Jewish community.

Some Jewish women undoubtedly preferred to handle their business in Jewish courts. Women from elite families might have stood to benefit from connections to local Jewish notables. Some women may have deliberately chosen to remain within Jewish courts because it seemed clear to them that Jewish law supported their position. Others might have preferred to rely on Jewish courts in marriage and divorce cases to ensure that their community would treat their marriage, divorce, or remarriage as fully legitimate.

Some women might not have had the legal knowledge or resources to look beyond their community for justice.

Two examples, one from Ashkenaz and one from Sepharad, offer some insight into the specific reasons why Jewish women might prefer to handle their legal troubles in Jewish courts. One case involves a young woman living in Frankfurt, who was forcibly converted to Christianity during the anti-Jewish riots of 1241. Before her conversion, she had been engaged; when she escaped, she went to Würzberg, where her fiancé lived. However, he claimed that he could not marry her on the grounds that she was presumed to have had sex with her Christian captors. In the meantime, he had already married another woman. The legal battle that ensued between the would-be couple appears to have remained entirely within the Jewish community (Furst 2008: 179–180). By staying within the Jewish court system, the woman may have sought to emphasize her history of good behavior and her continued allegiance to the Jewish community. By presenting herself as a good Jew and a woman of good character, she undermined the accusation that she had had sexual relations, consensual or otherwise, with her captors. In this case, however, avoiding Christian courts was also a matter of safety: reverting to Judaism after baptism, even baptism under duress, was illegal. If her conversion and return to Judaism were revealed in a Christian court, she might even have been executed.

The second example involves a messy divorce, between Esther Caravida of Girona and David Bonjorn of Perpignan, in 1337. Today, Girona is in northeastern Spain and Perpignan in southwestern France; in the mid-fourteenth century, however, the cities were on-and-off part of the same kingdom, spoke the same language (Catalan), and resembled one another culturally. David had entrusted certain valuable items, including books and scientific instruments, to his wife, and Esther and her mother Bonadona kept them in their home in Girona. They then used these goods as leverage to pressure David into granting Esther a divorce. David attempted to turn to a non-Jewish court to demand the return of his possessions. Bonadona countered by refusing to pursue the suit in a non-Jewish court on the grounds that it was the "rule and custom" to present such a case only before Jewish judges. The case ended up in a Jewish court—where Bonadona and Esther emerged victorious (Roth 2017: 549–553). Their insistence on pursuing the case in a Jewish court, whereas David had tried to move it to a Christian court, may have enabled Bonadona and Esther to make David seem less sympathetic to the Jewish judges who ultimately decided in their favor.

Jewish women in non-Jewish courts

Many scholars have been intrigued by the phenomenon of "court shopping" or "forum shopping," in which people selectively maneuvered between different legal systems in order to achieve their desired outcome. Court shopping took place in many contexts: for some cases, medieval Christians could choose between church courts and secular ones; medieval Muslims in some regions could move between courts associated with different schools of Islamic law. People who belonged to minority faiths in the medieval world could choose between courts linked to the governing authorities of the ruling faith, or the courts of their own community. Especially in the Mediterranean, east as well as west, extensive documentary evidence indicates that Jewish women were willing and able to turn to non-Jewish courts in their pursuit of justice. In medieval Egypt, in fact, a majority of the Jewish cases that went before Muslim courts involved a woman bringing a suit against a man (Zinger 2018: 164). However, going to non-Jewish courts also involved risk: in some cases, Jewish community leaders threatened to invalidate verdicts or even excommunicate Jewish women who went to non-Jewish courts.

Some women might have turned to non-Jewish courts because they thought that the law of the land would allow them to make claims that were not valid according to *halakhah*. Rabbi Solomon ibn Adret of Barcelona weighed in on a financial dispute that arose after a Jewish woman recovered her dowry from her husband in a non-Jewish court [*Doc. 22, p. 138*]. Such dowry recovery suits were fairly common among Catalan Christians—especially in cases like this one, where the husband's debts threatened to bankrupt the family (Kelleher 2010: 59–60). However, ibn Adret denied the validity of this financial move on the grounds that *halakhah* never justified the recovery of the dowry while the marriage lasted; the wife could only collect her dowry in the event of divorce or the husband's death. According to ibn Adret, the husband's Jewish creditor therefore could still demand repayment out of the wife's dowry wealth.

Jewish women and men also might have appreciated that some non-Jewish courts allowed them to offer their own interpretations of Jewish law without the intervention of rabbinic legal experts. In 1401, a Jewish woman in Crete, Channa Missini, sued her husband in a Venetian ducal court for having driven her from their home and taken a second wife, against local custom. Channa based her claims on local Jewish custom; her husband Joseph based his on Jewish law, even citing a specific passage from the Mishnah. The couple came to a compromise, according to which they would remain married, but Joseph would provide her a separate home from the new wife. This couple may have turned to a non-Jewish court in the hopes of finding just such a compromise, whereas a Jewish court might have pressured them to divorce. Intriguingly, however, the couple still wished to frame their arrangement as valid according to Jewish law (Lauer 2019: 142–145).

We should therefore not necessarily assume that women who turned to non-Jewish courts sought to circumvent Jewish law. Especially in medieval Egypt, some women might have considered themselves to be at a disadvantage in Jewish courts because they had fewer social connections than their male opponents. In the close-knit social and economic circles within Egyptian Jewish communities, judges and litigants often knew one another well. However, women rarely had close ties with men beyond their own relatives. Muslim courts therefore might have seemed more like a "level playing field" in which they could receive a genuinely impartial verdict, as neither Jewish women nor Jewish men necessarily had close ties to Muslim judges (Zinger 2018: 182–183).

Women in the Crown of Aragon who brought marriage and divorce cases to the royal court often would have had little luck if they were hoping to find a non-*halakhic* solution to their problems: the kings of Aragon often consulted rabbis before coming to a verdict. In some of these cases, the litigants might have relied on the royal court simply in the hopes of bringing additional pressure to bear on husbands reluctant to grant a divorce or pay alimony, even if they were required to do so under Jewish law (Assis 1997: 268–269).

Jewish women who went to non-Jewish courts varied in the motives that drove them and in the strategies that they pursued. Regardless, however, this practice highlights the interconnections between medieval Jewish communities and the surrounding Christian and Muslim communities. These women demonstrated their knowledge of both Jewish and non-Jewish legal systems, and their relative comfort in non-Jewish spaces. These court cases also demonstrate that religious identity did not always determine allegiance. Some Jewish women may have felt that the Jewish community and its courts did not represent their interests.

Responding to massacres

Over the course of the Middle Ages, local and regional Jewish communities on occasion suffered from violent attacks, in which many Jews lost their lives and others succumbed to conversion under duress. Massacres like these were far from everyday occurrences, but the threat of such extreme violence undoubtedly made Jews feel less secure. Most documented massacres were carried out by Christians and in places under Christian rule—for example, the Rhineland massacres in 1096 and the massacres that swept across the kingdoms of Castile and Aragon in 1391. However, occasional massacres occurred in Islamic lands as well—such as the massacre of the Jewish community of Muslim-ruled Granada, in the south of what is now Spain, in 1066.

The descriptions of these massacres do not always give particular attention to the specific experiences of women, who undoubtedly suffered and died alongside Jewish men. However, one of the most dramatic episodes recorded in the Chronicle of Solomon bar Simson, a twelfth-century account of the 1096 massacres, told the story of a Jewish woman named Rachel [*Doc. 23, p. 139*]. The chronicle emphasized the sacrificial martyrdom of the Jews of the Rhineland, who chose to commit suicide and slaughter their children rather than succumb to the attacking crusaders and accept Christianity. Rachel had four children, two sons and two daughters; rather than allow them to be converted and raised as Christians, she killed all four before allowing herself to be killed. The narrative praised Rachel for the strength of her faith and emphasized the pain she felt in killing her children. Strikingly, while the youngest boy, Aaron, hid after seeing that his older brother had been killed, Rachel's two daughters, Bella and Madrona, willingly offered themselves to be sacrificed. Although men as well as women died, committed suicide, and slaughtered others, Solomon bar Simson on a number of occasions emphasized the example set by women. Although he might have described real events, the focus on women probably also had a rhetorical function. If women had the strength to accept death rather than convert, and even choose death on behalf of their children, should not men be able to do the same?

Documentary and archaeological evidence also clearly indicates that Jewish women were slaughtered alongside men. The majority of the victims burned in a mass judicial murder in Blois, which I will discuss further below, were women; the list of victims specifies that at least one was pregnant (Einbinder 2002: 46). In the Catalan town of Tàrrega, where scholars have analyzed the remains of a mass grave linked to the massacres of Jews after the Black Death, half of all bodies—and the majority of those whose sex could be determined—belonged to women (Ruiz Ventura and Subirà de Galdàcano 2009: 131). In the Catalan capital of Barcelona, in contrast, the high numbers of widows working as moneylenders after their husbands' deaths could suggest that the massacres in the wake of the Plague killed more men than women. However, this evidence remains circumstantial and undoubtedly some women were slaughtered alongside the men of their community (Ifft Decker forthcoming).

Conversion, forced and voluntary

Although accounts like Solomon bar Simson's chronicle highlighted the martyrdom of Jews who chose death over conversion, many Jews made different choices. For a long time, historians contrasted the Jews who chose martyrdom in Ashkenaz with those who largely accepted conversion in Sepharad. Increasingly, however, scholars have challenged this dichotomy (Tartakoff 2015: 730). Both during the Crusade massacres and in later attacks, Jews in northern Europe converted under duress. In the Iberian Peninsula, some Jews chose martyrdom, while others accepted conversion but continued to practice Judaism in secret. Easy regional differences between converts and conversion have increasingly been undermined by new research.

Gender-based distinctions are complicated as well. Adolescent boys and young men may have been particularly susceptible to conversionary pressures, especially in northwestern Europe (Jordan 2001: 85). Educated male converts to Christianity were particularly prized; some of these converts came to play a prominent role in Christian anti-Jewish polemic and publicly staged disputations. Strikingly, however, Christian rhetoric often emphasized Jewish women's supposed susceptibility to conversion. The Castilian *Cantigas de Santa Maria* represented women as voluntarily choosing to convert after witnessing miracles performed on their behalf or those of their loved ones by the Virgin Mary. William Shakespeare's *The Merchant of Venice* vilified the male Jewish moneylender Shylock, but portrayed Shylock's daughter Jessica as willingly converting in order to marry her Christian lover.

A wide range of sources described the lived experiences of women who converted, whether by choice or under duress, as well as those women who actively resisted conversion. Real-life examples also attested to a link between marriage and conversion: some real Jewish women, like Shakespeare's imagined Jessica, converted so that they could marry or remain with significant others who were Christians, either by birth or by conversion. Jewish women hoping to marry Christian men received some support from Christian authorities, eager to encourage conversion, but they also risked losing the personal and financial support of their families. Jewish families often attempted, and sometimes even succeeded, in denying dowries to convert daughters (Toaff 1998: 33).

Women also converted to escape unhappy marriages. Husbands unwilling to grant their wives a divorce might have agreed in the wake of their conversion. In some cases, the Church even dissolved the marriages between convert women and their Jewish husbands so that they could marry Christian husbands (Tartakoff 2010). The woman from Seville, who sparked such anxiety in the communal leaders of Toledo [*Doc. 10, pp. 127–128*], probably used conversion strategically, as a means of obtaining a divorce from her husband and possibly marrying her lover as a Christian (Ifft Decker 2014: 45–46). The fear that Jewish women seeking divorces would not only turn to Muslim courts, but even convert to Islam, might have inspired rabbis in medieval Egypt to force husbands to divorce their "rebellious wives" (Grossman 2004: 241).

In some cases, Jewish women whose husbands had converted actively resisted subsequent pressures to convert. Conversion not only involved a change of faith, but a transformation of converts' everyday lives. The vast majority of converts changed their names, a dramatic symbol of their new identity. Converts were often pressured or required to leave their homes and avoid associations with Jews. Women's resistance to conversion therefore represents not only a statement of faith but also a sign of their connection to their community. Whether faith or community mattered most, women's resistance to conversion could also drastically change their lives and disrupt family dynamics. Tolrana, a Jewish woman of the Catalan city of Girona, in the wake of the massacres of 1391 refused to either convert to Christianity or to continue to live and remain married to her convert husband, who had taken the name Francesc after he became a Christian (Guerson and Lightfoot 2020: 350).

A husband's conversion created a variety of legal problems for a Jewish woman who sought to remain within her faith and community. Rashi, and other rabbis, firmly maintained the principle that "even though he has sinned, he is still of Israel" [*Doc. 24, pp. 139–140*]. In other words, converts still were legally considered Jews, which meant that halakhic rules still applied to them. That meant that if a Jewish woman wanted a divorce from her convert husband, she still needed to receive from him a bill of divorce. If a Jewish woman was widowed without children, she would still be required to either enter a Levirate marriage with her husband's brother or participate in the ritual of *chalitzah*—even if her brother-in-law had converted. Getting a convert to give his wife a bill of divorce or perform the *chalitzah* ritual was not always easy. Some converts were uninterested in doing anything linked with Jewish law, or worried that they could be punished by Christian authorities if their actions came to light. The conversion of a husband, or potential husband under the rules of Levirate marriage, could leave a woman an *agunah*.

In the wake of mass conversions, women played a crucial role in helping their families preserve Jewish practices. The records of the papal and Spanish Inquisitions in the Iberian Peninsula include many accusations and confessions directed at women. Women secretly practiced Judaism, and helped their families to do the same, by cleaning or providing clean clothes before the Sabbath and Passover, by removing blood and the sciatic nerve from meat, and by lighting candles on the Sabbath and festivals (Melammed 1999: 38–39). The need to practice Judaism in secret may have given an ever-greater importance to household-based rituals—and therefore specially positioned Jewish women as caretakers of their families' Jewish observance.

Ritual murder, blood libel, and host desecration accusations

Starting in the twelfth century, Christian denigration of Jews as Christ-killers took on a new form: Jews began to be accused of violently reenacting their alleged murder of Christ. The first **ritual murder** accusation, in which Jews were alleged to have ritually tortured and murdered a boy named William of Norwich in imitation of the death of Christ, arose in England in the mid-twelfth century (Rose 2015: 2). The **blood libel** accusation, which started to appear in the thirteenth century, introduced the claim that Jews also used the blood of murdered Christian boys for ritual purposes—in particular, in the making of matzah for Passover. Although popular devotions arose around some of these dead boys, none ever formally became recognized as saints. **Host desecration** accusations claimed that Jews sought to murder Christ once again by stabbing the consecrated Eucharistic wafers. According to Christian doctrine at the time (and Catholic doctrine today), the ceremony of the Eucharist brought about a process called transubstantiation: even though the wafer retained its appearance, it literally and physically transformed into the body of Christ. Jews thus very literally murdered Christ again in allegations of host desecration. Many such accusations also involved miracle stories, in which the hosts bled when stabbed, demonstrating that they were truly the body of Christ.

The protagonists—or antagonists—in most of the medieval ritual murder, blood libel, and host desecration accusations were men. The emphasis on wicked Jewish men in these allegations was not accidental. It reflected the fact that Christians perceived Jewish men as the leaders of their community and imagined the prototypical Jewish enemy as a man. Occasionally, however, women played a starring role in these accusations. In the northern French city of Blois, in 1171, a Christian thought he saw a Jewish man throw a murdered Christian boy into the Loire River. When he reported the matter to his lord, the lord saw in this accusation an opportunity to avenge himself upon a local Jewish woman, Pulcellina, who was powerful and respected by the count [*Doc. 25, p. 140*].

In response to this accusation, around 40 Jews were arrested, and over 30 Jews were executed. Pulcellina was not actually the person who the witness identified as having carried out the alleged crime. However, her influence with the count had apparently sparked resentment among many Christians; accounts of this ritual murder accusation claimed that the witnessed "murder" was only reported as a means of seeking vengeance against Pulcellina. Popular hatred of Pulcellina ensured that she was included in the accusation—and executed for it—along with many other Jewish women and men. The precise nature of Pulcellina's relationship with the count is not known. Some have suggested that her assurance that she has "the Count's love" referred to a romantic or sexual relationship, a theory further bolstered by the claim that the count's wife hated her. Susan Einbinder, however, has argued that Pulcellina was a moneylender who worked closely with the count and enjoyed his support, but questions the assumption that Pulcellina and the Count were romantically involved (Einbinder 1998: 29–33).

In the fifteenth century, the Jews of Trent, in northern Italy, were accused of ritually torturing and murdering a boy named Simon of Trent and then collecting his blood for use in the making of matzah. All the Jews arrested and ultimately executed for the alleged crime were men (Hsia 1992: 3, 47, 67). Yet a disturbing woodcut, in which nine Jews are depicted as acting together to circumcise and torture Simon, featured one Jewish woman (see Figure 9.1). She was erroneously labeled with the name Gruneta—the image probably was meant to refer to a woman named Brunetta, one of the women tangentially implicated in the ritual murder accusation but not convicted (Lipton 2014: 232). Like the men, "Gruneta"/Brunetta was visually marked as Jewish by a large hooked nose, a circular Jewish badge on her clothing, and a moneybag at her waist.

Figure 9.1 The Nuremberg Chronicle, Nuremberg, 1493, Simon of Trent © World
History Archive/Alamy Stock Photo.

The narrative that Christian authorities constructed about the alleged
murder, based on confessions obtained under torture, portrayed women as
playing at most a marginal role. A few women were interrogated and tortured, but, ultimately, they were not deemed guilty of the crime. The men's
testimonies either claimed that the woman had played no role whatsoever,
or that they knew of the crime but did not actively take part in it (Hsia
1992: 87, 108–111). Why, then, did this image, produced almost 20 years
later, portray "Gruneta"/Brunetta as an equal participant in the alleged
ritual murder of Simon?

The fifteenth century saw a growing visual emphasis on Jewish women,
as well as men, as enemies of Christianity. By the time this image was created in 1493, Jewish women were far more likely to be visually designated

as Jewish, both in Christian art and in the items of clothing or jewelry they were forced to wear (Lipton 2014: 233). Jewish women certainly did not participate equally in this artist's imagined version of the false ritual murder accusation: one Jewish woman appears alongside eight men. However, the presence of "Gruneta"/Brunetta indicates that Christian anti-Jewish vitriol increasingly targeted women as well as men.

Illness and epidemic

Illness and epidemic regularly threatened people's lives in the medieval world. While medieval medicine was not quite so ineffective as most people assume, Jews, Christians, and Muslims alike nevertheless found themselves at risk of losing their lives to disease and infection. People were deeply aware of their mortality. They made wills when they traveled, when they fell ill, when they became pregnant or were on the verge of childbirth. Medieval Jews made charitable donations that they hoped would help them in the world to come (Baumgarten 2014: 114). In the fourteenth and fifteenth centuries, images emphasizing the inevitability and universality of death became increasingly popular in Christian visual culture.

The best-known, and most devastating, medieval pandemic was the **Black Death**, which ravaged Asia, Europe, and Africa beginning in 1346. In some cities, it may have killed close to two-thirds of the population. The global trade networks that had contributed to prosperity in the thirteenth and early fourteenth centuries now allowed for the rapid travel of disease. In Christian Europe, Jewish men and women lost their lives not only to plague, but also to massacres. False accusations that Jews had poisoned the wells and thereby infected Christians with plague inspired attacks on Jewish communities across Europe (Benedictow 2004: 98). There is no evidence that massacres of Jews took place in Islamic lands affected by the plague, but some Muslim writers explained the outbreak of plague in Mecca as a divine punishment because city leaders had allowed nonbelievers, especially Jews, to live there (Benedictow 2004: 65).

There is no reason to think that plague affected women any less than men, and in places where scapegoating threatened Jewish lives, Jewish women were also slaughtered alongside men (Einbinder 2018: 44). Epitaphs on gravestones from the Iberian Peninsula memorialize some of the Jewish women who died during the Black Death pandemic. One woman, Sitbona, who lived in the city of Toledo, was described as "noble," "aristocratic," and "great." She was born into one elite family and had married into another. The epitaph expressed confidence in both her place in heaven and her eventual resurrection (Einbinder 2018: 98–100). Jacob ben Solomon, of Avignon, wrote extensively about the death of his 20-year-old daughter Esther from plague in 1383. His narrative detailed the tragedy of an incurable plague and emphasized his own close relationship with his lost daughter (Einbinder 2009: 112–136).

The women who did survive found new economic roles opened to them. In the cities of Barcelona and Girona, the proportion of loans extended by women jumped from around 2 percent of all Jewish loans to 20 and 10 percent, respectively. The massive number of deaths apparently left an unusual number of young widows, who were either childless or had only minor children. The high number of estates left in the hands of widows could indicate that, in those cities, more men than women died in the massacres. Alternatively, it could indicate some age disparity in the impact of the plague, as women were often younger than their husbands. It might even have been a chance result of the massive number of deaths. Regardless, for a brief period in the wake of the Black Death, Jewish women took on a newly prominent role as creditors. In order to justify their control of their husbands' estates, they also appealed to the legal norms of the Christian community around them. Christian women in Catalonia had the right to manage the estates of their late husbands for at least a year if they left their dowries and dowers uncollected; for the first time, Jewish women claimed the same right (Ifft Decker forthcoming).

Jewish women also lived with chronic illnesses, as well as caring for family members with such illnesses. Several responsa from Ashkenaz address situations involving women who were described as "mad" or "insane." Legal discussions often centered on questions of how to balance the need to protect women with mental illnesses with the needs of their husbands, and in particular their husbands' obligation to procreate. One man attempted to obtain an exemption from the ban of Rabbenu Gershom on polygyny, so that he could marry another woman and have children, but the local rabbis refused to grant it (Shoham Steiner 2014: 113). Women also sought to use their husbands' physical and mental illnesses as grounds on which to seek an exception to the general rule, but were not always successful. A woman in thirteenth-century Ashkenaz, for example, sought permission to obtain a divorce from her husband, whom she alleged was both dangerously violent and suffering from leprosy. However, while the rabbis told her that they would force a divorce if her husband beat her, they were hesitant to classify his illness as leprosy, and thus refused to grant a divorce on those grounds (Shoham Steiner 2014: 64–66).

Expulsion

The possibility of mass expulsions was one of the greatest insecurities faced by Jews in the medieval world. Expulsions were hardly everyday events, but medieval Jews knew it was possible that they could suddenly be told that they had to either leave homelands where they and their families had lived for centuries—or abandon their faith. Expulsions were traumatic experiences, lamented in poems and memorialized in chronicles. Families were disrupted: some members might remain in their homes and convert to the ruling faith; those who left might be scattered across cities or even countries. They often brought about economic losses as well as personal ones. Expelled Jews were in some cases prevented from bringing even movable valuables and cash, and any landed property had to be sold in a hurry, sometimes to buyers who prioritized their own gain over any sympathy they might have for members of the vulnerable Jewish minority.

Expulsions occurred more frequently in Christendom than under Islam. Jews were expelled from England in 1290; from France on several occasions, although the 1306 expulsion was one of the more far-reaching and traumatic; from several German cities over the course of the fourteenth and fifteenth centuries; and from a newly united Spain in 1492. However, the expulsion of *dhimmi* from Muslim territories was not entirely unknown; the Almohads required Jews and Christians to leave or convert when they conquered al-Andalus in the twelfth century.

Thus far, scholars have not identified any particularly striking ways in which Jewish women experienced expulsions differently from the men of their community. However, given women's heavy reliance on kinship ties as a form of social and economic support, they may have been particularly affected by the family separations caused by expulsions. Women who had begun their marriages living close to parents and siblings might find themselves separated from loved ones by both distance and borders. Hopefully, further research will ascertain more about Jewish women's experience of these crises.

Conclusion

Jews in the medieval world lived as members of a minority community, subject to distinct legal norms as well as religious ones, yet deeply interconnected with the Christian and Muslim communities around them. The lived experiences of medieval Jewish women were marked by their status as members of a minority faith—in many different ways. Belonging to a minority community positioned them to maneuver between legal norms and communities, whether by choosing a court in which to pursue justice or even embracing conversion. However, many Jewish women felt deeply connected to their faith, community, and family. Belonging to Jewish communities meant that women also experienced the same trials and tribulations that shaped the lives of the community as a whole, albeit sometimes in distinct ways.

PART III

Assessment

10 Conclusion

The underlying assumption of this book is that the study of Jewish women matters for our understanding of both women's history and Jewish history in the medieval world. Jewish women shared some experiences, rituals, and cultural norms with the Christian and Muslim women around them. At the same time, however, Jewish women's lives were shaped by belonging to a minority faith subject to certain legal disabilities, by the norms of *halakhah* that differed from local Christian and Muslim legal culture, and by the distinct religious and social practices of their community.

This book has also sought to draw attention to the fact that, often when we talk about Jews in the medieval world (and even sometimes in the modern world), we are first and foremost referring to Jewish men. Jewish women, as we have seen, observed Jewish rituals differently, were subject to different laws, and were perceived differently from Jewish men by the Christians and Muslims around them. If we are interested in the texture of Jewish everyday life in the medieval world, it is crucial that we acknowledge how gender as well as religious identity shaped the lives of medieval Jews.

The final pages of this book will be devoted to a brief discussion of some of the important recent developments in research on medieval Jewish women and some of the areas in which additional research might still expand our understanding of women's experiences. It will then conclude by addressing questions about change and continuity. Does the transition into early modernity represent a significant change for Jewish women? Or should we instead think about continuities in Jewish women's experiences as we move into the sixteenth and seventeenth centuries?

Directions for further research

A synthesis like this one would have been far more difficult to write 20 or even 10 years ago. Although scholars began to produce excellent work on the history of medieval Jewish women already in the 1980s and 1990s, the amount of work available, on Jewish communities stretching from England and France, to Muslim and Christian Spain, to Italy, to the Middle

DOI: 10.4324/9781003104964-13

East, has expanded dramatically over the first two decades of the twenty-first century. In particular, our understanding of this period has been enriched by studies that increasingly consider Jewish women in the context of the Christian and Muslim women around them, as well as within their own communities, and that draw on a wide range of sources in multiple languages.

Yet much work remains to be done. Women's relationships within their families—not only with their husbands, but with their parents, siblings, and children—still deserve further attention. Attention to nursing and childrearing practices in Jewish families has grown, but here too more attention is needed; regional studies that allow for comparisons between different times and places would be especially valuable. Jewish women's use of non-Jewish legal systems is a topic of interest, but given that clear distinctions have already been found between regions, additional local and regional studies have a great deal of potential to enrich our understanding of how and why Jewish women made use of Christian and Muslim courts and legal culture. The same can be said of Jewish women's work.

A 2008 special issue of the *Journal of Medieval History* called for more attention to the interactions between Jewish, Christian, and Muslim women in the medieval world. While some additional research has been done on this topic, interactions between women, especially women of different faiths, can be difficult to discover. Creative uses of a wide array of sources will hopefully contribute to our knowledge in this area.

Scholars have written a great deal about anti-Judaism, but have only begun to scratch the surface of the ways in which anti-Judaism was gendered. Were there distinct ways in which women experienced Jewish communities' most traumatic moments? How did Christians' rhetorical dismissal of Jewish women manifest in their interactions with Jewish women in practice? How were Jewish women portrayed in Muslim anti-Jewish rhetoric?

Change and continuity: Jewish women in the early modern world

In 1977, Joan Kelly-Gadol published an article whose title was a question: Did women have a Renaissance? Over the course of her essay, Kelly-Gadol argues that the economic, social, and cultural roles open to women narrowed with the dawn of the Renaissance (Kelly-Gadol 1977: 139). Stefanie Siegmund has argued that Jewish women also faced new restrictions in early modern Italy and Eastern Europe (Siegmund 2002: 138). In addition to a possible contraction in the social and economic opportunities available to Jewish women, they also experienced certain upheavals along with the other members of their community. With the expulsions of the late Middle Ages, the center of Jewish geography changed. The Jews of the Iberian Peninsula either succumbed to forced conversion—meaning that many Jewish women lived as crypto-Jews—or fled. Jewish communities in

Italy, North Africa, Eastern Europe, and the Middle East grew in size and significance.

Although a small number of Jewish men and women participated in the intellectual life associated with the Renaissance, overall the evidence does not point to any marked improvement in the lives of Jews in general or Jewish women in particular associated with the transition from the medieval to the early modern world. Both women and Jews faced new restrictions and saw little in the way of new opportunities.

Although scholars can point to some changes, often for the worse, in both Jewish history and women's history in the early modern world, scholars of women's history have also argued for continuity between the medieval and early modern periods. We should of course always remember that periodization is a construct. By convention, scholars choose dates that mark the end of the medieval period and the beginning of the Renaissance or early modern period—although depending on the scholar, or the book, or the region discussed, that date could be 1400 or 1453 or 1492 or 1500. Some of these dates are chosen because they are convenient round numbers. Others are associated with real dramatic or transformative moments: the Ottoman conquest of Constantinople in 1453, or the conjunction in 1492 of the Castilian-Aragonese conquest of Granada, Columbus' journey to the Americas, and the expulsion of the Jews from Spain. Even when the chosen date marks some concrete change, people's worldviews and identities did not transform overnight.

Additionally, Judith Bennett has suggested that women's history, in particular, is marked by continuity more than change. Bennett uses the term "patriarchal equilibrium" to describe the tendency of patriarchal ideas and institutions to resist change. Women's low status and limited opportunities look strikingly—and depressingly—similar in many different eras (Bennett 2006: 80). While there were moments in which we can attest to a more dramatic transformation in Jewish status—the Christianization of the Roman Empire, for example, or the emancipation of the Jews beginning in the late eighteenth century—the onset of early modernity is not one of those moments. Jews in 1550 lived in a set of places somewhat different from those of 1250, but they found themselves subject to a fairly similar range of regulations designed to create and reinforce interfaith boundaries and hierarchies. Readers should not therefore assume that the lives of Jewish women looked drastically different from what we have seen in the preceding pages after the date of 1500, which is where, for the sake of convenience, this book ends.

Documents

Unless stated otherwise, all translations are by the author of this book.

1. Eleazar of Worms, poetic elegy for his wife Dolce of Worms. Translated by Judith R. Baskin, reprinted with permission (Baskin 2001: 435–436). Citations in brackets indicate the verse of Proverbs 31:10–31 from which lines in italics are taken

What a rare find is a capable wife [31:10]: Such a one was my saintly wife, Mistress Dolce.

A capable wife [31:10]: the crown of her husband, the daughter of community benefactors. A woman who feared God, she was renowned for her good deeds.

Her husband put his confidence in her [31:11]: She fed him and dressed him in honor to sit with *the elders of the land* [31:23] and involve himself in Torah study and good deeds.

She was good to him, never bad, all the days of [31:12] his life with her. She made him books from her labor; her name [signifies] "Pleasant."

She looked for white *wool* for fringes; *and set her hand to them with a will* [31:13]. *She set her mind* [31:16] to fulfill divine commandments and all who observed her praised her.

She was like a merchant fleet [bringing her food from afar] [31:14] to feed her husband so that he might immerse himself in Torah. Her daughters saw her and *declared her happy* [31:29] *for her merchandise was excellent* [31:18].

She supplied provisions for her household [31:15] and bread to the boys.

How *her hands worked the distaff* [31:19] to spin threads for books. Vigorous in everything, she spun threads for phylacteries, and [prepared] sinews [to bind together] scrolls and books; she was as swift as a deer to cook for the young men and to fulfill the needs of the students.

She girded herself with strength [31:17] and stitched together some forty Torah scrolls. She prepared meat for special feasts and set her table for all of the community.

Judging wisely [31:18], she adorned brides and brought them [to the wedding] in appropriate [garments]. "Pleasant" bathed the dead and sewed their shrouds.

Her hands [31:19] stitched the students' garments and torn books. From her toil she often contributed to Torah scholars.

She gave generously to the poor [31:20] and fed her sons and daughters and her husband. She enthusiastically fulfilled the will of her Creator day and night.

Her lamp never went out at night [31:18]: she prepared wicks for the synagogue and the study rooms and she said psalms.

She sang hymns and prayers and recited supplications. Every day she extended her hands to say the prayers beginning *nishmat kol hai*, and *ve-khol ma'aminim*.

She invoked *pittum ha-qetoret* and the Ten Commandments. In all the cities she taught women, enabling their "Pleasant" intoning of songs.

She knew the order of morning and evening prayer; she came early to the synagogue and stayed late.

She stood throughout the Day of Atonement and chanted; she prepared the candles. She honored the Sabbath and festivals for those who devoted themselves to the study of Torah.

Her mouth was full of wisdom [31:26]: she knew what was forbidden and what was permitted. On the Sabbath she sat and listened to her husband's preaching.

Outstanding in her modesty, she was wise and well-spoken. Whoever was close to her was blessed. She was eager, pious, and amiable in fulfilling all the commandments.

She purchased milk for the students and hired teachers from her exertions. Knowledgeable and wise, she served her Creator in joy.

Her legs ran to visit the sick and to fulfill her Creator's commandments. She fed her sons and urged them to study, and the served the Holy One in reverence.

She was happy to do the will of her husband and never angered him. Her actions were "Pleasant." May the Eternal Rock remember her.

May her soul be enveloped in the wrappings of eternal life. *Extol her for the fruit of her hands* [31:31] in Paradise.

2. Alphabet of Ben Sira, Creation of Lilith, reprinted under fair use guidelines (Kvam, Schearing, and Ziegler 1998: 204)

When God created His world and created Adam, He saw that Adam was alone, and He immediately created a woman from earth, like him, for him, and named her Lilith. He brought her to Adam, and they immediately began to fight: Adam said, "You shall lie below" and Lilith said, "You shall lie below, for we are equal and both of us were [created] from earth." They did not listen to each other. When Lilith saw the state of things, she uttered the Holy Name and flew into the air and fled. Adam immediately stood in prayer before God and said: "Master of the universe, see that the woman you gave me has already fled away." God immediately sent three angels and told them: "Go and fetch Lilith; if she agrees to come, bring her, and if she does not, bring her by force." The three angels went immediately and caught up with her in the [Red] Sea, in the place that the Egyptians were destined to die. They seized her and told her: "If you agree to come with us, come, and if not, we shall drown you in the sea." She answered: "Darlings, I know myself that God created me only to afflict babies with fatal disease when they are eight days old; I shall have permission to harm them from their birth to the eighth day and no longer when it is a male baby; but when it is a female baby, I shall have permission to twelve days." The angels would not leave her alone, until she swore by God's name that wherever she would see them or their names in an amulet, she would not possess the baby [bearing it]. They then left her immediately. That is [the story of] Lilith who afflicts babies with disease.

3. Maimonides, Teshuvot ha-RaMBaM, no. 34: The Woman Teacher and Her Husband, Wife's Perspective

Question: Regarding a man who took as a wife a nine-year-old girl and she brought a portion [of property] held in common with her mother-in-law and her sister, and they all reside in one courtyard. The mother of the aforementioned man undertook in writing to support the aforementioned woman for ten years, and she supported her for seven years. After seven years, the mother-in-law said to her: "I am not able to support you." And the man does not have enough even for an hour, and he supported her for two months. The girl became pregnant and gave birth to a male child. And when [her husband] saw that it would be hard for him to support the household, he left the boy, who was nine months old, with his mother, and he traveled and remained absent for three years in the Land of Israel and in Damascus and other places, and he did not leave her even enough for either her or the baby to eat dinner that night.

He came back from his journey and did not have even a penny with him. The clerk who collects the head tax caught him, as he did not have with him the half-dirhem to pay it, until his father paid the tax on his behalf. His wife and his mother were obligated to pay the head tax for him, out of fear that he would be taken to jail, and he entered the courtyard with nothing at all. He dwelt in the city two years. The woman became pregnant and gave birth to another son, and the father left him with her when he was a year and a half and went back to traveling a second time; he did not leave her even enough for an hour, and he remained absent for another three years.

This woman reached the age of twenty-five years, in a state of immense humiliation due to her poverty, and she had with her two sons, who were more often starving than satiated. All the time that she was with [her husband], he could not light for her a lamp, neither on a weekday nor on the Sabbath nor on a holiday, and she would not see the light of a lamp unless she went to the home of his mother or brother, for she lives with them in the courtyard. Her strength was consumed by her poverty and by the awful state in which she found herself.

She has a brother who teaches scripture to children, and the woman is knowledgeable in scripture. She asked and petitioned her brother to let her teach the children scripture with him, so that she could acquire enough to sustain herself and her sons, as she was already near death from her pitiful circumstances, and [her husband] was absent. And he [her husband] came back from his journey and found her teaching children scripture at her brother's.

She taught scripture to children along with her brother for six years. Afterwards it happened that her brother went on a journey. She sat in his place and took the children and taught them scripture and continued doing this for four years. The oldest son grew and reached the age of seventeen years, and during those four years she brought him with her to teach scripture in her brother's place, so that he could speak with the men, whose sons were with her, and she could do the same for the women, when they came to ask after their children.

From the day these aforementioned sons were born, their father did not pay the head tax on their behalf nor tuition for them to learn at a house of Torah study, nor did he clothe them at all, not a garment nor a head covering nor even a shoe for their feet. The woman was under his authority for twenty-five years, and he did not but once buy a mat for the house to spread out beneath them, nor did he buy a blanket or a pillow or anything needed for their household, not even the linseed oil that she lights. If she had not bought it herself, she could not have managed to light a lamp. Neither she nor her children have any pleasure from him at all, not even in words, only curses and oaths.

He said to her: "Either stay home, like everyone else, or give me permission to marry another woman." The aforementioned woman said to him: "I was already afflicted by poverty, which I was in before, and I and my sons could not live until the day that I began teaching the children." And she said to him: "If you want a divorce, I will consent and I will not hold on to you. But allow you to marry another woman? I'll never do that."

Even though he can be found day and night at his mother's and if he buys anything, for some meager sum, it is for him and his mother, and his wife knows nothing of it—afterwards he complains about her to everyone in the city, that she is not fulfilling his needs and does not stay with him. She said to him: "We do not need this disgrace; let me take you from your mother's; should you sleep at home, I would not prevent you, and if you want, you could come live with me at the school and rent out the portion that I hold in common with your mother and my sister, and let the rent be paid to you, for I am divided between two courtyards; I pay 14 dirhems in rent to the school, and I get no profit for my portion in the courtyard, neither from the apartment nor the rent; I yield my benefit from it, solely out of generosity to you and your mother." And he said to her: "We will not rent it nor will I take the rent; sit at home like the other daughters of Israel or give me permission to marry another." Afterwards, as a subterfuge, he said to her: "I will borrow a dinar and I will buy you wheat with it, and you will sit at home." She said to him: "My profession is not like other professions, where if I left today, I could take it up tomorrow; if I abandoned my students even for a day, I would return and ask after them and would not find them, for their parents will have brought them to other schools. People do not bring their sons to our older son, who is only a boy, but to me. And our two sons have no trade other than the teaching of Torah, and if I stop teaching the children, the children will be lost and the wheat will run out and you will travel and go off like you always do, and I will stay here, along with the boys, and we will be lost, because they have no trade."

Holy eminence, may the Lord exalt you: must she agree to abandon her profession and return to what she had before? And must she undertake to fulfill his needs and serve him, when he does not provide her with food nor drink nor clothing and does not do for her anything that is specified in the Torah, and must she agree to give him permission to marry another woman? Make it known to us: what is the charge of the law with regard to all that is written above? Explain it well, as we have become accustomed to His grace; may your reward be doubled from heaven.

Answer: The law obligates the husband to fulfill his wife's needs, with regard to clothing and expenses and whatever else for which he is obligated, and if he is reluctant or unable to do so, he is forced to divorce her and to pay the delayed marriage portion, if he has it. He may prevent his wife from teaching a trade or reading. The way around this for the wife, if her words are words of truth, is for her to rebel and go out without the delayed marriage portion. He will then be compelled to divorce her, and she will be under her own authority and may teach whoever she wishes and do whatever she wants. So wrote Moses.

4. Maimonides, Teshuvot ha-RaMBaM, no. 45: The Woman Teacher and Her Husband, Husband's Perspective

Question: Our Rabbi, teach us regarding the case of a Jew, who has a wife, who has been with him for a number of years. In one of those years, it happened that he had a trip related to some of his affairs and his business, and he remained absent from his city intermittently for four years. Afterwards, when he returned home, he found that his brother-in-law, his wife's brother, had become a teacher of children, and that his sister—this man's wife—sits with her brother and teaches the children, since her husband taught her a little Torah and in her husband's absence, she studied the rest of the Torah alone.

Her husband said to her: "It is not at all fitting that you teach children, for I am afraid that their fathers will come to visit their children and it will be embarrassing for you, and I do not want this, neither for my sake nor for yours." And when this wife of his heard this from him, she harassed him and refrained from doing her duties, which Jewish women owe to their husbands: kneading and cooking and making the bed and honoring the house and washing clothes and fulfilling her duty to her sons. But she persisted in teaching the children at her brother's, from morning to evening. And if it happens that he needs to provide something for himself, cooking or kneading or washing clothes or the like, he needs to hire someone who will come provide this for him, at full pay. And this man has continued in this situation with this woman already for four years, and he is tired of it.

This woman holds a portion in part ownership with her sister and her mother-in-law, the mother of her husband, and he is afraid to divorce her, lest she take this portion and sell it and her sons will be left with nothing, for she will give it to whoever she marries. And this woman has it written concerning her husband in her marriage contract: That he may not marry another woman and he may not permit a maidservant whom she despises to stay with him, and if he does marry another or permit a maidservant whom she despises to stay with him, he must pay her delayed marriage portion completely and write for her a bill of divorce, so that by these means she may be free of him, even though she wants to divorce him and he does not want to divorce her. Your eminence, is it permitted for him to marry another woman in such a manner that the other remains under his authority, so that she will not rush to sell the portion, or not? Explain to us with a clear answer what is the judgment of the law in all these matters; may your recompense be doubled.

Answer: He is forbidden to marry another woman, except with her permission or if he pays her the delayed marriage portion. And he may forbid her from teaching children, and the court must rebuke her and forbid her from doing this. And if she demands a divorce, on account of the fact that her husband prevents her from teaching, she will not be granted this, but rather doors will be locked before her and paths blocked, and her affairs will be delayed for however long it takes until she returns and wishes to behave appropriately toward her husband. So wrote Moses.

5. Maimonides, Mishneh Torah, Ishut 12:1–3: The Obligations of Husbands and Wives

When a man marries a woman, whether she is a never-married maiden or a previously married woman, whether she is an adult or a minor, whether she is a daughter of Israel or a convert or a freed slave, he obligates himself to her for ten things and will receive from her four things.

Of the ten [obligations], three of them are from the Torah, and these are "*sh'arah, k'sutah,* and *onatah.*" *Sh'arah*: this is her food. *K'sutah*: literally, "covered" [clothing]. *Onatah*: to come upon her as is the way of all the earth [sexual intercourse]. [The other] seven are from the rabbis, and all are conditions [established by] the court. One of them is foundational to the marriage contract. The others are called conditions of the marriage contract; they are: To provide medical treatment for her if she falls ill. To redeem her if she is taken captive. To bury her if she dies. For her to be provided for from his estate. For her to dwell in his home after his death all the days of her widowhood. For their daughters to be provided for from his estate until they are betrothed. For their sons to inherit her *ketubah* in addition to their share of his estate, if they have brothers [half-brothers by other wives].

The four things that he receives [from his wife] are all from the rabbis, and they are: that the fruit of her hands [income from labor] will be his. That anything she finds will be his. That the usufruct of her property will be his during her lifetime. And if she dies in his lifetime, he will inherit from her. And he precedes all others as her heir.

6. A Jewish Marriage Contract, Written in Latin. Arxiu Històric de Girona, secció Girona-05, vol. 5, fol. 7v–9r. Girona, Catalonia, Spain, August 20, 1325

a Let it be known to all, having been done in the presence of the honorable Guillem Brun, judge ordinary of the city and bailiwick of Girona, that Bonjueu Saltell, Jew of Barcelona, present, holding paternal authority [*patria potestas*], liberated and established as independent his son Saltell Gracià, present, having reached the age of thirteen years, and seeking to be emancipated and liberated from paternal authority …. This was done on Tuesday, 13th of the Kalends of September [August 20], in the year of our Lord 1325, in the presence of witnesses Ramon Vidal of Anglès and Jaume Jalbert of Santa Eugènia.

b I, Bonjueu Saltell, Jew of Barcelona, acknowledge and recognize that I made an irrevocable grant between the living [*donatio inter vivos*] to you, Saltell Gracià, and yours, of my full half, undivided, of a certain large urban dwelling [*hospicium*], which I have and hold in the Jewish *Call major* [the larger section of the Jewish quarter] in the city of Barcelona, which on one side borders the *hospicium* of my late brother Llobell and the large synagogue [*scola maior judeorum*], and on another side the *hospicium* of Issach Bellshom and the Carrer dels Banys Freds, and on another side the *hospicium* of Jacob Darahi and that of Salomó de Bellquadre, and on the other side the public street Carrer del Call. Let it be known that this grant corresponds with that made with a Hebrew contract [*per instrumentum ebraycum*], which was completed on the 28th day of the Hebrew month called Shevat in the year 5078 [February 8, 1318] according to the reckoning of the Jews, and witnessed by Bonsenyor Gracià and Nassanell, Jews of Barcelona. I also acknowledge that after this had been done, I made to you, my son, and yours at the time of marriage an irrevocable *donatio inter vivos* of the same half of the *hospicium*, and that the aforementioned grant was clearly accomplished with a Hebrew instrument drawn up on the 23rd day of the Hebrew month called Tammuz in the year 5085 [July 3, 1325], according to the reckoning of the Jews, and that the aforementioned writ was drawn up by Abraham de Montsó and Nassanell, Jews of Barcelona, and that the grant was ratified and approved by *domina* Astruga, my wife, with a Hebrew instrument ....

c   I, Saltell Gracià, emancipated son of Bonjueu Saltell, Jew of Barcelona, Jew of Barcelona, neither deceived nor otherwise induced but freely and with secure knowledge ... acknowledge to you, my aforementioned father, that you made me a *donatio inter vivos* with two Hebrew writs, of your aforementioned half of a *hospicium*, which is in the Jewish *Call major* in the city of Barcelona, and that indeed afterward you made to me a ratification and approval of the transfer of the half-*hospicium*, as can be ascertained, with a public instrument drawn up by a notary .... And I, the aforementioned Saltell Gracià, and I, Reina, his wife, daughter of Bonjueu Cresques, Jew of Girona, with the will and express consent of my father, with both present and consenting, promise to you, Bonjueu Saltell, and yours, that without your consent we will not sell, grant, or otherwise alienate the aforementioned half-*hospicium* .... And for the aforementioned promises which we made and for which we obligated ourselves to you, we swear on the ten precepts of the Law to all and everything ratified above, and freely sign ....

d   Reina, daughter of Bonjueu Cresques, Jew of Girona, and his late wife Bonafilla, my mother, wife of Saltell Gracià, Jew of Barcelona, with the will and express consent of my husband, present and consenting, acknowledging that I have passed the age of 12 years, freely and with secure knowledge and fully apprised of my rights, I fully absolve and release you, the aforementioned Bonjueu Cresques, my father, and yours, from all share and any rights which I have or ought to have, or which are sought or should be sought on my behalf, either now or in the future, over all and each of the movable and immovable goods and other rights and claims, present and future, belonging to you or comprising the property of my late mother, on account of my share of both paternal and maternal inheritance and *legítima*, or any other claim against you or your goods, or those that belonged to my late mother .... Agreeing, et cetera, that for this release and concession, I have received from you 1,000 gold maravedis, which I gave and constituted as dowry at the time of marriage to my aforementioned husband, as is clearly stated in the Hebrew nuptial instrument drawn up for this purpose. Promising and swearing by God and by his Ten Precepts,

et cetera, I make and intend to have made to you this release and concession. In the case that you die intestate, on account of the present
release and concession, I release [you and your heirs] and renounce [any
claims] on my account, that have not previously been considered, in the
right of succession via intestacy ....

7. Babylonian Talmud, Kiddushin 41a. Discussion of the betrothal of minor girls

Mishnah: A man can betroth [a woman] by himself or through an agent. A
woman can be betrothed by herself or through an agent. A man can betroth
his daughter when she is a young woman (*na'arah*), by himself or through
an agent.

.... "A man can betroth his daughter when she is a young woman
(*na'arah*)." When she is a young woman, yes; when she is a minor girl
(*k'tanah*), no. This supports the position of Rav, as Rav Yehudah says that
Rav says, and some say Rabbi Eliezer said: "It is forbidden for a man to
betroth his daughter when she is a minor girl (*k'tanah*), until she grows up
and says "I want so-and-so.""

8. Rabbi Solomon ibn Adret, She'elot u-Teshuvot I.771: A Girl Refuses an Arranged Marriage

Reuven was asked to marry his daughter's daughter to the son of Simeon
and obligated himself to give him some amount of money as a fine and
swore to fulfill the conditions within a certain amount of time. After some
time had passed, he stood up and claimed that his daughter's daughter
would not marry the son of Simeon.

And he replied that the law is with him [Reuven], because it is a clear case
of *force majeure* if the girl does not want to marry the son of Simeon. And
what was he to do? You have no greater case of *force majeure* than this.
Even if he could resolve the matter with money, there is not even a condition that he should resolve if she refuses [to marry]. And as it says in [the
tractate of the Babylonian Talmud] Gittin: "Did he need to give her a vessel
of dinars [in order to satisfy her]?"* And do not respond to me that he
should have stipulated from the beginning that if the girl refuses, he would
be exempted [from paying the fine]—it is not so! The *force majeure*, which
is not common, is that all girls are willing [to marry] whoever their father
or relatives wish. And even if it were as common or uncommon as death
or illness, would you not agree that it is unavoidable and there is a case of
force majeure? But we would not say that about this, which is the cause of
the *force majeure*. And the heart knows whether it is done for a legitimate
purpose or out of perversity.

*A reference to a passage in the Babylonian Talmud (Gittin 30a) which
describes a situation in which a man promised his wife a conditional

divorce if he could not satisfy her. According to the opinion cited here, if he did everything in his power to satisfy her and she remained unsatisfied, the condition was met and the divorce was not valid.

9. Arxiu i Biblioteca Episcopal de Vic, Arxiu de la Curia Fumada, vol. 4592, fol. 81r–v: A Jewish Divorce Document, Written in Latin. Vic, Catalonia, Spain, December 8, 1307

Let it be known to all that I, Astrug Bonjuses de Vilamanya, son and universal heir of the late Bonjuses [...] Jew of Perpignan, of sure knowledge confess and acknowledge to you, Tolsana, daughter of the late David de Monellpell, Jew of [...], [formerly] my [wife] that I have given to you a writ of divorce [*libellum repudii*] signed in accordance with the rite of the Jews, as ought to be done on account of the fact that [....] between me and you. And that as I should do, have done, and wish to do, I restore her dowry of [illegible] marks of pure and fine silver, weighed in accordance with the custom of Perpignan, valued at 5,000 sous of Barcelona ....

10. Rabbi Solomon ibn Adret, She'elot u-Teshuvot, V.240: The Jewish Couple from Seville. Part of text is revised from previous translation by the author (Ifft Decker 2014: 43), reprinted under fair use guidelines

You also mentioned someone who came from Seville, and a woman with him. Witnesses testified about him that he had brought her out from under [the authority of] her husband in harlotry, and they both converted [to Christianity], and afterward she received a bill of divorce from her husband. And now they are in Toledo and go around under the presumption that they are Jews and that they are husband and wife, and it is in your power to inform on them to the royal authorities. What should be done with them?

Answer: You already knew that the woman committed harlotry while under [the authority of] her husband, and there are witnesses to the forbidden impurity, whether her husband or her lover. Whether she has children from her husband or from the defendant comes out of this or that. And even if they were repentant, one must compel them to bring her out by force and not allow her to dwell with him or in his neighborhood. But to inform on them to the royal authorities, this is not mine or yours [to do]. If you see in accordance with the testimony of the witnesses that this is the truth as was witnessed against them, that they converted and also that he brought out the woman in harlotry, and you see that there is a fence [as a means of prevention] in this matter to inform on him to the royal authorities, I already wrote to you about what will suffice in this matter. And if they will not be chastised, separate them and send them out from among you, one to one place and the other to another place, so that they will no longer copulate and return to their sin. And indeed I know that the elders and nobles of your city are resourceful in what they see and do, and it is permitted to them in accordance with the needs of the hour, as I said.

11. Maimonides, Mishneh Torah, Ishut 14:1–8: On Sex in Marriage

The aforementioned [obligation] of conjugal rights, from the Torah. To each and every man, in accordance with his strength and his trade. In what manner? Men who are healthy and soft and indulged, who do not have a trade that saps their strength, but who eat and drink and dwell in their homes—they should fulfill their conjugal rights every night. The workers like tailors and weavers and construction workers and similar trades: if they practice their trades in the city, they should fulfill their conjugal duties twice a week. If they practice their trades in another city, they should fulfill their conjugal duties once a week. Ass-drivers, once a week. Camel-drivers, once every thirty days. Seamen, once every sixty days. Torah scholars should fulfill their conjugal duties once a week, because the study of Torah exhausts their strength. It is the custom of Torah scholars to engage in sexual relations on Sabbath eve.

A wife may prevent her husband from leaving on business except to nearby places, so that he will not be prevented from his conjugal duties, and he may not leave except with her permission. And she may prevent him from going from a trade that requires him to fulfill his conjugal rights more often to a trade that requires him to fulfill his conjugal rights less often. For example, an ass-driver who seeks to become a camel-driver, or a camel-driver who seeks to become a seaman. Torah scholars may leave for Torah study without their wives' permission, for two or three years. So also, a wife cannot prevent her husband who is soft and indulged from becoming a Torah scholar.

A man may marry several wives, even one hundred, whether all at one time or one after the author, and his wife cannot hinder him. But he must be able to give each wife her food, clothing, and conjugal rights as is fitting. And he may not force them to dwell in one courtyard, but each one [may dwell] by herself.

And what are their conjugal rights? According to the number [of wives]. A laborer who has two wives should fulfill his conjugal duties to each once a week. If he has four wives, he is obligated to fulfill his conjugal duties to each one once every two weeks. If a seaman had four wives, he would be obligated to fulfill his conjugal rights to each one once every two years. Our sages therefore commanded that a man should not marry more than four wives, even if he has plenty of money, so that he may be able to fulfill his conjugal duties to each one once a month.

If he vows that his wife should tell others what he said to her, or what she said to him, of those words of folly and frivolity that a man might speak with his wife before they engage in sexual relations, he must divorce his wife and give her the *ketubah* money, for she should not [be forced] to be too bold and to relate disgraceful things to others. And so also if a man vows that she should do something during sexual relations to prevent pregnancy. Or if he vows that she should like a fool and do things that have no meaning at all but foolishness—he must divorce her and give her the *ketubah* money.

If he makes a vow keeping him from having sexual relations with his wife, they may wait one week. Beyond that, he must divorce her and give her his *ketubah* money or annul his vow—even if he is a seaman who only fulfills his conjugal duties once every six months, because his vow has made her sad and filled her with despair. How can a man make such a vow? If he says to her, "sexual relations are forbidden to you," or swears that he will not engage in sexual relations, his vow is invalid, and if he swears an oath [to this effect,] it is in vain because he is obligated to her. But if he says to her: "The pleasure of sexual relations with you is forbidden to me," this is a [valid] vow, and he is forbidden from having sexual relations with her, as one should not be fed something forbidden to him.

It is forbidden for a man to deny his wife her conjugal rights, and if he transgresses and deprives [her of her rights] in order to sadden her, he transgresses a negative commandment of the Torah, as it is said: "Do not deprive her of her food or clothing or conjugal rights." (Exodus 21:10). And if he becomes ill or his strength is diminished and he cannot engage in sexual relations, they should wait six months in case he regains his health, for he may not deprive her of conjugal rights for longer than this. And afterwards either she may grant permission [to him to remain married to her without sexual relations] or he must divorce her and give her the *ketubah* money.

A woman who denies her husband sexual intercourse is called a *moredet* ("rebellious"), and she is asked why she has rebelled. If she says, "He repulses me and I cannot voluntarily engage in sexual intercourse with him," her husband is forced to divorce her immediately, because she is not like a captive who must engage in sexual relations with someone she hates. She is divorced without any of the *ketubah* money at all but is entitled to whatever remains of the property that she brought to her husband, both that for which her husband is liable and that for which he is not liable. She is not entitled to anything at all that belongs to her husband, and even the shoe on her foot and the kerchief on her head that he gave her, she must return them to him, along with any gift that he gave her, for he did not give them to her on the assumption that she would take them and leave.

12. Zohar, Castile, 13th century, 1:49b–1:50a: The Kabbalist, His Wife, and the Shekhinah

Rabbi Simeon was once traveling to Tiberias, and with him were Rabbi Jose, Rabbi Judah, and Rav Hiyya. On their way, they saw Rabbi Pinchas coming toward them. When they had exchanged greetings, they dismounted and sat under a large tree on the hillside. Rabbi Pinchas said, "Now that we are seated, please instruct me further in the esoteric doctrine, which you teach every day."

Rabbi Simeon opened his teaching with the verse: "He went on his journeys from the Negev as far as Bethel, to the place where his tent had been at the beginning, between Bethel and Ai" (Genesis 13:3). It says, "he went on his journeys," not "his journey." Why? These journeys refer not only to his own journey, but also to that of the Shekhinah. From this we learn that every man must be "male and female" at all times, so that his faith might be firm, and so that he should not ever think or imagine that the Shekhinah forsakes him.

And if a man goes on a journey and his wife is not with him, would he no longer be "male and female"? But the Shekhinah is with him when he goes alone on a journey. He should direct his prayers to the Holy One, blessed be He, before he leaves, while he is still "male and female." Once the Shekhinah rests on him, he may then leave, for through his union with the Shekhinah he is "male and female." He is "male and female" at home, and he is "male and female" in the fields. And so it is written: "Righteousness will go before him, and will make a path for his steps" (Psalms 85:14).

Remark this. The whole time that a man is traveling, he should take particular care in his actions, lest his holy partner break off from him, and he be left imperfect, deprived of the union with the female. If it was needed when his wife was with him, how much more necessary is it when a heavenly partner is with him? And all the more so indeed since his heavenly partner acts as his guard all the time, until he returns home.

When he has returned home, it is his duty to give his wife pleasure, as she is the one who obtained for him this heavenly partner. There are two reasons that this is his duty: First, that this pleasure is a religious one, which also gives joy to the Shekhinah, and is a means of bringing peace into the world, as it is written: "You shall know that your tent is in peace, you shall visit your fold and you shall not sin" (Job 5:24). (It might be asked: if he fails to go to his wife, is it a sin? It is a sin, because his failure detracts from the honor of the heavenly partner, who was given to him on account of his wife.) Second, if his wife should conceive, the heavenly partner bestows upon the child a holy soul, for this covenant is called the covenant of the Holy One, blessed be He. Therefore a man should be as zealous in pursuit of this joy as in his pursuit of the joy of the Sabbath, which is the partner of the Sages. And thus "You shall know that your tent is in peace," since the Shekhinah accompanies you and dwells in your house, "and you shall visit your fold and you shall not sin," by carrying out in gladness the religious duty to have conjugal intercourse in the presence of the Shekhinah.

It is in this manner that the students of Torah, who are away from their wives for all six days of the week while they devote themselves to study, in this period are attached to a heavenly partner, so that they might not cease to be "male and female." When the Sabbath comes, it is fitting for the students of Torah to bring their wives joy for the honor of the heavenly partner, and to seek to do the will of their Master, as has been said.

Likewise, when a man's wife is observing her days of separation, in all those days while he waits for her, he has with him his heavenly partner, so that he might continue to be "male and female." When his wife is purified, it is his duty to bring her joy through the joyful fulfillment of his religious obligation. The same reasons that we have given apply also to this case. According to the esoteric doctrine, all the men of true faith are bound to devote their whole mind and purpose to this one [the Shekhinah].

It could be objected that according to what has been said, a man is in a state of great honor when he is on a journey than when he is at home, on account of the heavenly partner who is with him. That is not so, for when he is at home, his wife is the foundation of the home, because it is on account of her that the Shekhinah does not depart from the home. Thus it is written: "and Isaac brought her into the tent of his mother Sarah" (Genesis 24:67); our masters interpret this to mean that the Shekhinah came into Isaac's house with Rebecca.

According to the esoteric doctrine, the supernal Mother is together with the male only when the house is prepared, and the male and female are joined. At this time blessings are showered forth upon them by the supernal Mother. And so also the lower Mother is found together with the male only when the house is prepared, and the male goes to the female and they are joined, then the blessings of the mother are showered forth upon them.

Therefore two females encompass the male in his house, like the Male above. This is alluded to in the verse: "Unto ['ad] the desire of the everlasting hills (Genesis 49:26). This 'ad is the object of desire of the "everlasting hills," by which is meant the supreme female, who is to make ready for him and bring him bliss and bless him, and also the lower female, who is joined with him and is supported by him.

And so also below, when the man is married, the desire of the "everlasting hills" is for him, and two females, the upper and the lower, are to bring him bliss—the upper one by showering upon him blessings, and the lower one by receiving support from him and from joining with him. And so it is with the man in his home.

But when he is on a journey, while the supernal Mother is still with him, the lower wife remains behind. And therefore when he returns home, it is fitting that he take measures to encompass himself with two females, as we have said.

13. Poem by the wife of Dunash ben Labrat, al-Andalus, 10th century, reprinted under fair use guidelines (Cole 2007: 27)

Will her love remember his graceful doe,
her only son in her arms as he parted?
On her left hand he placed a ring from his right,

on his wrist she placed her bracelet.
As a keepsake she took his mantle from him,
and he in turn took hers from her.
Would he settle, now, in the land of Spain,
if its prince gave him half his kingdom?

14. Babylonian Talmud, Shabbat 65a-b: Sexual Relations between Women

[Mishnah]: "Girls may go out with ribbons." The father of Shmu'el did not allow his daughters to go out with ribbons, and he did not allow them to lie next to one another, and he made ritual baths for them in the days of [the month of] Nissan and [placed] mats in the river in the days of [the month of] Tishrei. "He did not allow them to go out with ribbons"—but did not we learn [in the Mishnah]: "Girls may go out with ribbons"?! The daughters of the father of Shmu'el had colorful ones [that they might have removed to show to others].

"He did not allow them to lie next to one another"—this may support the opinion of Rav Huna, as Rav Huna said: Women who rub with one another [out of sexual desire] are unfit for [marrying into] the priesthood. No—he [the father of Shmue'el] holds that they should not become accustomed to [sleeping with] a foreign body [as it could encourage sexual desire].

15. A Refugee Woman from Jerusalem Writes from Tripoli, reprinted under fair use guidelines (Goitein 1975: 80–83)

[My lord and] illustrious master, may God make your welfare and happiness permanent. [I have to convey] to you, my dear boy, something which I shall immediately describe .... Abu 'l-Khayr was with al-Muntasir. Al-Muntasir died and Abu 'l-Khayr disappeared. Consequently, we are lacking clothing and food to a degree I am unable to describe. But [our relative] Joseph was not remiss in providing us with cash, wheat, and other things. Moreover, he returned to me the collaterals, which I had given him, so that I could place them with someone else. God the exalted, deserves thanks and has imposed on us to thank Him. You must write him a letter of thanks ....

I learned that Abu 'l-Wafa' was taken by the Bedouins at the time when his brother disappeared. I am a luckless young woman, suffering both by the hunger of the family, and especially the baby girl, who are with me, and by the bad news I heard about my boy. If my lord, the Nagid, has sworn that he would not go to my aid and visits on me the iniquities committed by Abu 'l-Khayr, have mercy upon me you, your sister, and your mother, as far as you are able to do so.

As far as I am concerned, by our religion, it is better to be captured by the Rum [the Crusaders], for the prisoners find someone who gives them food and drink, but I, by our religion, am completely without clothing, and I and my children are starving.

Now, do not neglect me. Be mindful of the family bonds and the blood. Show your affection for me by writing to me.

The brother of this man [her husband] was not remiss towards him, when he first arrived here, until he sued them for an inheritance. This led to a complete rupture between them, and no one of them talks to me ... Miserable days have come upon me. Must it be so? At the time when I was in Jerusalem, your letters and contributions came to me plentifully, as is proper between two sisters, but now you cut me ....

16. Rabbi Asher ben Yehiel, Shut haRosh, 17.7: Obligations of Mothers and Wetnurses

We will learn: Rachel was impregnated by Reuven; afterward, he married her and she gave birth to a son and he gave the son to a wetnurse. Subsequently, he abandoned her and went to another city and married another woman. And she hired herself out to be a wetnurse to another master, in order to support herself, and lives in the infant's house, and undertook the obligation to breastfeed him for a certain amount of time, with a large fine [if she breaks the contract]. And eight or nine months passed, and the infant knows her and does not want to nurse from anyone else. Then the wetnurse who was nursing her son stopped nursing him, because her son's father went to another city and no one is paying her. And the court tells her [Rachel] that she should nurse her own son. And she says that she cannot, because she is obligated to nurse the son of her master, and her master says that he will not give her up because he has already paid her salary, and moreover his son will not nurse from another woman, and one soul cannot take precedence over another. Moreover, that she is not obligated to nurse her son because she is not [the father's] wife, with *chuppah* [the wedding canopy, referring to marriage] and *kiddushin* [consecration or betrothal].

Answer: The law is with the father of the [second] infant, because she contracted herself to nurse him and is obligated to nurse him so as not to kill the infant. And she is not commanded to breastfeed her son, even if she were married, because the father of the child does not provide her maintenance, and she cannot be left to starve to death. All the more so in this case, as she is not married and is not obligated to nurse his son. What's more, her son is already accustomed to nurse from another woman, and this infant [the child of her employer] is accustomed to her milk and will not nurse from another woman, and one soul cannot take precedence over another. Instead, the court should hire a wetnurse for him and force the father of the child to pay her salary, and if the court cannot force him, it should pay her salary.

17. Rabbi Meir of Rothenburg, She'elot u-Teshuvot ha-Maharam, Prague, no. 502: A Jewish Businesswoman

You asked about a widow who lived for ten years or more after the death of her husband. Her husband's heirs came and claimed from her all she had, because they said that it remained from her husband. She said that it did not in fact remain from her husband, except for 9 *qav* of grain. She claims that she sold it and increased its value [by using the sum to make other business deals] and also borrowed from others and earned more with this money, and that now she has about thirty pounds. And now she wishes to swear on the Torah that she increased the value [of her property] with her *ketubah* and *tosefet ketubah*.

18. Jewish Women in Credit Contracts from Medieval Catalonia

a Barcelona, Arxiu Capitular de Barcelona, pergamins, 1—6—1896. April 8, 1277.

Latin: Let it be known to all that I, Bonafilla, wife of the absent Vidal Gracià, acknowledge and recognize to you, Jaume de Santa Eugènia, sacrist major, that on account of the price of the houses and censals and their belongings, which you bought from Berenguer de Sanahuja, you are released by me, on account of the command of the same Berenguer, from 70 sous de tern of the good and proper money of Barcelona, which the aforementioned Berenguer de Sanahuja received in a loan, with an interest rate of 4 pence per pound per month, from my aforementioned husband, with a public instrument, which Pere de Termes, public notary of Barcelona, caused to be written and concluded on the 10th of the Kalends of March in the year of the Lord 1273 [February 20, 1274]. Also you are released by me for the interest on the aforementioned debt, 26 sous of the aforementioned coinage, and thus I acknowledged that I have and have received from you, between capital and interest, 96 sous; thus, renouncing any exception not enumerated in money, I make to you, and to the aforementioned Berenguer de Sanahuja, in my name and that of my aforementioned husband, a good and perpetual agreement of not seeking [further financial claims]. So that this may be better said and understood, for your security and good understanding, as well as that of the aforementioned Berenguer de Sanahuja and of his [kin], I hand over to you the aforementioned instrument of the aforementioned debt. Moreover, I promise to you, the aforementioned sacrist, that I will bring about and take care that my aforementioned husband will ratify, confirm, and approve for you the aforementioned release, which I made to you from the aforementioned debt and its interest, and that he will never take legal action against you or the aforementioned Berenguer de Sanahuja over the aforementioned [debt and interest], in court or outside the courts. On account of this, I obligate all my movable and immovable goods, which I have or will have, to you and to the aforementioned Berenguer de Sanahuja. In addition, I give to you a guarantor, Salomó Gracià, who with me or without me will complete and cause the aforementioned things to be completed. Therefore I, the aforementioned guarantor, voluntarily taking upon myself this responsibility as guarantor ... agree and promise to you, the aforementioned sacrist, that with or without the aforementioned Bonafilla, I will bring about and seek that the aforementioned Vidal Gracià will approve and confirm to you the aforementioned release made to you by the aforementioned Bonafilla, from the aforementioned debt and its interest, and that he will never take legal action against you or the aforementioned Berenguer de Sanahuja over the aforementioned matters. On account of this, I obligate my goods to you and to the aforementioned Berenguer. This was done on the 6th of the Ides of April in the year 1277 [April 8, 1277]. Signature of the aforementioned Bonafilla, that I approve and confirm this.

Hebrew: That the above was done, I, Roven, witness, acknowledge this, and I, Bonafilla acknowledge, that I have done what is written above, and I sign my name orally through Roven, witness.

Latin: The witnesses to this matter are Jaume Sabater, Deuslosal Bonjueu, and Roven Jaffia. Signature of Pere Març, notary public of Barcelona, that I confirm this. Signature of Jaume de Fontfoll, sworn scribe under Pere Març, notary public of Barcelona, that at his order I wrote and concluded this on the day and year above.

b Vic, Arxiu i Biblioteca Episcopal de Vic, Arxiu de Curia Fumada 4591, fol. 6v. February 17th, 1294.

We, Ferrer de Mercadal and his wife Bernarda of Vic, confess that we owe you, Reina, daughter of Bonmacip, Jew of Vic, 80 sous de tern of Barcelona, for which we were released by your father, to whom we owed this sum for a debt of 77 sous of capital and its interest, which we owed with an instrument, and also with pledges specified in that instrument, which stipulated to you that [the debt] would be repaid on the Feast of Santa Maria in August without interest, and [with interest] if [repaid] beyond [that date]. And for these matters, Berenguer Fiquer of Vic and Berenguer Martí of the parish of Vic act as guarantors. And the debtors swear and renounce. Witnesses, Berenguer de Terreres and Guillem de Manlleu.

c Girona, Arxiu Històric de Girona, Girona-6, vol. 9bis, fol. 33v. July 15, 1334.

I, Bonadona, widow of Astrug Caravida, Jew of Girona, confess and acknowledge to you, Ramon de Prades, present, that Bellshom Scapat, Jew of Girona, for me and in my name, held and received in the table of Feliu Gener, moneychanger of Girona, 6 pounds of Barcelona, which I receive in repayment and on account of those debts which you owed, as the principal party and without guarantor or guarantors, to the aforementioned Astrug (deceased), who made me a grant of his [outstanding] loans and his goods, with a Hebrew writ. This was done, et cetera. Witnesses: Berenguer Batlle of Ramis and Guillem d'Albrisser of Girona

d Barcelona, Arxiu Capitular de Barcelona, Notaris, vol. 221, fol. 97v. May 12, 1349.

I, Pere Bonet, of the parish of Sant Vicenç de Cervelló, confess and acknowledge that I owe you, Starona, widow of Salomó Abraham, 15 sous, under penalty of land, on account of a loan of capital. I promise to repay it, without interest by the Feast of All Saints, and when this time has passed, I will give you interest at a rate of 4 denarii per pound per month. I therefore renounce, et cetera. And I obligate, et cetera. And [I give as] a guarantor Berenguer de Ragers, of the same parish. Witnesses Pere d'Almoina and Jaume d'Amigdal, scribe.

19. Simcha ben Samuel of Vitry, Mahzor Vitry, #498

And there are women who take special care not to enter the synagogue during the period of time when they are menstruating. And they do not need to do so [i.e. to refrain from entering the synagogue]. So, why do they do this? If it is because they believe that the synagogue is like the Temple—even after immersion, why should they be able to enter [the synagogue]? Is it not the case that a sacrifice is required, after which one immerses and then waits until the sun has set, and if they enter before then they are excommunicated? If so, one should not enter [the synagogue] at all, until a sacrifice is brought in the future to come [after the arrival of the Messiah]. And if the synagogue is not like the Temple, they should certainly enter. Moreover, all of us men are indeed impure, because of nocturnal emissions and impurity of death and insects, and we enter the synagogue. So we learn that the synagogue is not like the Temple, and they may enter. But in any event, [the synagogue] is a place of purity, and what they do is praiseworthy.

20. Rabbi Meir of Rothenburg, She'elot u-Teshuvot ha-Maharam, Prague, no. 108: Women's Aliyot in a Town of Cohanim

In a city in which all the inhabitants are *cohanim* [of priestly lineage], except for two or three Israelites, *cohanim* should not read [from the Torah] in place of Israelites in order to complete the quorum of seven. A *cohen* should not read after another *cohen*, because it implies a defect in the first one, and certainly should not read the fourth or fifth portion of the Torah, because it implies a defect in both of them. It implies a defect in the first one because those who leave after the second *cohen* reads will say that the prayer-leader just learned that the first is invalid, and the order must start over by calling another *cohen*. And even if the prayer-leader does not say "Rise, so-and-so the *cohen*," why does it matter? Is it required to call out "the *cohen*"? Even though it is now the custom to recite the name of those called up to the Torah, it is because otherwise they might argue. In any event, one is not obligated to mention the *cohen* by name; and what's more, one does not even need to mention his name, but merely beckon him with a hand to come up. I have heard that this is what Rabbi Shmuel of Bamberg, may his name be as a blessing, did .... In a city in which all the inhabitants are *cohanim*, and there is not in it even one Israelite, it seems to me that the *cohen* should read twice and then they should call up women, because anyone can complete the quorum of seven, even a male or female slave or a child. Rabbi Simcha, may his name be as a blessing, explained that this is not just for the quorum of seven, but even for the quorum of three [when reading from the Torah on some weekday mornings], as the Mishnah states that a child may read from the Torah and recite the translation. Nevertheless, it is the case that the sages say that a woman should not read from the Torah, because of the honor of the congregation. But if there is no other option, the honor of the congregation is superseded by the implication that there is a defect in the *cohanim* who read from the Torah, so that none may say that they are the sons of divorcées [whom people of priestly lineage were forbidden to marry].

21. Will of Regina, wife of Bondia Coras, Jew of Puigcerdà (Catalonia, Spain), October 23, 1306. Translation based on edited document (Burns 1996: 177–178)

Regina, widow of Bondia Coras, Jew, given that I am ill, etc., I make and establish my testament concerning my goods, disposing, etc. First of all, I order that my body be buried.

And I order that 100 sous be given to Iuceff Choen, which I leave to him. Also I distribute 30 sous to Issach de Soall. Also to the heirs of the late Iuceff de Soall, Jew, 30 sous. Also 20 sous to Momet, Jew. Also I distribute 100 sous to Mancosa, widow of Abraham de la Rotxela, Jew.

Also I distribute to Aster, sister of the aforementioned Mancosa, 50 sous. Also I order that charity be given for my soul, on the day of my death; I assign and distribute 100 sous for this to be done.

Also I distribute to Aster, my daughter, wife of Fagim Bonet, Jew, for the portion and inheritance that belongs and ought to belong to her from my goods, 100 sous of Barcelona; with this [money] and with her dowry which she had at the time of the marriage of her and her aforementioned husband, I institute her as my heir, and unless otherwise, etc.

Also I distribute to Gaux, my daughter and that of my late husband, for the portion and right that belongs to her from my goods, 100 [sous]; with this [money] and with the dowry which she had at the time of the marriage of her and her husband Astruch Iuceff, I institute her as my heir, and unless otherwise, etc.

Also I distribute as alms for the Jews of Puigcerdà, for my soul out of the love of God, my bed with all its bedclothes and furnishings, which will stand in the *scola* (school or synagogue) of the aforementioned Jews. And I constitute as my executor, who will carry out my testament, Astrug Jucef, Jew, to whom I give license, etc.

As for the rest of my goods, wherever and whatever they be, I institute as my universal heirs Bondia and Jucef, my grandsons, sons of the late Astrug Bondia, Jew. This however etc.

Witnesses: Matheus de Oliana, Arnaldus Payleres, Raimundus Rahedor, Astruch de Besalu, Iacob Abrahe Choen, Bernardus Duran, Iuceff Abrahe, and Vitalis son of Astruch Crexent.

Astruch Iuceff owes 5 sous.

22. Rabbi Solomon ibn Adret, She'elot u-Teshuvot, VI.4: Responsum on Jewish Law, Dowry Restitution, and Christian Courts

Question: Reuven owed 1,000 dinars with a debt contract to a non-Jew. And his wife did not sign it [the contract]. And the non-Jew came to confiscate the property of Reuven. Reuven's wife brought her *ketubah* [marriage contract], which preceded the debt contract, to the non-Jewish courts, and she collected all the assets of her *ketubah* that were found in the possession of her husband Reuven. Now, Simeon [a Jewish creditor] brought out a debt contract against Reuven, and brought suit against him in the Jewish courts. And Reuven claimed that he had nothing, as his wife had collected all his possessions, which the treasurer of their courts had returned to her. And Simeon claims that her collection was not in accordance with the law, in accordance with the principle that the *ketubah* is not collected in the lifetime [of the husband]. With whom is the law?

Answer: It is the case that the law is with Simeon. He spoke truth, that her collection was not in accordance with the law, and what she collected was not to be collected. As a creditor, he first collects from him [the debtor] what he has not collected. As for the *ketubah*, it may never be collected if she [the wife] dies in the lifetime of her husband. And what of the Rav Ba'al Ha-Ittur, who states that the *nedunya* [dowry] may be collected in the lifetime [of the husband]? I do not agree with this. All are possessions of the husband, which he will not pay except in either widowhood or divorce. Moreover, the sum of the *ketubah* is considered to be the *nedunya* [dowry] and the supplement to the *ketubah* [dower granted by husband] together, and there is no division between the two at the time of payment. This seems clear to me.

23. The Chronicle of Solomon bar Simson, ed. and trans Shlomo Eidelberg (Eidelberg 1996: 35–36), reprinted under fair use guidelines

Who has seen or heard of an act like the deed of the righteous and pious young Mistress Rachel, daughter of Isaac, son of Asher, and wife of Judah? She said to her friends: "Four children have I. Have no mercy on them either, lest those uncircumcised ones come and seize them alive and raise them in their ways of error. In my children, too, shall you sanctify the Holy Name of God." One of her friends came and took the knife to slaughter her son. When the "mother of the sons" saw the knife, she cried loudly and bitterly and smote her face and breast, and said: "Where is Your grace, O Lord?" With an embittered heart she [the mother] said to her companions: "Do not slaughter Isaac before his brother Aaron, so that he [Aaron] will not see the death of his brother and flee." A friend took the boy and slew him .... The lad Aaron, upon seeing that his brother had been slaughtered, cried: "Mother, do not slaughter me," and fled, hiding under a box.

She also had left two daughters, Bella and Madrona, modest and beautiful maidens. The maidens took the knife and sharpened it, so that it would have no notch. They extended their throats, and the mother sacrificed them to the Lord, God of Hosts, Who commanded us not to depart from His pure doctrine, and to remain wholehearted with him, as it is written: "Thou shalt be wholehearted with the Lord thy God."

When this pious woman had completed sacrificing her three children to their Creator, she raised her voice and called to her son: "Aaron, Aaron, where are you? I will not spare you either, or have mercy on you." She drew him out by his feet from under the box where he had hidden and slaughtered him before the Exalted and Lofty God. Then she placed them all on her arms, two children on one side and two on the other, beside her stomach, and they quivered beside her, until finally the enemy captured the chamber and found her there sitting and lamenting over them. They said to her, "Show us the money you have in your sleeves"; but when they saw the slaughtered children, they smote and killed her upon them, and her pure soul expired.

24. Rabbi Solomon Yitzhaki (Rashi), Shut ha-Rashi, #173: Levirate Marriage and Conversion

Rashi responded: On the case of the Levirate marriage [the marriage between a widow and her late husband's brother] that fell to a man who has converted: the ritual of *chalitzah* is needed. There is no difference, whether the husband betrothed her and then the brother-in-law converted, or if he converted before the betrothal. For indeed, a convert is like a Jew who is suspected in all matters, as it is said: "Israel has sinned"—even though he has sinned, he is still of Israel (Babylonian Talmud, Sanhedrin 44a). There is no exception made for him from the laws of Israel, but he is not believed in matters relating to prohibitions, as he is suspected regarding them; and his wine is like the wine of the idolaters, since he is suspected of idolatry. But his betrothal is indeed betrothal and his *chalitzah* is indeed *chalitzah*. As a general rule, he is as a suspected Jew. A responsum, found among the responsa of the Ge'onim, stated that if he had converted at the time of the betrothal, she does not need *chalitzah*, for the first betrothal and marriage bind her to *chalitzah* or Levirate marriage—this cannot be relied on, for its words contradict one another. For if his bond is a bond and his *chalitzah* is *chalitzah* after he converted, why would it matter if she were betrothed before or after the conversion? For he is still considered completely to be a Jew, and his *chalitzah* is *chalitzah*. Therefore, there is no remedy but *chalitzah*, and may the Rock of Israel light our eyes with the light of Torah. Shlomo bar Yitzchak.

25. Ephraim of Bonn, Sefer Zekhira, pp. 30–31, reprinted under fair use guidelines (Einbinder 1998: 33): Pulcellina of Blois

Now, he [the servant] knew of his lord that he would rejoice in disaster, because he hated a certain haughty [or high-ranking] Jewish woman in town, and that is why he spoke this way. Then he [the lord] answered, "Now I shall take my revenge on Madame So-and-so, Madame Pu[l]cellina." The next morning, he rode to the count of the city, that is Thibaut the Evil the son of Thibaut He is Worthy of Cursing—evil curses and bitterness on his head!—the ruler who hearkens to the lies of his evil servants! When he [Thibaut] heard, he grew angry and took all the Jews in Blois and put them in prison. Then Madam Pu[l]cellina encouraged them all, for she trusted in the Count's love, since he had loved her greatly. until now. But Jezebel his wife, the enemy, incited him, because she, too, hated Madame Pu[l]cellina. Now all of them were in chains except for her. But the count's servants who were guarding her would not let her speak to the count at all, lest she change his mind.

Glossary

Abrahamic faiths

Monotheistic religious traditions that specifically worship the God of Abraham. These faiths generally claim spiritual and sometimes biological descent from Abraham. Abraham also features prominently in the scriptures of such faiths—as he does in the Hebrew Bible, accepted by Christians as their Old Testament, and in the Qur'an. Judaism, Christianity, and Islam are all Abrahamic faiths.

Agunah (plural *agunot*)

"Chained woman." A woman who wants a divorce, but her husband either refuses to divorce her or has disappeared without giving her a *get*. Because divorce under Jewish law is unilateral, a woman in this position is thus "chained" to her marriage.

Anti-Judaism

A term often used by historians in lieu of the more common "anti-Semitism" to refer to pre-modern, primarily religiously based, hostility toward Jews and Judaism.

Ashkenaz

A term drawn from the Hebrew Bible, where it is used as both a personal name and the name of a kingdom, which medieval Jews came to associate with the regions of what is now Germany and northern France. The Jews of England, who for the most part came from northern France, and the Jews of Eastern Europe, many of whom had emigrated there from north and central Europe, are also referred to as Ashkenazi Jews.

Babylonian Talmud

The interpretive commentary on the Mishnah developed in Babylonia in the sixth and seventh centuries CE. It would become the more authoritative version of the Talmud, as compared with the Palestinian Talmud.

Black Death
A medieval pandemic that raged across Asia, the Middle East, North Africa, and Europe from 1347 to 1353, and continued to strike in recurrent, slightly less deadly outbreaks through the seventeenth century. Medical explanations and prevention efforts coexisted alongside supernatural explanations and scapegoating inspired by bigotry. Despite the fact that Jews died alongside Christians, some Christian communities slaughtered and burned Jews accused of causing plague by poisoning the wells.

Blood libel
A version of the ritual murder accusation. Blood libel accusations falsely claimed that Jews had not only slaughtered Christian children, but also used their blood for ritual purposes, for example using it in the making of matzah for Passover. These false accusations were made despite the fact that Jewish dietary laws forbade all consumption of blood.

Bogeret
A girl who has reached physical and sexual maturity. According to Jewish law, the *bogeret* was no longer subject to her father's authority, even if she was still unmarried.

Cairo Genizah
A *genizah* is a special repository that Jews use to deposit books or papers that have written on them the name of God, which cannot be simply thrown in the trash with other kinds of refuse. In medieval Cairo, Jews placed a wide array of materials, including personal letters, contracts, and inventories, in their *genizah*. Most were written in Hebrew characters but did not necessarily include the name of God. The Cairo Genizah has become an invaluable source for the communal, social, religious, and economic history of medieval Egypt.

Caliph
Arabic word meaning "successor," referring to the successors of Muhammad designated as rulers of the Islamic world. In theory,

there was meant to be only a single caliph; in practice, starting in the tenth century, some local rulers declared independent caliphates.

Consumption loans Loans of small sums of money, intended to meet immediate needs. They were often meant to be repaid relatively quickly.

Conversa Spanish word, literally meaning a female convert. It typically is used to refer to those women in the Iberian Peninsula who converted, often under duress, during the 1391 massacres or in the wake of the 1492 Expulsion, along with their descendants.

Dar-al-harb The "abode of war," referring to territory not under Muslim rule, where Muslims could and should wage war.

Dar-al-Islam The "abode of Islam," referring to territory under Muslim rule.

Dhimmi Literally, "protected people." A category describing non-Muslim monotheists with written sacred scriptures, which initially included Jews and Christians but was also sometimes expanded to include other groups, for example Zoroastrians. People who belonged to this category could continue to practice their faith and live protected under Islamic rule as long as they obeyed certain conditions designed to reinforce religious boundaries and hierarchies.

Dowry The wealth that a bride received from her family and granted to her husband. The dowry could come in the form of cash, movable goods, land, or some combination of all three. The husband controlled the dowry for the duration of the marriage, but the wife could recover it if she were widowed or bequeath it to her heirs if she died before her husband. Jewish contracts and legal texts often referred to the dowry with the Aramaic word *nedunya*.

Get A bill of divorce, which the husband delivers to his wife either personally or through an agent. The delivery and receipt of the *get* in itself makes the divorce legally valid.

Eucharist	The wafer consecrated and consumed during the Christian Mass. According to medieval Christian doctrine (as well as Catholic doctrine today), the Eucharist not only represented the body of Christ, but was in its inner substance physically transformed into the body of Christ in the ceremony of communion.
Haggadah	Book containing a guide to the procedure for celebrating the seder, the ritual meal of Passover, as well as the narrative of the Exodus story read as part of the seder celebration.
Halakhah	Literally "the way," this term refers to Jewish law. It encompasses not only religious or spiritual laws, but also civil and even criminal law. Medieval Jewish communities could generally govern themselves in accordance with *halakhah* in matters of both religious and civil law, and sometimes even in criminal law.
Host desecration	The false accusation that Jews stole and in some manner defiled consecrated Eucharistic wafers. Many host desecration accusations referenced alleged miracles, in which a stabbed or burned host bled, revealing that it was truly the body of Christ.
Inquisition	An institution established by the papacy in the thirteenth century with the aim of rooting out heresy. The early inquisition focused in particular on a group called the Cathars, based in southern France. The Inquisition did not formally have jurisdiction over Jews, for the most part, nor did it seek to convert Jews to Christianity. However, if a convert to Christianity reverted to Judaism, that convert's Jewish practice would now be considered a Christian heresy, and their case would be subject to the Inquisition. The Inquisition also sometimes pursued cases against Jews accused of "judaizing," attempting to bring converts back to Judaism. In 1478, King Ferdinand II of Aragon and Queen Isabella I of Castile received permission from the

Pope to establish the Spanish Inquisition, which was especially dedicated to rooting out crypto-Judaism among converts and their descendants. Prior to 1478, references to the Inquisition always refer to the papal Inquisition, which also remained in power in Catholic regions outside Spain through the early modern era.

Intersectionality	A term coined by scholar Kimberlé Williams Crenshaw to describe the interconnections between categories of identity like race, class, and gender. The way people experience privilege and disadvantage, in the past and today, depends on their intersectional identities.
Kabbalah	Jewish mystical tradition that arose in Spain and southern France in the twelfth century.
Karaites	A Jewish sect that arose in Baghdad around the seventh century, known for their rejection of the Oral Law. The name stems from the Hebrew word meaning "to read," and Karaites are often portrayed as literal readers of scripture.
Ketubah	A Jewish marriage contract, written in a combination of Aramaic and Hebrew. The *ketubah* created a valid marriage and recorded the couple's financial commitments and personal obligations to one another. The same term also refers to the sum of money the husband granted to his wife.
Levirate marriage	A marriage between a childless widow and her late husband's brother. The offspring of this union would legally be considered the child of the deceased first husband. Childless widows were expected to enter Levirate marriages if a brother were available and could only be released through the performance of a special ceremony, called *chalitzah*.
Mamzer	A child born of a forbidden sexual relationship, like adultery or incest. According to Jewish law, a *mamzer* remained a member of the community, but could only marry

	another *mamzer*. This status would in turn be passed on to their children.
Midrash (plural *midrashim*)	A genre of rabbinic biblical interpretation, often intended to fill in gaps or explain problems in the biblical text. Some *midrashim* are written in the form of narratives or stories.
Mikveh	A Jewish ritual bath. Immersion in the *mikveh* restores ritual purity; medieval Jewish women (and some Jewish women today) immerse in the *mikveh* after menstruation and childbirth. Immersion in the *mikveh* also forms part of the conversion ceremony; medieval Jews who returned to their original faith were not legally required to immerse in the *mikveh*, but in some places local custom encouraged immersion, and some rabbinic authorities even believed it was required.
Mishnah	A written codification of the Oral Law compiled by rabbis active around 200 CE.
Mitzvah (plural Mitzvot)	A commandment, namely one of the 613 commandments said to be prescribed in the Torah. The term is sometimes also used less literally to refer to a good deed.
Monotheism	The belief in only one God, who is often portrayed as the creator of the world and as an omnipotent figure.
Moredet	"Rebellious wife." The *moredet* "rebelled" by refusing to have sexual intercourse with her husband and/or perform household tasks. Medieval Jewish courts would force a husband to divorce a *moredet*, but she would generally forfeit her *ketubah* money.
Nedunya	See **Dowry**.
Niddah	A term that refers both to a menstruating woman and to the laws and rituals surrounding menstrual impurity.
Notary	A public official, appointed by a king or local ruler. Especially in the Western Mediterranean, the notaries became important both as legal professionals who knew how to draw up valid contracts and as officials whose authority turned private arrangements into legally enforceable facts.

Palestinian Talmud	The interpretive commentary on the Mishnah developed in Palestine in the fourth and fifth centuries CE. It is sometimes referred to as the Jerusalem Talmud; however, that term is inaccurate: no Jews lived in Jerusalem at this time, and the sages who produced this work were largely based in the Galilee.
Polygyny	Marrying multiple wives. This text deliberately uses the word "polygyny" rather than "polygamy," which literally means multiple *spouses* (non-gendered), to highlight the fact that Jewish men (at least in some regions) could marry more than one wife, but Jewish women could never legally marry more than one husband.
Qur'an	Sacred scriptures of Islam, considered to be the written version of the divine revelations given to Muhammad.
Rabbanites	In places like the Middle East with a significant Karaite presence, Jews who continued to accept and adhere to the Oral Law were referred to as Rabbanites.
Rabbi	The word "rabbi" literally means my teacher, and was initially used as a title of respect to refer to teachers and sages. The term would come to refer to those people who specialized in the reading and interpretation of scripture, as well as the production and interpretation of the Oral Law. Beginning in the third century, rabbis often held positions as communal leaders or judges. In the Middle Ages, rabbis both held formal positions of authority in specific communities and commanded respect more widely as legal and ritual experts.
Responsa	A genre of rabbinic literature, composed of both questions sent to important rabbis and the rabbis' responses. Responsa of individual rabbis have been compiled into collections, which later rabbis consulted as precedent. They usually describe real cases, and sometimes quite specific ones, but often omit identifying information, like the real names or even specific location of the people involved.

Ritual murder	The false charge that Jews, in an effort to reenact their alleged murder of Christ, ritually slaughtered Christian boys.
Sepharad	A place name drawn from the Hebrew Bible, which medieval Jews came to associate with the Iberian Peninsula—today, the countries of Spain and Portugal. After the expulsion of the Jews from Spain in 1492 and Portugal in 1497, Sephardi Jews immigrated all over the known world, creating early modern Sephardic Jewish communities in North Africa, Turkey, Palestine, Greece, Italy, and the Netherlands.
Shekhinah	A feminine manifestation of God's presence in the world, especially in the mystical tradition of kabbalah.
Supersession	A doctrine claiming that Christians had replaced Jews as God's chosen people.
***Takkanah* (plural *takkanot*)**	Ordinances issued by rabbinic courts. Although some *takkanot*, like the ban on polygyny, were linked with particularly illustrious rabbis, the authority of the *takkanot* ultimately stemmed from that of Jewish communal governments, not the prestige of individual rabbis—although such prestige might explain why the *takkanah* of Rabbenu Gershom came to be accepted beyond his own community. Members of the community who violated *takkanot* could be excommunicated.
TaNaKH	Acronym used by Jews to refer to the Hebrew Bible, based on the three sections into which it is traditionally divided: Torah (the Five Books of Moses), *Nevi'im* (Prophets—a category that includes the books of 1-2 Kings and prophets like Jeremiah and Amos), and *Ketuvim* (Writings—a broad-ranging category that includes the books of Esther and Ruth, Psalms, and Song of Songs, among others).
Tkhines	Prayers written in Yiddish for women, and sometimes by women. Many were printed during the early modern period, but it is likely that women's prayers like these existed earlier, perhaps only or primarily in oral form.

Toledot Yeshu	Literally, the "deeds of Jesus." A Jewish polemical retelling of the Christian Gospels, which claimed that Mary had been tricked into adulterous sex while she was menstruating. Jesus was therefore portrayed as a bastard conceived during menstruation, representing two different taboos.
Torah	Speaking precisely, the word "Torah" refers to the Five Books of Moses: Genesis (Hebrew *Bereshit*), Exodus (*Sh'mot*), Leviticus (*Vayikra*), Numbers (*Bamidbar*), and Deuteronomy (*D'varim*). In practice, however, Jews in the Middle Ages and today often use the word Torah more broadly to refer to the entire Hebrew Bible or even to the entire spectrum of Jewish learning.
Tosefet ketubah	Literally, the supplement or addition to the *ketubah*. As the monetary gift of the *ketubah* became a relatively small symbolic sum, many husbands committed to grant their wives a more substantial gift, made up of the *ketubah* plus a supplement.
Transubstantiation	The Christian doctrine that held that the Eucharistic wafer and the wine consecrated in communion not only symbolized the body and blood of Christ, respectively, but also transformed physically into the body and blood of Christ, even while they retained their outward appearance. Affirmed at the Fourth Lateran Council of 1215.
Usury	A polemical term used for the lending of money at interest, particularly at interest rates considered unreasonable or extortionate, or deemed illegal.
Wetnurse	A woman hired to breastfeed a child in place of the birth mother.
Zohar	Central work of the Jewish mystical movement known as Kabbalah. Although it was attributed to the second-century sage Rabbi Simeon bar Yohai, in reality it was composed in thirteenth-century Castile, probably by Kabbalist Moses de Leon.

Guide to further reading

Primary sources

Students interested in embarking on research projects on medieval Jewish women and gender can turn to a few primary source collections. A wide array of primary sources related to pre-modern Jewish communities in Europe can be found in Marc Saperstein's updated version of Jacob Rader Marcus' classic sourcebook, *The Jews in Christian Europe: A Source Book, 315–1791* (Cincinnati: Hebrew Union College Press, 2015). When possible, students may also want to look for earlier editions of the same sourcebook, under the title *The Jew in the Medieval World: A Source Book, 315–1791* (Cincinnati: Hebrew Union College Press, 1999). Earlier versions included a slightly different selections of primary texts, including some from the Islamic East. However, students seeking more extensive source material from the Islamic world would do better to turn to Norman Stillman's *The Jews of Arab Lands: A History and Source Book* (Philadelphia: The Jewish Publication Society of America, 1979), as well as to published documents from the Cairo Genizah in numerous articles by S.D. Goitein. Lawrence Fine's collection *Judaism in Practice* (Princeton: Princeton University Press, 2001) includes primary sources with introductory essays related to Jewish faith and culture in the medieval and early modern world. Students in search of primary sources on women's history more broadly should consult Emilie Amt's *Women's Lives in Medieval Europe: A Sourcebook* (New York: Routledge, 2010).

Students who have developed more specific interests can also find a variety of primary source texts in other designated sourcebooks. Those who are especially interested in delving more deeply into the writings of Maimonides, both legal and philosophical, can turn to Isidore Twersky's *A Maimonides Reader* (Springfield, NJ: Behrman House, 1972). Students interested in further exploring queer Jewish history, from antiquity to the present, can take advantage of an excellent new sourcebook edited by Noam Sienna, *A Rainbow Thread* (Philadelphia: Print-O-Craft Press, 2019). The Jewish communities of medieval Spain and Portugal are extensively documented in Olivia Remie Constable's *Medieval Iberia* (Philadelphia: University of

Pennsylvania Press, 2012). Several excellent collections will be of use to students interested in the Hebrew poetry of al-Andalus and the portrayal of women in that tradition. Peter Cole's *The Dream of the Poem* (Princeton: Princeton University Press, 2007) and Raymond Scheindlin's *Wine, Women, and Death: Medieval Hebrew Poems on the Good Life* (Oxford: Oxford University Press, 1999) are particularly valuable anthologies.

Students who have Hebrew skills and wish to do independent research involving responsa, ethical literature, legal codes, and other medieval Jewish texts might wish to see if their institution has a subscription to the Bar-Ilan Responsa Database, a searchable database of thousands of pre-modern and modern Jewish texts.

Medieval Jewish history

Students who wish to learn more background about medieval Jewish history can turn to several wide-ranging surveys. On Christian Europe, Kenneth Stow's *Alienated Minority: The Jews of Medieval Latin Europe* (Cambridge: Harvard University Press, 1991) and Robert Chazan's *Reassessing Jewish Life in Medieval Europe* (New York: Cambridge University Press, 2010) offer useful overviews. For more information on the Jewish communities of the medieval Islamic world, Stillman's *The Jews of Arab Lands* (see previous section) pairs primary sources in translation with a survey text. Mark R. Cohen's *Under Crescent and Cross: The Jews in the Middle Ages* (Princeton: Princeton University Press, 2008) offers a comparison of Jewish life under Muslim and Christian rule, although the somewhat more complicated case of the Iberian Peninsula often gets left out.

Numerous monographs, some of them extensive multi-volume studies, provide more detailed and nuanced discussions of the Jewish communities of specific regions. S.D. Goitein's *A Mediterranean Society: The Jews of the Arab World as Portrayed in the Documents of the Cairo Genizah* (Berkeley: University of California Press, 1967–1993) provides immense detail, organized thematically. Those who wish for a somewhat broader overview might appreciate his one-volume abridgment (Berkeley: University of California Press, 2003). On the Iberian Peninsula, see Eliyahu Ashtor, *The Jews of Moslem Spain* (Philadelphia: The Jewish Publication Society of America, 1993); Yitzhak Baer, *A History of the Jews of Christian Spain* (Philadelphia: The Jewish Publication Society of America, 1961–1966); Yom Tov Assis, *The Golden Age of Aragonese Jewry: Community and Society in the Crown of Aragon, 1213–1327* (Oxford: The Littman Library of Jewish Civilization, 1997); Elka Klein, *Jews, Christian Society, and Royal Power in Medieval Barcelona* (Ann Arbor: University of Michigan Press, 2006); and Maya Soifer Irish, *Jews and Christians in Medieval Castile: Tradition, Coexistence, and Change* (Washington, DC: Catholic University Press, 2016). On Ashkenaz, see David Malkiel, *Reconstructing Ashkenaz: The*

Human Face of Franco-German Jewry, 1000–1250 (Stanford: Stanford University Press, 2009). On Italy, see Ariel Toaff, *Love, Work, and Death: Jewish Life in Medieval Umbria* (London: Littman Library of Jewish Civilization, 1998).

Medieval women and gender

Several surveys can provide students with a broader understanding of women and gender in the medieval world. Joan Scott's classic essay, "Gender: A Useful Category of Historical Analysis" in *The American Historical Review* 91:5 (1986): 1053–1075 provides a useful basis for students to understand why historians study gender. *The Oxford Handbook of Women and Gender in Medieval Europe*, edited by Judith M. Bennett and Ruth Mazo Karras (Oxford: Oxford University Press, 2016) includes a wide range of articles, mostly focused on Christian women, but also incorporating general discussion of Jewish and Muslim women in the medieval world. Overviews that also discuss methodologies in gender and women's histories will be especially useful to students. Judith Bennett's *History Matters: Patriarchy and the Challenge of Feminism* (Philadelphia: University of Pennsylvania Press, 2006) convincingly explains why studying medieval women should matter for both medievalists and feminists. Patricia Skinner's *Studying Gender in Medieval Europe: Historical Approaches* (London: Palgrave, 2018) introduces students to some of the theories and methods historians use when studying women and gender in the Middle Ages. For more on women in the Islamic world, see Gavin R. Hambly's edited collection *Women in the Medieval Islamic World* (New York: St. Martin's Press, 1988).

Students in search of additional overviews on medieval Jewish women should consult Judith R. Baskin's *Jewish Women in Historical Perspective* (Detroit: Wayne State University Press, 1991; second edition published 1998), which includes survey articles on Jewish women in a range of times and places from antiquity to the modern world. Readers of this work are especially encouraged to consult the essays on late antiquity, the Middle Ages, and early modernity by Judith Romney Wegner, Judith R. Baskin, Renée Levine Melammed, Howard Adelman, and Chava Weissler. The classic survey on medieval Jewish women is Avraham Grossman's *Pious and Rebellious: Jewish Women in Medieval Europe* (Waltham, MA: Brandeis University Press, 2004). Grossman's work of course does not incorporate the extensive research that has been done since 2004 but is able to offer greater detail than this survey. Students interested in constructions of gender in Jewish culture should consult Judith R. Baskin's *Midrashic Women: Formations of the Feminine in Rabbinic Literature* (Hanover: Brandeis University Press, 2002) for an overview of gender in rabbinic *midrash*, as well as Shaye D. Cohen's *Why Aren't Jewish Women Circumcised? Gender and Covenant in Judaism* (Berkeley: University of California Press,

2005), for a discussion of ancient and medieval discussions of gender and circumcision.

The remainder of this guide will be organized thematically, following the structure set forth in the chapters of this book, and will incorporate not only works on medieval Jewish women, but also relevant scholarship on Christian and Muslim women, for students interested in pursuing comparative research.

Marriage, divorce, and widowhood

Discussions of marriage, divorce, and widowhood are so foundational to medieval Jewish life, especially Jewish women's lives, that they are interwoven throughout numerous scholarly works. For the Islamic East, the third volume of Goitein's *Mediterranean Society* discusses marriage and divorce extensively. Eve Krakowski's *Female Adolescence, Jewish Law, and Ordinary Culture* (Princeton: Princeton University Press, 2018) offers a detailed discussion of age at marriage and of how young women experienced the transition to married life. Rebecca Winer extensively discusses marriage and widowhood in *Women, Wealth, and Community in Perpignan, c. 1250–1300: Christians, Jews, and Enslaved Muslims in a Medieval Mediterranean Town* (Aldershot: Ashgate Publishing, 2006). Judith R. Baskin's article "Mobility and Marriage in Two Medieval Jewish Societies," in *Jewish History* 22 (2008): 223–243, provides a useful comparison between marriage practices in Ashkenaz and the Islamic East. For discussion of divorce cases in medieval Catalonia, see Pinchas Roth, "'My Precious Books and Instruments': Jewish Divorce Strategies and Self-Fashioning in Medieval Catalonia," in *Journal of Medieval History* 43:5 (2017): 548–556, and Sarah Ifft Decker, "Jewish Divorce and Latin Notarial Culture in Fourteenth Century Catalonia," in Thomas Barton, Susan McDonough, Sara McDougall, and Matthew Wranovix (eds.), *Boundaries in the Medieval and Wider World. Festschrift in Honor of Paul Freedman* (Turnhout, Belgium: Brepols), pp. 45–60. For analysis of a specific intriguing marital conflict in medieval Egypt, detailed in Documents 3 and 4 of this volume, see Renée Levine Melammed's article "He Said, She Said: A Woman Teacher in Twelfth-Century Cairo," *AJS Review* 22:1 (1997): 19–35.

The scholarship on marriage practices in Christian Europe is far too extensive to discuss fully here, but interested students should consult Diane Owen Hughes' foundational article, "From Brideprice to Dowry in Mediterranean Europe," *Journal of Family History* 3:3 (1978): 262–296. As just a brief selection of important scholarship on Christian marriage practices in different regions of Europe, see Barbara Hanawalt's *The Wealth of Wives: Women, Law, and Economy in Late Medieval London* (Oxford: Oxford University Press, 2007) for England; Martha Howell's *The Marriage Exchange: Property, Social Place, and Gender in the Cities of the*

Low Countries, 1300–1550 (Chicago: The University of Chicago Press, 1998) on the Netherlands; Dana Wessell Lightfoot's *Women, Dowries, and Agency: Marriage in Fifteenth-Century Valencia* (Manchester: Manchester University Press, 2013) on the Crown of Aragon; and Christiane Klapisch-Zuber's *Women, Family, and Ritual in Renaissance Italy*, translated by Lydia G. Cochrane (Chicago: The University of Chicago Press, 1985), on Italy. On marriage and divorce in the Islamic world, see Yossef Rapoport's *Marriage, Money, and Divorce in Medieval Islamic Society* (Cambridge: Cambridge University Press, 2005).

Sex and sexuality

For discussions of the place of sex and sexuality in Jewish tradition, students should begin with David Biale's *Eros and the Jews: From Biblical Israel to Contemporary America* (New York: Basic Books, 1992) and Daniel Boyarin's *Carnal Israel: Reading Sex in Talmudic Culture* (Berkeley: University of California Press, 1993). The most detailed overview of sources relating to real-life sexual activity in a medieval Jewish community can be found in Yom Tov Assis' 1988 article "Sexual Behavior in Mediaeval Hispano-Jewish Society," in Ada Rapoport-Albert and Steven J. Zipperstein (eds.), *Jewish History: Essays in Honor of Chimen Abramsky* (London: Peter Halban Publishers), pp. 25–59. Students especially interested in discussions of sex and sexuality as related to Jewish-Christian relations should consult David Nirenberg's *Communities of Violence: Persecution of Minorities in the Middle Ages* (Princeton: Princeton University Press, 1996), especially pp. 127–165, and Rachel Furst's article "Captivity, Conversion, and Communal Identity: Sexual Angst and Religious Crisis in Frankfurt, 1241," in *Jewish History* 22:1/2 (2008): 179–221.

On women's sexual and reproductive health, see Carmen Caballero-Navas, "The Care of Women's Health and Beauty: An Experience Shared by Medieval Jewish and Christian Women," in *Journal of Medieval History* 34 (2008): 146–163, as well as the work of Monica Green, especially her volume of reprinted collected essays, *Women's Healthcare in the Medieval West: Texts and Contexts* (Aldershot: Ashgate Variorum, 2000). On sex and women's healthcare in the Islamic world, see Basim Musallam, *Sex and Society in Islam: Birth Control before the Nineteenth Century* (Cambridge: Cambridge University Press, 1983).

Family, childbirth, and childrearing

For discussion of Jewish family structures, see in particular Kenneth Stow's article "The Jewish Family in the Rhineland in the High Middle Ages: Form and Function," *The American Historical Review* 92:5 (1987): 1085–1110, for Ashkenaz; Winer's *Women, Wealth, and Community* on the Crown of Aragon; and both volume III of Goitein's *Mediterranean Society* and

Krakowski's *Coming of Age* on the Middle East. For those interested in the institution of guardianship, Winer's discussion is by far the richest available; see in particular pp. 107–132.

Rich discussion of motherhood, childcare, and nursing practices can be found in Elisheva Baumgarten's groundbreaking *Mothers and Children: Jewish Family Life in Medieval Europe* (Princeton: Princeton University Press, 2004). For more on how wetnursing crossed interfaith boundaries, see Rebecca Lynn Winer's article "Conscripting the Breast: Lactation, Slavery, and Salvation in the Realms of Aragon and Kingdom of Majorca, c. 1250–1300," *Journal of Medieval History* 34 (2008): 164–184.

Jewish women's work

Jewish women's work differed across regions of the medieval world. Students interested in this topic are encouraged to pay attention to regional differences as well as different forms of labor. For Jewish women's role in credit, those interested in England should consult Suzanne Bartlet's biography of the exceptional and intriguing figure of Licoricia of Winchester, *Licoricia of Winchester: Marriage, Motherhood, and Murder in the Medieval Anglo-Jewish Community* (Edgware: Vallentine Mitchell, 2009). For a more general overview, see Victoria Hoyle's article "The Bonds that Bind: Money Lending between Anglo Jewish and Christian Women in the Plea Rolls of the Exchequer of the Jews, 1218–1280," *Journal of Medieval History* 34 (2008): 119–129. On France, William Chester Jordan's "Jews on Top: Women and the Availability of Consumption Loans in Northern France in the Mid-Thirteenth Century," *Journal of Jewish Studies* 29:1 (1978): 39–56 explores Jewish women's moneylending using court records. For central Europe, students should consult Martha Keil's "Public Roles of Jewish Women in Fourteenth and Fifteenth-Century Ashkenaz: Business, Community, and Ritual," in Christoph Cluse (ed.), *The Jews of Europe in the Middle Ages (Tenth to Fifteenth Centuries): Proceedings of the International Symposium held at Speyer, 20–25 October, 2002* (Turnhout, Belgium: Brepols, 2004), pp. 317–330. On the Crown of Aragon, useful works include Winer's *Women, Wealth, and Community*; Anna Rich Abad's "Able and Available: Jewish Women in Medieval Barcelona and Their Economic Activities," *Journal of Medieval Iberian Studies* 6:1 (2014): 71–86; and Sarah Ifft Decker's "Jewish Women, Christian Women, and Credit in Thirteenth-Century Catalonia," *The Haskins Society Journal* 27 (2016): 161–178.

Several works offer important reassessments of the role Jews played in the credit industry. In his book *Shylock Reconsidered: Jews, Moneylending, and Medieval Society* (Berkeley: University of California Press, 1989), Joseph Shatzmiller encourages readers to avoid assuming that relations between Jewish creditors and Christian debtors were always marked by hostility. Julie Mell's two-volume study, *The Myth of the Medieval Jewish*

Moneylender (Cham, Switzerland: Palgrave Macmillan, 2017–2018) argues that Jews played only a minor role in credit and the traditional narrative should be fully discarded. Those interested in Jews' mercantile activities in the Islamic East should consult Jessica Goldberg's *Trade and Institutions in the Medieval Mediterranean: The Geniza Merchants and their Business World* (Cambridge: Cambridge University Press, 2012).

Readers especially interested in Jewish women's role in medical practice should look into Shatzmiller's survey, *Jews, Medicine, and Medieval Society* (Berkeley: University of California Press, 1994). The particularly intriguing case of the Jewish midwife Floreta d'Ays is discussed in detail by Monica Green and Daniel Lord Smail in their article "The Trial of Floreta d'Ays (1403): Jews, Christians, and Obstetrics in Later Medieval Marseille," *Journal of Medieval History* 34 (2008): 185–211. On gender and medicine in late medieval and early modern Europe, see Katherine Park's *Secrets of Women: Gender, Generation, and the Origins of Human Dissection* (New York: Zone Books, 2006).

Students interested in the topic of women's work should also consult some of the groundbreaking studies on Christian women's work in medieval Europe: Martha Howell's *Women, Production, and Patriarchy in Late Medieval Cities* (Chicago: The University of Chicago Press, 1986); Judith Bennett's *Ale, Beer, and Brewsters in England: Women's Work in a Changing World, 1300–1600* (New York: Oxford University Press, 1996), and Sharon Farmer's *Surviving Poverty in Medieval Paris: Gender, Ideology, and the Daily Lives of the Poor* (Ithaca: Cornell University Press, 2002) and *The Silk Industries of Medieval Paris: Artisanal Migration, Technological Innovation, and Gendered Experiences* (Philadelphia: University of Pennsylvania Press, 2016).

Gender, faith, and worship

By far the most important work of scholarship on Jewish women's piety is Elisheva Baumgarten's *Practicing Piety in Medieval Ashkenaz: Men, Women, and Everyday Religious Observance* (Philadelphia: University of Pennsylvania Press, 2014), which compares Jewish women's pious practices with those of both Jewish men and Christian women. Baumgarten's previous book, *Mothers and Children*, also details women's rituals centered around childbirth and infancy. More work is needed on medieval women's prayers; readers should consult Chava Weissler's *Voices of the Matriarchs: Listening to the Prayers of Early Modern Jewish Women* (Boston: Beacon Press, 1998) on early modern *tkhines* from Ashkenaz.

For more on menstruation and ritual purity, Charlotte Fonrobert's *Menstrual Purity: Rabbinic and Christian Reconstructions of Biblical Gender* (Stanford: Stanford University Press, 2000) offers an excellent discussion of rabbinic discourse, along with a comparison with Christianity. Readers seeking a comparison with Islam are encouraged to look into

Marion Katz's work, particularly her article "Scholarly Authority and Women's Authority in the Islamic Law of Menstrual Purity," in Firoozeh Kashani-Sabet and Beth S. Wenger (eds.), *Gender in Judaism and Islam: Common Lives, Uncommon Heritage* (New York: NYU Press, 2014), pp. 73–104.

A great deal has been written on women's sanctity and piety in medieval Christendom. A small selection of recommended scholarly works includes Caroline Walker Bynum's *Holy Feast and Holy Fast: The Religious Significance of Food to Medieval Women* (Berkeley: University of California Press, 1987); Walter Simons' *Cities of Ladies: Beguine Communities in the Medieval Low Countries* (Philadelphia: University of Pennsylvania Press, 2001); Fiona J. Griffiths' *The Garden of Delights: Reform and Renaissance for Women in the Twelfth Century* (Philadelphia: University of Pennsylvania Press, 2007); and Jeffrey Hamburger and Susan Marti's edited volume *Crown and Veil: Female Monasticism from the Fifth to the Fifteenth Centuries* (New York: Columbia University Press, 2008).

Jewish women between communities

On Jewish women choosing between Jewish and non-Jewish courts, see Rena Lauer's excellent discussion of Jewish legal culture in Venetian Crete, *Colonial Justice and the Jews of Venetian Crete* (Philadelphia: University of Pennsylvania Press, 2019). On the Islamic world, Oded Zinger's article "'She Aims to Harass Him': Jewish Women in Muslim Legal Venues in Medieval Egypt," *AJS Review* 42:1 (2018): 159–192, is especially interesting. For an example from the early modern period, see Lois C. Dubin's "Jewish Women, Marriage Law, and Emancipation: The Civil Divorce of Rachele Morschene in Late Eighteenth-Century Trieste," in David N. Myers, Massimo Ciavolella, Peter H. Reill, and Geoffrey Symcox (eds.), *Acculturation and Its Discontents: The Italian Jewish Experience Between Exclusion and Inclusion* (Toronto: University of Toronto Press, 2008), pp. 119–147. Christian women also behaved strategically in courtrooms; Marie Kelleher's *The Measure of Woman: Law and Female Identity in the Crown of Aragon* (Philadelphia: University of Pennsylvania Press, 2010) offers an excellent example of how Christian women negotiated legal culture.

The study of links between gender, anti-Judaism, and the crises faced by the Jewish community is still a developing field, but students interested in this topic should start with Susan Einbinder's works: *Beautiful Death: Jewish Poetry and Martyrdom in Medieval France* (Princeton: Princeton University Press, 2002); *No Place of Rest: Jewish Literature, Expulsion, and the Memory of Medieval France* (Philadelphia: University of Pennsylvania Press, 2009) and *After the Black Death: Plague and Commemoration among Iberian Jews* (Philadelphia: University of Pennsylvania Press, 2018). For a more general introduction on medieval

Christian anti-Judaism, students are encouraged to consult Miri Rubin's *Gentile Tales: The Narrative Assault on Late Medieval Jews* (Philadelphia: University of Pennsylvania Press, 2004).

Paola Tartakoff's work offers an excellent starting point for readers interested in learning more about Jewish and Christian attitudes toward conversion in medieval Christendom. Her article "Testing Boundaries: Jewish Conversion and Cultural Fluidity in Medieval Europe, c. 1200–1391," *Speculum* 90:3 (2015): 728–762 includes a rich historiographical overview on conversion in both Sepharad and Ashkenaz, along with a new approach that encourages attention to similarities rather than differences between the regions. Those interested in Iberian *conversa* women are encouraged to turn to Renée Levine Melammed's *Heretics or Daughters of Israel? The Crypto-Jewish Women of Castile* (New York: Oxford University Press, 1999), which offers extensive analysis as well as a number of translated inquisitorial records.

Bibliography

Primary sources

Amt, Emilie (2010). *Women's Lives in Medieval Europe: A Sourcebook*. 2nd edn. New York: Routledge.

Baskin, Judith R. (2001). "Dolce of Worms: The Lives and Deaths of an Exemplary Medieval Jewish Woman and Her Daughters," in Lawrence Fine (ed.), *Judaism in Practice; From the Middle Ages through the Early Modern Period*. Princeton: Princeton University Press, pp. 429–437.

Cole, Peter (2007). *The Dream of the Poem: Hebrew Poetry from Muslim and Christian Spain, 950–1492*. Princeton: Princeton University Press.

Constable, Olivia Remie (2012). *Medieval Iberia: Readings from Christian, Muslim, and Jewish Sources*. Philadelphia: University of Pennsylvania Press.

Eidelberg, Shlomo (ed. and trans.) (1996). *The Jews and the Crusaders: The Hebrew Chronicles of the First and Second Crusades*. Hoboken, NJ: Ktav Publishing House.

Glückel of Hameln (2012). *The Life of Glückel of Hameln: A Memoir, ed. and trans. Beth Zion Abrahams*. Philadelphia: The Jewish Publication Society of America.

Kvam, Kristen E., Linda S. Schearing, and Valarie H. Ziegler (1998). *Eve and Adam: Jewish, Christian, and Muslim Readings on Genesis and Gender*. Bloomington: Indiana University Press.

Rader Marcus, Jacob and Marc Saperstein (eds.) (2015). *The Jews in Christian Europe: A Source Book, 315–1791*. Cincinnati: Hebrew Union College Press.

Scheindlin, Raymond (1999). *Wine, Women, and Death: Medieval Hebrew Poems on the Good Life*. Oxford: Oxford University Press.

Sienna, Noam (2019). *A Rainbow Thread: An Anthology of Queer Jewish Texts from the First Century to 1969*. Philadelphia: Print-O-Craft Press.

Stillman, Norman (1979). *The Jews of Arab Lands: A History and Source Book*. Philadelphia: Jewish Publication Society of America.

Twersky, Isidore (1972). *A Maimonides Reader*. Springfield, NJ: Behrman House.

Secondary sources

Adelman, Howard (1991). "Rabbis and Reality: Public Activities of Jewish Women in Italy during the Renaissance and Catholic Restoration," *Jewish History* 5:1, pp. 27–40.

Aranoff, Deena (2019). "Mother's Milk: Child-Rearing and the Production of Jewish Culture," *Journal of Jewish Identities* 12:1, pp. 1–17.

Ashtor, Eliyahu (1993). *The Jews of Moslem Spain*, 3 vols. Philadelphia: The Jewish Publication Society of America.

Assis, Yom Tov (1988). "Sexual Behavior in Mediaeval Hispano-Jewish Society," in Ada Rapoport-Albert and Steven J. Zipperstein (eds.), *Jewish History: Essays in Honor of Chimen Abramsky*. London: Peter Halban Publishers, pp. 25–59.

Assis, Yom Tov (1997). *The Golden Age of Aragonese Jewry: Community and Society in the Crown of Aragon, 1213–1327*. Oxford: The Littman Library of Jewish Civilization.

Baer, Yitzhak (1961–1966). *A History of the Jews of Christian Spain*, 2 vols. Philadelphia: The Jewish Publication Society of America.

Bartlet, Suzanne (2009). *Licoricia of Winchester: Marriage, Motherhood, and Murder in the Medieval Anglo-Jewish Community*. London: Vallentine Mitchell.

Baskin, Judith R. (ed.) (1991). *Jewish Women in Historical Perspective*. Detroit: Wayne State University Press.

Baskin, Judith R. (ed.) (1998a). *Jewish Women in Historical Perspective*. 2nd edn. Detroit: Wayne State University Press.

Baskin, Judith R. (1998b). "Jewish Women in the Middle Ages," in Judith R. Baskin (ed.), *Jewish Women in Historical Perspective*. 2nd edn. Detroit: Wayne State University Press, pp. 101–127.

Baskin, Judith R. (2002). *Midrashic Women: Formations of the Feminine in Rabbinic Literature*. Hanover: Brandeis University Press.

Baskin, Judith R. (2008). "Mobility and Marriage in Two Medieval Jewish Societies," *Jewish History* 22:1–2, pp. 223–243.

Baumgarten, Elisheva (2004). *Mothers and Children: Jewish Family Life in Medieval Europe*. Princeton: Princeton University Press.

Baumgarten, Elisheva (2014). *Practicing Piety in Medieval Ashkenaz: Men, Women, and Everyday Religious Observance*. Philadelphia: University of Pennsylvania Press.

Benedictow, Ole J. (2004). *The Black Death, 1346–1353: The Complete History*. Woodbridge, Suffolk: The Boydell Press.

Bennett, Judith M. (1996). *Ale, Beer, and Brewsters in England: Women's Work in a Changing World, 1300–1600*. New York: Oxford University Press.

Bennett, Judith M. (2006). *History Matters: Patriarchy and the Challenge of Feminism*. Philadelphia: University of Pennsylvania Press.

Bennett, Judith M. and Ruth Mazo Karras, eds. (2016). *The Oxford Handbook of Women and Gender in Medieval Europe*. Oxford: Oxford University Press.

Biale, David (1992). *Eros and the Jews: From Biblical Israel to Contemporary America*. New York: Basic Books.

Boyarin, Daniel (1993). *Carnal Israel: Reading Sex in Talmudic Culture*. Berkeley: University of California Press.

Brundage, James (1988). "Intermarriage between Christians and Jews in Medieval Canon Law," *Jewish History* 3, pp. 25–40.

Burns, Robert I. (1996). *Jews in the Notarial Culture: Latinate Wills in Mediterranean Spain, 1250–1350*. Berkeley: University of California Press.

Bynum, Caroline Walker (1987). *Holy Feast and Holy Fast: The Religious Significance of Food to Medieval Women*. Berkeley: University of California Press.

Caballero-Navas, Carmen (2008). "The Care of Women's Health and Beauty: An Experience Shared by Medieval Jewish and Christian Women," *Journal of Medieval History* 34, pp. 146–163.

Chazan, Robert (2010). *Reassessing Jewish Life in Medieval Europe*. New York: Cambridge University Press.

Chojnacki, Stanley (2000). *Women and Men in Renaissance Venice: Twelve Essays on Patrician Society*. Baltimore: The Johns Hopkins University Press.

Cohen, Mark R. (2008). *Under Crescent and Cross: The Jews in the Middle Ages*. Princeton: Princeton University Press.

Cohen, Mark R. (2009). *Poverty and Charity in the Jewish Community of Medieval Egypt*. Princeton: Princeton University Press.

Cohen, Shaye D. (2005). *Why Aren't Jewish Women Circumcised? Gender and Covenant in Judaism*. Berkeley: University of California Press.

Cuffel, Alexandra (20007). *Gendering Disgust in Medieval Religious Polemic*. Notre Dame, IN: University of Notre Dame Press.

Efron, John, Matthias Lehman, and Steven Weitzman (2019). *The Jews: A History*. 3rd edn. New York: Routledge.

Einbinder, Susan (1998). "Pulcellina of Blois: Romantic Myths and Narrative Conventions," *Jewish History* 12:1, pp. 29–46.

Einbinder, Susan (2002). *Beautiful Death: Jewish Poetry and Martyrdom in Medieval France*. Princeton: Princeton University Press.

Einbinder, Susan (2009). *No Place of Rest: Jewish Literature, Expulsion, and the Memory of Medieval France*. Philadelphia: University of Pennsylvania Press.

Einbinder, Susan (2018). *After the Black Death: Plague and Commemoration among Iberian Jews*. Philadelphia: University of Pennsylvania Press.

Elliott, Dyan (1993). *Spiritual Marriage; Sexual Abstinence in Medieval Wedlock*. Princeton: Princeton University Press.

Epstein, Marc Michael (2011). *The Medieval Haggadah: Art, Narrative and Religious Imagination*. New Haven: Yale University Press.

Farmer, Sharon (2002). *Surviving Poverty in Medieval Paris: Gender, Ideology, and the Daily Lives of the Poor*. Ithaca: Cornell University Press.

Farmer, Sharon (2016). *The Silk Industries of Medieval Paris: Artisanal Migration, Technological Innovation, and Gendered Experiences*. Philadelphia: University of Pennsylvania Press.

Fonrobert, Charlotte Elisheva (2000). *Menstrual Purity: Rabbinic and Christian Reconstructions of Biblical Gender*. Stanford: Stanford University Press.

Furst, Rachel (2008). "Captivity, Conversion, and Communal Identity: Sexual Angst and Religious Crisis in Frankfurt, 1241," *Jewish History* 22: 1/2, pp. 179–221.

Goitein, S.D. (1967–1993). *A Mediterranean Society: The Jewish Communities of the Arab World as Portrayed in the Documents of the Cairo Geniza*, 5 vols. Berkeley: University of California Press.

Goitein, S.D. (1975). "Tyre-Tripoli-'Arqa: Geniza Documents from the Beginning of the Crusader Period," *The Jewish Quarterly Review* 66:2, pp. 69–88.

Goitein, S.D. (2003). *A Mediterranean Society: An Abridgment in One Volume*, ed. Jacob Lassner. Berkeley: University of California Press.

Goldberg, Jessica (2012). *Trade and Institutions in the Medieval Mediterranean: The Geniza Merchants and their Business World*. Cambridge: Cambridge University Press.

Green, Monica (1996). "The Development of the *Trotula*," *Revue d'Histoire des Textes* 26, pp. 119–203.

Green, Monica and Daniel Lord Smail (2008). "The Trial of Floreta d'Ays (1403): Jews, Christians, and Obstetrics in Later Medieval Marseille," *Journal of Medieval History* 34, pp. 185–211.

Grossman, Avraham (2004). *Pious and Rebellious: Jewish Women in Medieval Europe*. Waltham, MA: Brandeis University Press.

Guerson, Alexandra and Dana Wessell Lightfoot (2020). "A Tale of Two Tolranas: Jewish Women's Agency and Conversion in Late Medieval Girona," *Journal of Medieval Iberian Studies* 12:3, pp. 344–364.

Hambly, Gavin R. (ed.). (1988). *Women in the Medieval Islamic World*. New York: St. Martin's Press.

Hanawalt, Barbara (2007). *The Wealth of Wives: Women, Law, and Economy in Late Medieval London*. Oxford: Oxford University Press.

Hezser, Catherine (2007). "Roman Law and Rabbinic Legal Composition," in Charlotte Elisheva Fonrobert and Martin S. Jaffee (eds.), *The Cambridge Companion to the Talmud and Rabbinic Literature*. Cambridge: Cambridge University Press, pp. 144–164.

Hoyle, Victoria (2008). "The Bonds that Bind: Money Lending between Anglo Jewish and Christian Women in the Plea Rolls of the Exchequer of the Jews, 1218–1280," *Journal of Medieval History* 34: pp. 119–129.

Howell, Martha (1986). *Women, Production, and Patriarchy in Late Medieval Cities*. Chicago: The University of Chicago Press.

Howell, Martha (1998). *The Marriage Exchange: Property, Social Place, and Gender in the Cities of the Low Countries, 1300–1550*. Chicago: The University of Chicago Press.

Hsia, R. Po-Chia (1992). *Trent 1475: Stories of a Ritual Murder Trial*. New Haven: Yale University Press.

Hughes, Diane Owen (1978). "From Brideprice to Dowry in Mediterranean Europe," *Journal of Family History* 3:3, pp. 262–296.

Hughes, Diane Owen (1986). "Distinguishing Signs: Ear-rings, Jews, and Franciscan Rhetoric in the Italian Renaissance City," *Past and Present* 112, pp. 3–59.

Iancu-Agou, Daniele (1987). "Une vente de livres hébreux à Arles en 1434: Tableau de l'elite juive arlesienne au milieu de XVe siècle," *Revue des études juives* 146, pp. 5–62.

Ifft Decker, Sarah (2014). "Conversion, Marriage, and Creative Manipulation of Law in Thirteenth-Century Responsa Literature," *Journal of Medieval Iberian Studies* 6:1, pp. 42–53.

Ifft Decker, Sarah (2015). "The Public Economic Role of Catalan Jewish Wives, 1250–1350," *Tamid* 11, pp. 45–66.

Ifft Decker, Sarah (2016). "Jewish Women, Christian Women, and Credit in Thirteenth-Century Catalonia," *The Haskins Society Journal* 27, pp. 161–178.

Ifft Decker, Sarah (2017). "Jewish Divorce and Latin Notarial Culture in Fourteenth Century Catalonia," in Thomas Barton, Susan McDonough, Sara McDougall, and Matthew Wranovix (eds.), *Boundaries in the Medieval and Wider World. Festschrift in Honor of Paul Freedman*. Turnhout, Belgium: Brepols, pp. 45–60.

Ifft Decker, Sarah (2019a). "Between Two Cities: Jewish Women and Exogamous Marriage in Medieval Catalonia," *Journal of Medieval History* 45:4, pp. 481–503.

Ifft Decker, Sarah (2019b). "Minding Manors: Gender, Acculturation, and Jewish Women's Landholding in Medieval Catalonia," *Hispania Judaica* 14, pp. 15–38.

Ifft Decker, Sarah (forthcoming). *The Fruit of Her Hands: Jewish and Christian Women's Work in Medieval Catalan Cities*. University Park, PA: Pennsylvania State University Press.

Jordan, William Chester (1978). "Jews on Top: Women and the Availability of Consumption Loans in Northern France in the Mid-Thirteenth Century," *Journal of Jewish Studies* 29:1, pp. 39–56.

Jordan, William Chester (2001). "Adolescence and Conversion in the Middle Ages: A Research Agenda," in Michael A. Signer and John van Engen (eds.), *Jews and Christians in Twelfth-Century Europe*. Notre Dame, IN: University of Notre Dame Press.

Katz, Marion (2014). "Scholarly Authority and Women's Authority in the Islamic Law of Menstrual Purity," in Firoozeh Kashani-Sabet and Beth S. Wenger (eds.), *Gender in Judaism and Islam: Common Lives, Uncommon Heritage*. New York: NYU Press, pp. 73–104.

Keil, Martha (2004). "Public Roles of Jewish Women in Fourteenth and Fifteenth-Century Ashkenaz: Business, Community, and Ritual," in Christoph Cluse (ed.), *The Jews of Europe in the Middle Ages (Tenth to Fifteenth Centuries): Proceedings of the International Symposium held at Speyer, 20–25 October, 2002*. Turnhout, Belgium: Brepols, pp. 317–330.

Kelleher, Marie (2010). *The Measure of Woman: Law and Female Identity in the Crown of Aragon*. Philadelphia: University of Pennsylvania Press.

Kelly-Gadol, Joan (1977). "Did Women Have a Renaissance?" in Renate Bridenthal and Claudia Koonz (eds.), *Becoming Visible: Women in European History*. Boston: Houghton Mifflin.

Klapisch-Zuber, Christiane (1985). *Women, Family, and Ritual in Renaissance Italy, tr. Lydia G. Cochrane*. Chicago: The University of Chicago Press, 1985.

Klein, Elka (1993). "Protecting the Widow and the Orphan: A Case Study from Thirteenth Century Barcelona," *Mosaic* 14, pp. 65–81.

Klein, Elka (2006a). *Jews, Christian Society, and Royal Power in Medieval Barcelona*. Ann Arbor: University of Michigan Press.

Klein, Elka (2006b). "Public Activities of Catalan Jewish Women," *Medieval Encounters* 12:1, pp. 48–61.

Krakowski, Eve (2018). *Coming of Age in Medieval Egypt: Female Adolescence, Jewish Law, and Ordinary Culture*. Princeton: Princeton University Press.

Langer, Ruth (1995). "The *Birkat Betulim*: A Study of the Jewish Celebration of Bridal Virginity," *Proceedings of the American Academy for Jewish Research* 61, pp. 53–94.

Lauer, Rena (2019). *Colonial Justice and the Jews of Venetian Crete*. Philadelphia: University of Pennsylvania Press.

Lehman, Marjorie (2014). "Dressing and Undressing the High Priest: A View of Talmudic Mothers." *Nashim* 26, pp. 52–74.

Lightfoot, Dana Wessell (2013). *Women, Dowries, and Agency: Marriage in Fifteenth-Century Valencia*. Manchester: Manchester University Press.

Lipton, Sara (2008). "Where are the Gothic Jewish Women? On the Non-Iconography of the Jewess in the *Cantigas de Santa Maria*," *Jewish History* 22, pp. 139–177.

Lipton, Sara (2014). *Dark Mirror: The Medieval Origins of Anti-Jewish Iconography*. New York: Metropolitan Books.

Lipton, Sara (2016). "Isaac and Antichrist in the Archives," *Past and Present* 232:1, pp. 3–44.

Malkiel, David (2009). *Reconstructing Ashkenaz: The Human Face of Franco-German Jewry, 1000–1250*. Stanford: Stanford University Press.

Marcus, Ivan (1996). *Rituals of Childhood: Jewish Acculturation in Medieval Europe*. New Haven: Yale University Press.

McDonough, Susan (2021). "Moving Beyond Sex: Prostitutes, Migration and Knowledge in Late-Medieval Mediterranean Port Cities," *Gender and History*, pp. 1–19, https://doi.org/10.1111/1468-0424.12574.

Meacham, Tirzah (1999). "Appendix," in Rahel R. Wasserfall (ed.), *Women and Water: Menstruation in Jewish Life and Law*. Hanover: Brandeis University Press, pp. 255–261.

Melammed, Renée Levine (1997). "He Said, She Said: A Woman Teacher in Twelfth-Century Cairo," *AJS Review* 22:1, pp. 19–35.

Melammed, Renée Levine (1999). *Heretics or Daughters of Israel? The Crypto-Jewish Women of Castile*. New York: Oxford University Press.

Mell, Julie (2017–2018). *The Myth of the Medieval Jewish Moneylender*, 2 vols. New York: Palgrave Macmillan.

Musallam, Basim (1983). *Sex and Society in Islam: Birth Control before the Nineteenth Century*. Cambridge: Cambridge University Press.

Nirenberg, David (1996). *Communities of Violence: Persecution of Minorities in the Middle Ages*. Princeton: Princeton University Press.

Nirenberg, David (2007). "Deviant Politics and Jewish Love: Alfonso VIII and the Jewess of Toledo," *Jewish History* 21:1, pp. 15–41.

Park, Katherine (2006). *Secrets of Women: Gender, Generation, and the Origins of Human Dissection*. New York: Zone Books.

Rapoport, Yossef (2005). *Marriage, Money, and Divorce in Medieval Islamic Society*. Cambridge: Cambridge University Press.

Rich Abad, Anna (1999). *La comunitat jueva de Barcelona entre 1348 i 1391 a través de la documentació notarial*. Barcelona: Fundació Noguera.

Rich Abad, Anna (2014). "Able and Available: Jewish Women in Medieval Barcelona and Their Economic Activities," *Journal of Medieval Iberian Studies* 6:1, pp. 71–86.

Romney Wegner, Judith (1998). "The Image and Status of Women in Classical Rabbinic Judaism," in Judith R. Baskin (ed.), *Jewish Women in Historical Perspective*. 2nd edn. Detroit: Wayne State University Press, pp. 73–100.

Rose, E.M. (2015). *The Murder of William of Norwich*. New York: Oxford University Press.

Roth, Pinchas (2017). "'My Precious Books and Instruments': Jewish Divorce Strategies and Self-Fashioning in Medieval Catalonia," *Journal of Medieval History* 43:5, pp. 548–561.

Ruiz Ventura, Jordi and M. Eulàlia Subirà de Galdàcano (2009). "Reconstrucció antropòlogica del pogrom de 1348 a Tàrrega," *Urtx: revista cultural de l'Urgell* 23, pp. 126–137.

Rustow, Marina (2008). *Heresy and the Politics of Community: The Jews of the Fatimid Caliphate*. Ithaca, NY: Cornell University Press.

Safran, Janina (2013). *Defining Boundaries in al-Andalus: Muslims, Christians, and Jews in Islamic Iberia*. Ithaca: Cornell University Press.

Schraer, Michael (2019). *A Stake in the Ground: Jews and Property Investment in the Medieval Crown of Aragon*. Leiden: Brill.

Scott, Joan (1986). "Gender: A Useful Category of Historical Analysis," *The American Historical Review* 91:5, pp. 1053–1075.

Shatzmiller, Joseph (1989). *Shylock Reconsidered: Jews, Moneylending, and Medieval Society*. Berkeley: University of California Press.

Shatzmiller, Joseph (1994). *Jews, Medicine, and Medieval Society*. Berkeley: University of California Press.

Shoham-Steiner, Ephraim (2014). *On the Margins of a Minority: Leprosy, Madness, and Disabiltiy among the Jews of Medieval Europe*, tr. Haim Watzman. Detroit: Wayne State University Press.

Siegmund, Stefanie (2002). "Gendered Self-Government in Early Modern Jewish History: The Florentine Ghetto and Beyond," in Marc Lee Raphael (ed.), *Gendering the Jewish Past*. Williamsburg, VA: Department of Religion, The College of William and Mary, pp. 137–155.

Skinner, Patricia (2018). *Studying Gender in Medieval Europe: Historical Approaches*. London: Palgrave.

Soifer Irish, Maya (2016). *Jews and Christians in Medieval Castile: Tradition, Coexistence, and Change*. Washington, DC: Catholic University Press.

Stow, Kenneth R. (1987). "The Jewish Family in the Rhineland in the High Middle Ages: Form and Function," *The American Historical Review* 92:5, pp. 1085–1110.

Stow, Kenneth R. (1991). *Alienated Minority: The Jews of Medieval Latin Europe*. Cambridge: Harvard University Press.

Taitz, Emily, Sondra Henry, and Cheryl Tallan (2003). *The JPS Guide to Jewish Women: 600 BCE–1900 CE*. Philadelphia: The Jewish Publication Society.

Tallan, Cheryl (1991). "Medieval Jewish Widows: Their Control of Resources," *Jewish History* 5:1, pp. 63–74.

Tartakoff, Paola (2010). "Jewish Women and Apostasy in the Medieval Crown of Aragon, c. 1300–1391," *Jewish History* 24, pp. 7–32.

Tartakoff, Paola (2015). "Testing Boundaries: Jewish Conversion and Cultural Fluidity in Medieval Europe, c. 1200–1391," *Speculum* 90:3, pp. 728–762.

Toaff, Ariel (1998). *Love, Work, and Death: Jewish Life in Medieval Umbria*. London: The Littman Library of Jewish Civilization.

Trivellato, Francesca (2009). *The Familiarity of Strangers: The Sephardic Diaspora, Livorno, and Cross-Cultural Trade in the Early Modern Period*. New Haven: Yale University Press.

Weissler, Chava (1998). *Voices of the Matriarchs: Listening to the Prayers of Early Modern Jewish Women*. Boston: Beacon Press.

Winer, Rebecca Lynn (2006). *Women, Wealth, and Community in Perpignan, c. 1250–1300: Christians, Jews, and Enslaved Muslims in a Medieval Mediterranean Town*. Aldershot: Ashgate Publishing.

Winer, Rebecca Lynn (2008). "Conscripting the Breast: Lactation, Slavery, and Salvation in the Realms of Aragon and Kingdom of Majorca, c. 1250–1300," *Journal of Medieval History* 34, pp. 164–184.

Winer, Rebecca Lynn (2011). "Marriage, Family, and the Family Business: Links Between the Jews of Medieval Perpignan and Girona," in Sílvia Planas Marcé (ed.), *Temps i espais de la Girona jueva: Actes del Simposi Internacional celebrat a Girona 23, 24, i 25 de març de 2009*. Girona Judaica 5. Girona: Patronat Call de Girona, pp. 243–256.

Zinger, Oded (2018). "'She Aims to Harass Him': Jewish Women in Muslim Legal Venues in Medieval Egypt." *AJS Review* 42:1, pp. 159–192.

Index

Printed in the USA
CPSIA information can be obtained
at www.ICGtesting.com
LVHW020616250823
756160LV00003B/90

9 780367 612726